International Linkages and Consortia of the Elementary Education Program in the College of Teacher Education, University of Northern Philippines-UNESCO Heritage City of Vigan

Christopher Fuster Bueno, PhD

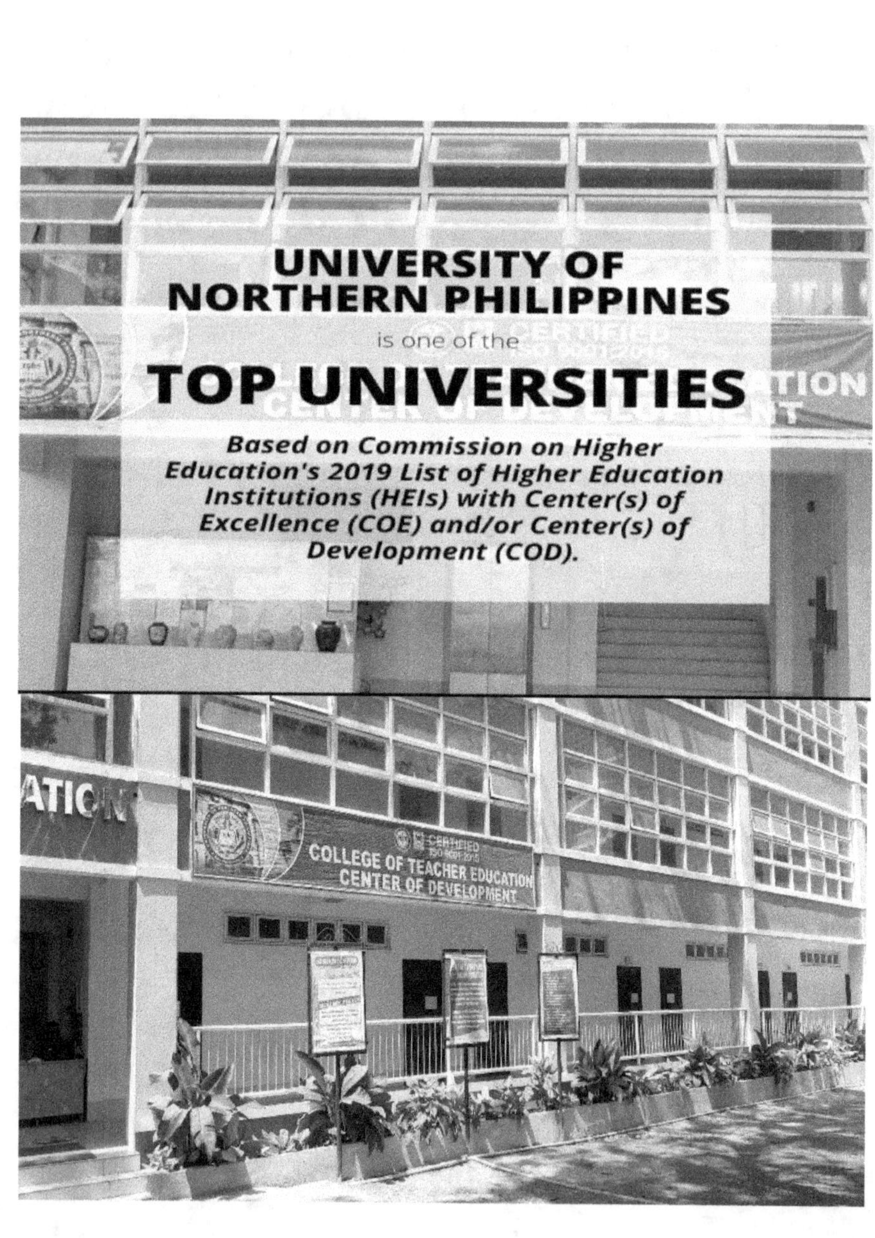
UNIVERSITY OF
NORTHERN PHILIPPINES
is one of the
TOP UNIVERSITIES
Based on Commission on Higher
Education's 2019 List of Higher Education
Institutions (HEIs) with Center(s) of
Excellence (COE) and/or Center(s) of
Development (COD).
COLLEGE OF TEACHER EDUCATION
CENTER OF DEVELOPMENT

CONTENTS

FOREWORD

In this COVID-19 pandemic, the college has done its best to ensure its safety and continuously serving the fullest capacity of the college to produce future teachers with the vision to be globally competitive graduates who will work with compassion, love, and commitment to serve the humanity. Since 2016 the College has been granted the Center of Development, ISO 9001:2015 certified with Level IV (Phase 2) accreditation and we are moving forward to ensure that we give the best education to train the future teachers.

As Center of Development (COD), the educational metamorphosis of the teacher education programs for the last five years has reached its pinnacle of sustainable quality education to all the graduates. It assures to give the best service for quality and excellence in the teacher education programs. The granting of the Center of Development award, ISO Certification, and Level IV (Phase 2) Accreditation connotes the achievement of academic excellence within the ambit of highly qualified and competent teachers, who possess the multi-dimensional talent to sustain quality instruction, innovative research, and professional commitment with unique individual expertise in the field of pedagogy, technology and specialized knowledge in the teacher education program

For those who are enrolled in the elementary education program with a specialization in early childhood education, general education, and special education we have already reached its peak of 90 percent LET rating for first takers. The graduates have been at the top of their careers as we ensure the branding of *taktak* UNP-CTE of its best in doing the pedagogical practices in the field of basic education. The Special Education and Inclusive Education programs have proved their competence with the only national topnotcher in Region 1.

In the elementary education program, they are trained to become globally competent with the pedagogical knowledge in making innovative action research, an expert in making lesson plan, doing contextualized MTB-MLE program, and ensure that you will be future leaders as principals, department heads, supervisors and schools division superintendent in the Department of Education. For those who are enrolled in Secondary Education, the Senior faculty of the university which most of them are associate professors and professors have all the expertise in the field of Social Studies, Sciences, Mathematics, Filipino, English, and Physical Education. to contribute to a knowledge-based society.

Finally, the Bachelor of Technology and Livelihood Education (BTLED) and Bachelor of Technical Vocational Teacher Education (BTVTEd) provide the best education in the field of industrial research imbued with teaching competence in technological development particularly in electronic technology with emphasis on a digital utility model.

In the continuing quest for academic excellence, the college continues to achieve global recognition in the teacher education program not only as Center of Development, ISO Certified, Level IV (Phase 2) accreditation but also with a high passing mark of 90 percent of the elementary and secondary programs for first takers for almost five years now. The college is no longer behind in achieving quality and excellence for the post-graduate programs. The current educational reforms that we are doing with the support of the high faculty profile and doctorate holders have been emerging to be the competitive graduate programs that can deliver what is expected to be globally competitive graduates.

It has been established to develop the graduate students to critically and innovatively think as effective managers in the field of educational management. The post-advanced education has been changing its graduate education These are the expected graduate education outcomes that you will be able to achieve for PQF Level 8 (for MA programs) and 9 (for Doctorate program). We have the best graduate faculty to engage in professional development and creative works. perspectives to achieve a globally recognized university. Likewise, the ISO mantra provides us the compassion to genuinely serve beyond our calling. Wherein we are committed to provide excellent services towards the development of competitive graduates for the total satisfaction of the stakeholders. Our COD response for quality and excellence contributed to the LEVEL IV status which continuously demonstrates excellent performance in advanced education in the areas of instruction, research and publication, extension and linkages, and institutional qualifications.

ACKNOWLEDGMENTS

This is to acknowledge the academic contributions of the ever-committed, dedicated, compassionate, and resilient faculty members of the undergraduate and graduate programs whose professional competence in the teacher education program has inspired their students to work hard and maintain an average BLEPT rating of more than 80 percent for the last five years. (2015-2019) .

The *taktak* UNP branding of the College of Teacher Education (CTE) graduates has been admired by the teacher of the Department of Education and other Higher Education Institutions for their professional productivity in dealing with all the basic education affairs. The feedbacks coming from the employer have shown their high regards in the implementation of the Pedagogical, Technological, Content Knowledge in the mainstream of the basic education program.

The CTE faculty members are the purveyors of the pinnacle of success in the articulation, innovation, and compassion in the delivery of the 21st-century skills of the Teacher Education Program. Likewise, the hard-working CTE faculty has been engrossed with so many academic tasks (Level IV accreditation, ISO Certification, COPC, Institutional Accreditation, etc.) that almost impossible to finish are always able to deliver with exemplary performance

In the name of academic excellence and global competitiveness, let this acknowledgment represents all the blueprints of the book publications for the College of Teacher Education, University of Northern Philippines... to recognize and showcase the genuine meaning of professional competence, commitment, and dedication in the Teacher Education Program....

Chapter 1
Overview of the Accomplishments in Academic Excellence and International Linkages of the Colleges of Teacher Education, University of Northern Philippines

The College of Teacher Education (CTE) has been designated as the Center of Development for Teacher Education Program per (CMO No 17, Series of 2016). This recognition has paved the way for the CTE to be a potent catalyst for world class scholarships, best practices, innovative curriculum, research and extension and professional development in the Teacher Education program.

The University of Northern Philippines has been granted a Registration Certificate by the AJA Registrars (now SOCOTECH) and registered against the requirements of ISO 9001:2015. The scope of registration includes the provision of tertiary education services in the **College of Teacher Education** covering the admission and enrollment process of promotion and conferment of degrees. The certification is valid from December 5, 2018, to December 6, 2021. The college was also awarded a GRANT of FOUR MILLION PESOS under CMO No. 33, S. 2016 in the K to 12 Transition Program, for the engagement entitled: Sustaining Academic Excellence in the Teacher Education Program through Inclusive Education and Sustainable Development

I. CHED Quality Assurance of the Teacher Education Programs

Based on the guidelines for the implementation of CMO No. 46 s. 2012, the Policies, Standards and Guidelines for the Teacher Education program implements the "shift to learning competency-based standards/outcomes-based education in response to the 21st Century Philippine Teacher Education framework.

The learning outcomes of the teacher education are the following:
a. Articulate the rootedness of education in philosophical, socio-cultural historical, psychological and political contexts.
b. Demonstrate mastery of subject matter/discipline.
c. Facilitate learning using a wide range of teaching methodologies and delivery modes appropriate to specific learners and their environments.
d. Develop innovative curricula, instructional plans, teaching approaches, and resources to diverse learners.
e. Apply skills in the development and utilization of ICT to promote quality, relevant and sustainable educational practices.

f. Demonstrate a variety of thinking skills in planning, monitoring, assessing and reporting learning processes and outcomes.

g. Practice professional and ethical teaching standards sensitive to the local, national and global realities.

h. Pursue lifelong learning to personal and professional growth through varied experiential and field-based opportunities.

The Teacher Education graduates have the common standard learning outcomes under the Philippine Qualification Frameworks (PQF) :

a. Articulate and discuss the latest developments in the specific field of practice (PQF level 6 descriptor)

b. Effectively communicate in English and Filipino both orally and in writing.

c. Work effectively and collaboratively with a substantial degree of independence in multi-disciplinary and multi-cultural teams (PQF level 6 descriptor)

d. Act in recognition of professional, social and ethical responsibility.

e. Preserve and promote "Filipino historical and cultural heritage" based on (RA 7722)

II. Undergraduate Programs of the Teacher Education

This is anchored on the Undergraduate degree programs in the Philippines are located in Level VI of the Philippine Qualifications Framework (https://pqf.gov.ph/Home/Details/16) Their graduates must be able to demonstrate broad and coherent knowledge and skills in their field of study for professional work; apply their knowledge in professional/creative work or research in a specialized field of discipline and/or further study; and be able to work with a substantial degree of independence and or/in teams of individuals in related fields with minimal supervision.

Apart from acquiring undergraduate degrees, passing the licensure examination is an additional PQF Level VI requirement for graduates of disciplines regulated by the Professional Regulation Commission. Without a license, such graduates are not eligible to work in their chosen regulated profession in the Philippines although their baccalaureate degree may qualify them for employment in related professions or in the same profession in countries that do not require a professional license.

The undergraduate degree programs have the following descriptions and specifications:

A. Elementary Education Programs (General Education, Early Childhood Education and Special Needs)

This undergraduate teacher education program is designed to prepare individuals intending to teach in the elementary level for General Education, Early Childhood Education and Special Needs. It aims to develop highly motivated and competent teachers specializing in the content and pedagogy for elementary education.

The BEEd program also draws from various disciplines (allied fields) like social sciences, science, math, technology, languages, and humanities to ensure that he graduates have a multi-disciplinary preparation in content and pedagogy. After successful completion of all academic requirements of the degree/program graduates of BEEd should be able to practice the teaching profession in the elementary level.

1. Bachelor of Elementary Education (BEEd-CMO No. 74 Series of 2017))

This undergraduate teacher education program is designed to prepare individuals intending to teach in the elementary level for General Education, Early Childhood Education and Special Needs. It aims to develop highly motivated and competent teachers specializing in the content and pedagogy for elementary education.

The specific program outcomes of the Elementary Education are the following:

    a. Demonstrate in-depth understanding of the diversity of learners in various learning areas.

    b. Manifest meaningful and comprehensive pedagogical content knowledge (PCK) of the different subject areas.

    c. Utilize appropriate assessment and evaluation tools to measure learning outcomes.

    d. Manifest skills in communication, higher order thinking and use of tools and technology to accelerate learning and teaching.

    e. Demonstrate positive attributes of a model teacher both as an individual and as a professional.

    f. Manifest a desire to continuously pursue personal and professional development

2. Bachelor of Early Childhood Education (BECEd-CMO No. 76 Series of 2017)

The BECEd is a four-year program. Specifically, this program provides students with fundamental understanding and application of the principles of early childhood care and education, as well as experience in the application of these principles. It is designed to prepare students for teaching and supporting young children's development. A broad range of employment opportunities are available by fulfilling the degree requirements. Completion of the appropriate program will qualify graduates for employment in government or private institutions.

The specific program outcomes of the Early Childhood Education are the following:

a. Demonstrate high level of content and pedagogical knowledge.
b. Demonstrate appreciation for diversity.
c. Manifest collaborative skills.
d. Demonstrate innovative thinking skills.
e. Possess critical and problem-solving skills.
f. Advocate for children's

3. Bachelor of Special Needs Education-Generalists (BEEd-CMO No. 77 Series of 2017)

The BSNEd program prepares teachers who will instruct and manage students with additional needs in inclusive and segregated educational settings its graduates will be equipped to teach the basic education curriculum and alternate curricula depending on the needs of the students. Those who will teach in the elementary level will be trained across different subject areas. Those who will teach in the secondary level will provide educational support to students with additional needs in inclusive classrooms or provide educational services to students who may be enrolled in special education centers.

A graduate of this degree program should be able to teach in regular and special education schools education schools as a teacher provided that he/she passes the Licensure Examination for Teachers in his/her subject area of specialization. After completion of all academic requirements of the program, graduates of Bachelor of Special Needs Education (BSNEd) should be able to practice the teaching profession in the field of Special Needs Education.

Graduates of the Generalist BSNEd may be employed in special education centers/ clinics as special education teachers, therapists, or clinicians. They can also work in regular schools that practice inclusion as learning support staff and as special education teachers.

B. Secondary Education Programs

The Bachelor of Secondary Education (BSEd) is an undergraduate teacher education program designed to equip learners with adequate and relevant competencies to teach in their chosen area of specialization in secondary level. It aims to develop highly motivated and competent teachers specializing in the content and pedagogy for secondary education.

1. **Bachelor of Secondary Education** (BSEd -CMO No. 75 Series of 2017)) major in English, Filipino, Mathematics, Sciences, and Social Studies.

The specific program outcomes in the different filed of specializations of the Secondary Education are the following:

1.1 Bachelor of Secondary Education major in English
   a) Possess broad knowledge of language and literature for effective learning.
   b) Use English as a glocal language in a multilingual context as it applies to the teaching of language and literature.
   c) Acquire extensive reading background in language, literature, and allied fields.
   d) Demonstrate proficiency in oral and written communication.
   e) Show competence in employing innovative language and literature teaching approaches, methodologies, and strategies.
   f) Use technology in facilitating language learning and teaching.
   g) Inspire students and colleagues to lead relevant and transformative changes to improve learning and teaching language and literature.
   h) Display skills and abilities to be a reflective and research-oriented language and literature teacher.

1.2 Bachelor of Secondary Education major in Filipino

a) Nagpapamalas ng mataaas na antas ng kaalaman sa pagtuturo ng wika at panitikang Filipino.

b) Nagpapakita ng malawak at malalim nap ag-umawa at kaalaman sa ugnayan ng wika, kultura, at lipunan.

c) Nakakagamit ng iba'tibang kasanayan at kaalaman sa proseso ng pagtututro-pagkatuto.

d) Nagtataglay ng kaalaman hinggil sa usapin ng kultural at linggwistikong dibersidad ng bansa.

e) Nakapagididisenyo ng malikhain, inobatibo, at integratibong mga alternatibong dulog sa pagtuturo at pagkatuto.

f) Nakagagawa ng pananaliksik ukol sa ikauunlad ng wikang Filipino bilang wikang panturo.

1.3 Bachelor of Secondary Education major in Mathematics

a) Exhibit competence in mathematical concepts and procedures.

b) Exhibit proficiency in relating mathematics to other curricular areas.

c) Manifest meaningful and comprehensive pedagogical content knowledge (PCK) of mathematics.

d) Demonstrate competence in designing, constructing and utilizing different forms of assessment in mathematics.

e) Demonstrate proficiency in problem-solving by solving and creating routine and non-routine problems with different levels of complexity.

f) Use effectively appropriate approaches, methods, and techniques in teaching mathematics including technological tools.

g) Appreciate mathematics as an opportunity for creative work, moments of enlightenment, discovery and gaining insights of the world.

1.4 Bachelor of Secondary Education major in Science

a) Demonstrate deep understanding of scientific concepts and principle.

b) Apply scientific inquiry in teaching and learning.

c) Utilize effective science teaching and assessment methods

1.5 Bachelor of Secondary Education major in Social Studies

a) Utilize appropriate various socio-cultural and historical materials in explaining current issues.

b) Organize communities towards self-reliance and self-sufficiency

c) Demonstrate leadership skills that will help in teaching or training students who will empower their communities.

d) Integrate local and global perspectives in teaching the principle of the common good.
e) Employ principles of sustainable development in teaching and learning.
f) Show scholarship in research and further learning.
g) Display the qualities of an innovative teacher who was has mastery of the subject matter.

C. Industrial Education (Technical-Vocational Education Programs)

Quality pre-service teacher education is a key factor in the quality of Philippine education. In the Philippines, the pre-service preparation of teachers is a very important function and responsibility that has been assigned to higher education institutions. All efforts to improve the quality of education in the Philippines are dependent on the service of teachers who are properly prepared to undertake the various important roles and functions of teachers. As such, it is of utmost importance that the highest standards are set in defining the objectives, components, and processes of the pre-service technical teacher education curriculum.

Based on CMO No.79, Series of 2017, the Bachelor of Science in Industrial Education has migrated to the Bachelor of Technical-Vocational Teacher Education (BTVTEd) and Bachelor of Technology Livelihood Education.(BTVLEd).

Bachelor of Technical-Vocational Teacher Education (BTVTEd) with Specialization in Electronic Technology, Civil and Construction Technology, Food and Service Management and Garments, Fashion and Design.

The main concern of the BTVTEd program is the preparation of teachers in TLE for Grade 9-10, senior high school for the Technical-Vocational Livelihood (TVL) track, Technical-Vocational Education and Training (TVET) and for Higher Education Institutions offering BTVTEd and other allied programs.

This group of teacher is equipped not only with strong theoretical understanding of teaching and technology, but also with practical exposure in industry. Specifically, the BTVTEd Program is expected to produce teachers who can assume the following major roles:

a) Effective synthesizers of organized knowledge to allow analytical and critical thinking.
b) Efficient and effective promoters and facilitators.
c) Committed humanist whose clear understanding and appreciation of human ideals and values inspire learners to realize their potential.
d) Model teachers with high regard for learning imbued with proper work attitude and values as practiced in industry.
e) Nationally certified trainers in their field of specialization.
f) Implementers of TVTE innovative approaches/insights , best practices in the context f K-12 TVL Track.

II. Graduate Programs for the Teacher Education

The Graduate Education has the CHED Policy Standards guidelines that constitute a level or stage of academic work that is considered an advanced program of study.

It is focused on a particular or interdisciplinary academic discipline or profession and involves certain objectives :
1) rigorous evaluation of work and interaction with professors and peers;
2) professional experience via internships, teaching, and research; and
3) production of original research or creative work. (RCW)

Across all orientations and levels of graduate work, the ultimate goal is to contribute to the process of knowledge acquisition, generation, sharing, and exchange Its outcome is the mastery of a specialized field of study, the development of original and critical thinking, and the demonstration of problem-solving skills that prepares the holder of the degree for advanced instruction and leadership positions in the areas of research, creative work, as well as the practice of his or her profession. Thus, the CTE graduate students are trained to engage in the instructional development materials that will be contributed to the knowledge-based society which is expected to share the best practices and innovative ideas to enhance the school programs.

It is expected the theory-based educational leadership of the graduate programs is applied The leadership potentials are harnessed by the theory-driven management that applied to real-life situations with the educational outcome to introduce new management styles.The graduate students are mainly trained on educational researches that endowed to produce the development of new ideas that can be published in refereed journals.

It is expected in the MA programs that you will be able to achieve PQF Level 7 Descriptor that would demand the following from graduate students:

1) Advance knowledge and skills in a specialized, interdisciplinary, or multidisciplinary field of study for professional practice;
2) Self-directed research;
3) Lifelong learning with a highly substantial degree of independence that involves individual work or teams of interdisciplinary or multidisciplinary experts in the field; and
4) Application of these skills in research, professional, or creative work

III. International Linkages and Consortia for the Teacher Education Program in the Foreign Universities and Foundations

The College of Teacher Education was able to sustain the international linkages that have significant program outcomes in the areas of twinning agreement on research and facilitation of teacher education experiences. It has a significant educational impact on the stakeholders' adoption of the best practices of educational administration along with language proficiency, cultural diversity, pedagogical practices, and 21st-century education. The program outcomes in the vertical articulation of the graduate and undergraduate programs in teacher education resulted in the award of the Center of Development and paradigm shift of documentation process under the ISO 9001: 2015.

The university mainly supports the education programs through the Center for International Studies in the Blended Education System for Foreign Students as approved by the UNP Board Resolution No. 19, s.2012. This is CHED compliant advanced education program with customized EdD programs for foreign students who hold high positions in the national and local government agencies as well as private entities. The complementation process of the Blended Education System integrates the international linkages and partnerships with the support of the Romchatra Foundation with the academic exchange program connected with the Maritime Silk Road Confucius

Institute through the ASEAN Universities. These have been the continuing academic exchange such as Tan Trao University, Suan Dusit University, and Rajamagala Universities of Thailand.

In the case of technical assistance on book publication, the Romchatra Foundation has a high level of educational impact in the relevant areas of Asian Culture, History and Tradition were five books published particularly in support with the Maritime Silk Road Confucius Institute disseminated in the ASEAN universities. The academic exchange provided a greater understanding of Confucian Philosophy, ASEAN Cultural Diversity, Chinese Culture and Tradition, Asian Economic, and Political Development. For the academic collaboration, it has the program outcome of the enhancement of academic collaboration by providing complimentary exchange and assistance in the different school activities.

These are the research presentation, lecture, and conferences provided by the different partner agencies that have contributed to the understanding of the cultural diversity, career development, and ASEAN integration particularly in the area of inclusivity of higher education program Finally, the academic visit and benchmarking highlighted the enhancement of the curricular support in the inclusion of higher education lesson on ASEAN integration, cultural and educational exchange, language proficiency program and another line of academic interest.

Furthermore, the implementation of the international linkages and partnership revolved in the presentation of the technical papers relevant to the cultural heritage and ASEAN Integration. The internationalization efforts of the education program provided the research utilization of the strategic opportunity of the location of the university to share the academic experience is the engineering structural conservation management of the UNESCO Heritage City of Vigan. It also presented an overview of the ASEAN Integration and Technology.

The College of Teacher Education) has the following objectives in networking, linkages, and consortia: (1) connect the graduate education program with a development partner in the academe, national government agencies, and the local government units in the international community ; (2) enable education programs on basic education, instructional competence, educational management and supervision, and others to become responsive to local and national thrusts through linkages in foreign countries; (3) benchmark standards (

local and international) for integration in the education programs in advanced higher education; and (5) transfer educational models through the product of research and linkages for the enhancement of the education program.

A. NATIONAL AWARDS ON ACADEMIC EXCELLENCE AND QUALITY ASSURANCE CERTIFICATION

1. The College of Teacher Education was designated as **Center of Development** under CHED Memorandum Order No. 17, Series 2016.

2. **ISO- 9001: 2015 Certification Award** granted a Registration Certificate by the AJA Registrars (now SOCOTECH) and registered against the requirements of ISO 9001:2015. The scope of registration includes the provision of tertiary education services in the College of Teacher Education covering the admission and enrollment process of promotion and conferment of degrees. The certification is valid from December 5, 2018, to December 6, 2021.

3. **"Sustaining Academic Excellence in the Teacher Education Program through Inclusive Education and Sustainable Development "**- Grantee under CMO No. 33, series of 2016 Approved Budget of P 4,000,000.00. This project with a budget of Php 4,000,000.00 would further assist the SUCs and HEIs in the province of Ilocos Sur to implement Teacher Education programs through inclusive education and sustainable development to enhance the basic education program. The general objective of the project is to sustain academic excellence and to cascade the best practices of the Teacher Education program anchored on inclusive education and sustainable development excellence in the Teacher Education Program in the province of Ilocos Sur.

B. National Topnotcher Awards

1. The 10th Placer in the 2016 Licensure Examination for Teachers (LET) as laudable achievement of Darigold P. Apopo (BSEd 2016- Magna Cum Laude). The only BSEd Topnotcher in Region I that exemplifies the excellent academic programs of BSEd major in Social Science including high percentage passing of Filipino, English, Mathematics and MAPEH.

2. Jonathan del Castillo, magna cum laude 2018 graduate of the Bachelor of Elementary education, major in Special Education has landed in the illustrious top 10 of the September 2018 Licensure for Licensure Examination for Teachers (BEEd Category) with a rating of 87.60%.

C. National and Regional Award

1. Plaque of Distinction Award for being the **Center of Development in Teacher Education** given by CHED Regional Office last 2016 Regional Higher Education Conference held at Fort Ilocandia, Laoag City last June 8, 2016.

2. **SUCTEA Award for the Center of Development**. The College of Teacher Education (CTE) has been designated as the Center of Development for Teacher Education Program per (CMO No 17, Series of 2016). This recognition has paved the way for the CTE to be a potent catalyst for world-class scholarships, best practices, innovative curriculum, research and extension, and professional development in the Teacher Education program.

3. **National Award for Graduate Cultural Education** and **Sentro ng Wika** for the Graduate Diploma for Cultural Education accredited by the Philippine Cultural Education of NCCA.

D. International Awards for Linkages and Collaboration

1. **ASEAN Internship Academy Award** for its invaluable partnership it has forged to implement CHED's Students Internship Abroad Program in Thailand by the ASEAN Internship Academy (October 9, 2017)

2. **Student Exchange Tan Trao Award** for the Student Internship Program awarded by the Tan Trao University, Vietnam .In partnership with the UNP Center for International Studies, the College of Teacher Education accepted ten students from the Tan Trao University for exposure on May 5-30, 2017. The students were accompanied by their professor. They were exposed to the CTE Best Practices in classroom instruction, co-curriculum activities, extra-curricular activities, extension, and lectures on orthography and culture heritage. The said Vietnamese students underwent a rigid selection process so that the best 10 excellent

students were sent to the UNP-CTE to undergo the May 5-30, 2017 exposure.

3. **Romchatra Foundation Award for** Traimit Educational Model. The Romchatra Foundation through Phromomankachalan has expanded the international linkages of the UNP to be a partner of the academic publications including cultural exchange activities under Hanban that recognized the effort of the CTE to bring the forefront of scholarly publication through the ASEAN Community. The forging of agreement on Academic and cultural collaboration with the assistance of the Center of International Studies became the Best Practices of International linkages on Academic and Cultural Exchange program through the Confucius Maritime Silk Road of the Romchatra Foundation.

4. **SEAMEO-SEA Teacher Award for Student Internship**. The University of Northern Philippines implemented the twinning student exchange program for their academic exposures with extra-curricular activities, cultural heritage experiences in the UNESCO Heritage City of Vigan. The participating Foreign Universities for the Pre-service Student Teachers Exchange Program in Southeast Asia.
    1. Indonesia University of Education (UPI), Bandung Indonesia
    2. Sebelas Maret University (UNS), Surukarta, Indonesia,
    3.Nakon S. Thammarat Rajabhat (NSTRU), Thammarat,Thailand
    4. Buriram Rajabhat University (BRU), Buriram University

IV. Educational Reforms in Achieving Academic Excellence

Based on the trending analysis of the Licensure Examination of Teachers (LET), the college has been implementing innovative practices and admission policies to ensure the support of the Center of Development. The College of Teacher Education (CTE) has been designated as the Center of Development for Teacher Education Program per (CMO No 17, Series of 2016). This recognition has paved the way for the CTE to be a potent catalyst for world-class scholarships, best practices, innovative curriculum, research and extension, and professional development in the Teacher Education program.

The instructional recognition must be addressed to the current needs to put curricular and policy reform for the learning management to ensure the increasing trend analysis for the Licensure Examination for Teachers (LET). The research findings have been the basis to enhance the academic reforms to support the Center of Development granted in 2016.

These were the considerations for the academic policies based on the empirical result of the previous research on academic performance and the result of the Licensure Examinations since 2016:

1. All of the cum laude graduates (An average of 50 Graduates every year for the last four years from 2016-2019) have successfully passed the Licensure Board Examination for Teachers.

2. Those who passed in the TAT and with high average grades in their professional, major, and general education subjects were successful graduates who passed the licensure examination.

3. The College Admission Test (CAT) and Teaching Aptitude Test (TAT) found out to be significantly related in passing the Licensure Examination for Teachers:

It can be noted that all the personal profile of the graduates significantly correlates with LET performance. This means that the respondents who obtained higher UNP- CAT rating, TAT result, practicum performance, and those who attended the LET review classes tend to perform better in the LET. This implies that these variables contribute significantly to the success of graduates in taking the LET.

1. This supports the findings of Bañez and Pardo (2016) who found that UNP-CAT score and attendance in LET review classes significantly correlate with LET performance. (Rabanal and Manzano, 2018)
2. The general average in the LET of all the batches of the BEEd graduates shows a passing performance. The passing performance in the LET of the BEEd graduates is an indication of a relatively strong foundation in both the general and professional education courses. This further implies that the faculty who handled these courses were able to impart the essential knowledge and develop the necessary skills among these graduates. (Rabanal and Manzano, 2018)

Based on the conclusions established in the studies of the Licensure Examination for Teachers, the following recommendations are made: (Rabanal and Manzano, 2018)

(1) The university may consider intensifying its admission and retention policies to admit only the most qualified students.

(2) An enhancement and an intensive review program may be undertaken to better prepare graduates for the licensure examination.

(3) The university may consider reviewing the teacher education curriculum to include varied professional development activities as well as the specialization courses to better prepare the graduates for the licensure examination.

Based on the recommendations from the empirical studies of academic performance and results of the Licensure Examination for Teacher implemented the academic reforms for the admission policies in School Year 2016-2017 to sustain the grant of Center of Development in the Teacher Education:

1. The admission and retention policies admitted only the most qualified applicants based on the required of 78 percent for the College Admission Test and passing of the Teaching Aptitude Tests (TAT)

2. The LET intensive review program has been a part of the better preparation of the BEEd graduates. The local LET review was conducted by the senior faculty who were national reviewers in CBRC and the national topnotcher of the LET Edmar Paguirigan (8th Placer, 2014). In addition to this local review, the Memorandum of Agreement was signed by the Carl Balita Review Centers (CBRC) to conduct the intensive review for the graduates.

3. The varied professional activities in the Teacher Education program such as the active participation of the professional organizations of SUCTEA and other teacher education organizations contribution to the enhancement of the pedagogical skills of the faculty members.

4. The international linkage exposures for the ASEAN countries particularly Romchatra Foundation widened the horizon of educational training of the students. It embarked on the participation of the Student Exchange Programs and Student Internship Abroad in the foreign universities and SEAMEO has given the opportunity to enhance the content knowledge and experiential learnings of the students.

5. The Center of Development provided the opportunity to get additional funding for the action research capability building and other in-service training of the Fiduciary Funds of the college.

As a result of the substantial accomplishments in the academic activities through the admission policies on College Admission Tests (CAT), Teaching Aptitude Test (TAT), Student Internship Abroad, Student Exchange Program, SEA Teacher, INSET SUCTEA participation, CHED external fund, and Local Review and collaboration with the CBRC, the college achieved the highest licensure examination performance of the elementary education in 2019 with the present administration of President Erwin Cadorna in achieving the Agenda Goal No. 1. Develop ethical leaders through academic excellence with the strategic direction for the ethical leaders through academic excellence adopted the systems-based approach in teaching and training students to become innovators and ethical leaders for tomorrow.

With the continuing academic reforms and policy implementation of quality and excellence, the College of Teacher Education has achieved its highest LET rating of 92.38 for first-time takers with a national passing rate of 31.34. Surprisingly, the elementary education graduates surpassed the LET passers of the SUCs offering Teacher Education Program (The Center of Excellence -MMSU, DMMSU, and PSU)The administration of President Erwin Cadorna immediately achieved the ethical leaders through academic excellence that surpasses the SUCs offering Teacher Education in the whole Region I:

The College of Teacher Education submitted the accomplishment report (December 2, 2019) of the Board Licensure Examination for Professional Teachers (BLEPT) conducted last September 2019 for the Bachelor of Elementary Education:

The performance of the elementary, secondary, and industrial education to appreciate the academic impact of the innovations and reforms conducted by the college for the last four years (2016-2019) in academic admission, maintain quality and excellence in the Teacher Education program.

This justifies the existence of the Center of Development for Teacher Education Program per (CMO No 17, Series of 2016) as the potent catalyst for world-class scholarships, best practices, innovative curriculum, research and extension, and professional development in the Teacher Education program. The evidence-based LET for first-time takers provided the continuing quest to innovate academic programs and policies to support the higher education advocacy on quality and excellence.

V. Exemplary Accomplishments and Contributions in the Teacher Education Program

The College of Teacher Education was able to sustain the international linkages that have significant program outcomes in the areas of twinning agreement on research and facilitation of teacher education experiences. It has a significant educational impact on the stakeholders' adoption of the best practices of educational administration along with language proficiency, cultural diversity, pedagogical practices, and 21st-century education. The program outcomes in the vertical articulation of the graduate and undergraduate programs in teacher education resulted in the award of the Center of Development and paradigm shift of documentation process under the ISO 9001: 2015.

The university mainly supports the education programs through the Center for International Studies in the Blended Education System for Foreign Students as approved by the UNP Board Resolution No. 19, s.2012. This is CHED compliant advanced education program with customized EdD programs for foreign students who hold high positions in the national and local government agencies as well as private entities. The complementation process of the Blended Education System integrates the international linkages and partnerships with the support of the Romchatra Foundation with the academic exchange program connected with the Maritime Silk Road Confucius Institute through the ASEAN Universities. These have been the continuing academic exchange such as Tan Trao University, Suan Dusit University, and Rajamagala Universities of Thailand.

In the case of technical assistance on book publication, the Romchatra Foundation has a high level of educational impact in the relevant areas of Asian Culture, History and Tradition were five books published particularly in support with the Maritime Silk Road Confucius Institute disseminated in the ASEAN universities. The academic exchange provided a greater understanding of Confucian Philosophy, ASEAN Cultural Diversity, Chinese Culture and Tradition, Asian Economic, and Political Development. For the academic collaboration, it has the program outcome of the enhancement of academic collaboration by providing complimentary exchange and assistance in the different school activities.

These are the research presentation, lecture, and conferences provided by the different partner agencies that have contributed to the understanding of the cultural diversity, career development, and ASEAN integration particularly in the area of inclusivity of higher education program Finally, the academic visit and benchmarking highlighted the enhancement of the curricular support in the inclusion of higher education lesson on ASEAN integration, cultural and educational exchange, language proficiency program and another line of academic interest.

Furthermore, the implementation of the international linkages and partnership revolved in the presentation of the technical papers relevant to the cultural heritage and ASEAN Integration. The internationalization efforts of the education program provided the research utilization of the strategic opportunity of the location of the university to share the academic experience is the engineering structural conservation management of the UNESCO Heritage City of Vigan. It also presented an overview of the ASEAN Integration and Technology.

The College of Teacher Education) has the following objectives in networking, linkages, and consortia: (1) connect the graduate education program with a development partner in the academe, national government agencies, and the local government units in the international community ; (2) enable education programs on basic education, instructional competence, educational management and supervision, and others to become responsive to local and national thrusts through linkages in foreign countries; (3) benchmark standards (local and international) for integration in the education programs in advanced higher education; and (5) transfer educational models through the product of research and linkages for the enhancement of the education program.

4. NATIONAL AWARDS ON ACADEMIC EXCELLENCE AND QUALITY ASSURANCE CERTIFICATION

1. The College of Teacher Education was designated as **Center of Development** under CHED Memorandum Order No. 17, Series 2016.

2. **ISO- 9001: 2015 Certification Award** granted a Registration Certificate by the AJA Registrars (now SOCOTECH) and registered against the requirements of ISO 9001:2015. The scope of registration includes the provision of tertiary education services in the College of Teacher Education covering the admission and enrollment process of promotion and conferment of degrees. The certification is valid from December 5, 2018, to December 6, 2021.

3. **"Sustaining Academic Excellence in the Teacher Education Program through Inclusive Education and Sustainable Development"**- Grantee under CMO No. 33, series of 2016 Approved Budget of P 4,000,000.00. This project with a budget of Php 4,000,000.00 would further assist the SUCs and HEIs in the province of Ilocos Sur to implement Teacher Education programs through inclusive education and sustainable development to enhance the basic education program. The general objective of the project is to sustain academic excellence and to cascade the best practices of the Teacher Education program anchored on inclusive education and sustainable development excellence in the Teacher Education Program in the province of Ilocos Sur.

4. National Topnotcher Awards

a) The 10th Placer in the 2016 Licensure Examination for Teachers (LET) as laudable achievement of Darigold P. Apopo (BSEd 2016- Magna Cum Laude). The only BSEd Topnotcher in Region I that exemplifies the excellent academic programs of BSEd major in Social Science including high percentage passing of Filipino, English, Mathematics, and MAPEH.

b) Jonathan del Castillo, magna cum laude 2018 graduate of the Bachelor of Elementary education, major in Special Education has landed in the illustrious top 10 of the September 2018 Licensure for Licensure Examination for Teachers (BEEd Category) with a rating of 87.60%.

5. National and Regional Award

a) Plaque of Distinction Award for being the **Center of Development in Teacher Education** given by CHED Regional Office last 2016 Regional Higher Education Conference held at Fort Ilocandia, Laoag City last June 8, 2016.

b) **SUCTEA Award for the Center of Development.** The College of Teacher Education (CTE) has been designated as the Center of Development for Teacher Education Program per (CMO No 17, Series of 2016). This recognition has paved the way for the CTE to be a potent catalyst for world-class scholarships, best practices, innovative curriculum, research and extension, and professional development in the Teacher Education program.

c) **National Award for Graduate Cultural Education** and **Sentro ng Wika** for the Graduate Diploma for Cultural Education accredited by the Philippine Cultural Education of NCCA.

6. International Awards for Linkages and Collaboration

a) **ASEAN Internship Academy Award** for its invaluable partnership it has forged to implement CHED's Students Internship Abroad Program in Thailand by the ASEAN Internship Academy (October 9, 2017)

b) **Student Exchange Tan Trao Award** for the Student Internship Program awarded by the Tan Trao University, Vietnam. In partnership with the UNP Center for International Studies, the College of Teacher Education accepted ten students from the Tan Trao University for exposure on May 5-30, 2017. The students were accompanied by their professor. They were exposed to the CTE Best Practices in classroom instruction, co-curriculum activities, extra-curricular activities, extension, and lectures on orthography and culture heritage. The said Vietnamese students underwent a rigid selection process so that the best 10 excellent students were sent to the UNP-CTE to undergo the May 5-30, 2017 exposure

c) **Romchatra Foundation Award for** Traimit Educational Model. The Romchatra Foundation through Phromomankachalan has expanded the international linkages of the UNP to be a partner of the academic publications including cultural exchange activities under Hanban that recognized the effort of the CTE to bring the forefront of scholarly publication through the ASEAN Community. The forging of agreement on Academic and cultural collaboration with the assistance of the Center of International Studies became the Best Practices of International linkages on Academic and Cultural Exchange program through the Confucius Maritime Silk Road of the Romchatra Foundation.

d) **SEAMEO-SEA Teacher Award for Student Internship.** The University of Northern Philippines implemented the twinning student exchange program for their academic exposures with extra-curricular activities, cultural heritage experiences in the UNESCO Heritage City of Vigan. The participating Foreign Universities for the Pre-service Student Teachers Exchange Program in Southeast Asia.
   (1) Indonesia University of Education (UPI), Bandung Indonesia
   (2) Sebelas Maret University (UNS), Surukarta, Indonesia,
   (3).Nakon S. Thammarat Rajabhat (NSTRU), Thammarat, Thailand
   (4) Buriram Rajabhat University (BRU), Buriram University

IV. Educational Reforms in Achieving Academic Excellence

Based on the trending analysis of the Licensure Examination of Teachers (LET), the college has been implementing innovative practices and admission policies to ensure the support of the Center of Development. The College of Teacher Education (CTE) has been designated as the Center of Development for Teacher Education Program per (CMO No 17, Series of 2016). This recognition has paved the way for the CTE to be a potent catalyst for world-class scholarships, best practices, innovative curriculum, research and extension, and professional development in the Teacher Education program.

The instructional recognition must be addressed to the current needs to put curricular and policy reform for the learning management to ensure the increasing trend analysis for the Licensure Examination for Teachers (LET). The research findings have been the basis to enhance the academic reforms to support the Center of Development granted in 2016.

These were the considerations for the academic policies based on the empirical result of the previous research on academic performance and the result of the Licensure Examinations since 2016:

1. All of the cum laude graduates (An average of 50 Graduates every year for the last four years from 2016-2019) have successfully passed the Licensure Board Examination for Teachers.

2. Those who passed in the TAT and with high average grades in their professional, major, and general education subjects were successful graduates who passed the licensure examination.

3. The College Admission Test (CAT) and Teaching Aptitude Test (TAT) found out to be significantly related in passing the Licensure Examination for Teachers:

It can be noted that all the personal profile of the graduates significantly correlates with LET performance. This means that the respondents who obtained higher UNP- CAT rating, TAT result, practicum performance, and those who attended the LET review classes tend to perform better in the LET. This implies that these variables contribute significantly to the success of graduates in taking the LET.

1. This supports the findings of Bañez and Pardo (2016) who found that UNP-CAT score and attendance in LET review classes significantly correlate with LET performance. (Rabanal and Manzano, 2018)

2. The general average in the LET of all the batches of the BEEd graduates shows a passing performance. The passing performance in the LET of the BEEd graduates is an indication of a relatively strong foundation in both the general and professional education courses. This further implies that the faculty who handled these courses were able to impart the essential knowledge and develop the necessary skills among these graduates. (Rabanal and Manzano, 2018)

Based on the conclusions established in the studies of the Licensure Examination for Teachers, the following recommendations are made: (Rabanal and Manzano, 2018)

(1) The university may consider intensifying its admission and retention policies to admit only the most qualified students.

(2) An enhancement and an intensive review program may be undertaken to better prepare graduates for the licensure examination.

(3) The university may consider reviewing the teacher education curriculum to include varied professional development activities as well as the specialization courses to better prepare the graduates for the licensure examination.

Based on the recommendations from the empirical studies of academic performance and results of the Licensure Examination for Teacher implemented the academic reforms for the admission policies in School Year 2016-2017 to sustain the grant of Center of Development in the Teacher Education:

1. The admission and retention policies admitted only the most qualified applicants based on the required of 78 percent for the College Admission Test and passing of the Teaching Aptitude Tests (TAT)

2. The LET intensive review program has been a part of the better preparation of the BEEd graduates. The local LET review was conducted by the senior faculty who were national reviewers in CBRC and the national topnotcher of the LET Edmar Paguirigan (8th Placer, 2014). In addition to this local review, the Memorandum of Agreement was signed by the Carl Balita Review Centers (CBRC) to conduct the intensive review for the graduates.

3. The varied professional activities in the Teacher Education program such as the active participation of the professional organizations of SUCTEA and other teacher education organizations contribution to the enhancement of the pedagogical skills of the faculty members.

4. The international linkage exposures for the ASEAN countries particularly Romchatra Foundation widened the horizon of educational training of the students. It embarked on the participation of the Student Exchange Programs and Student Internship Abroad in the foreign universities and SEAMEO has given the opportunity to enhance the content knowledge and experiential learnings of the students.

5. The Center of Development provided the opportunity to get additional funding for the action research capability building and other in-service training of the Fiduciary Funds of the college.

As a result of the substantial accomplishments in the academic activities through the admission policies on College Admission Tests (CAT), Teaching Aptitude Test (TAT), Student Internship Abroad, Student Exchange Program, SEA Teacher, INSET SUCTEA participation, CHED external fund, and Local Review and collaboration with the CBRC, the college achieved the highest licensure examination performance of the elementary education in 2019 with the present administration of President Erwin Cadorna in achieving the Agenda Goal No. 1. Develop ethical leaders through academic excellence with the strategic direction for the ethical leaders through academic excellence adopted the systems-based approach in teaching and training students to become innovators and ethical leaders for tomorrow.

With the continuing academic reforms and policy implementation of quality and excellence, the College of Teacher Education has achieved its highest LET rating of 92.38 for first-time takers with a national passing rate of 31.34. Surprisingly, the elementary education graduates surpassed the LET passers of the SUCs offering Teacher Education Program (The Center of Excellence -MMSU, DMMSU, and PSU)The administration of President Erwin Cadorna immediately achieved the ethical leaders through academic excellence that surpasses the SUCs offering Teacher Education in the whole Region I:

The College of Teacher Education submitted the accomplishment report (December 2, 2019) of the Board Licensure Examination for Professional Teachers (BLEPT) conducted last September 2019 for the Bachelor of Elementary Education:

> *The performance of the elementary, secondary, and industrial education to appreciate the academic impact of the innovations and reforms conducted by the college for the last four years (2016-2019) in academic admission, maintain quality and excellence in the Teacher Education program.*

Chapter 2
The International Linkages and Consortia in the Bachelor of Elementary Education Program: An Executive Summary

The College of Teacher Education for Bachelor of Elementary Education (BEEd) implemented the international linkages and partnership in response to the teacher education program on the academic excellence on the faculty and students' exchange program, international conferences research collaboration, book publication, socio-cultural ASEAN integration, cultural diversity (MTB-MLE), other basic education programs. The internationalization efforts of the education program provided the research utilization of the strategic opportunity of the location of the university to share the academic experience is the engineering structural conservation management of the UNESCO Heritage City of Vigan. It also presented an overview of the ASEAN Integration and Technology.

These sustained international linkages and consortia provide the academic excellence in the BEEd program that consequently granted the Center of Development in the College of Teacher Education. The international best practices became a world-class engagement to become a potent catalyst of the professional and academic development in the elementary education program.

1. It has fully been realized by supporting culture-based education. With the foundation of the MTB-MLE and academic collaboration of the SEAMEO for the young children (Kindergarten to Grade 3 of the K to 12 enhanced curricula), and academic collaboration with the foreign universities in the ASEAN region.

2. It integrates the international linkages and partnerships with the support of the SEAMEO student exchange program, the Cultural Diversity, and the Experience of the primary school–future teachers of partner universities were also enhanced. Partnership with different ASEAN Schools such as Romchatra Foundation with the academic exchange program connected with the Maritime Silk Road Confucius Institute. Thus, ASEAN Universities had opened the eyes of one of our students to diversity by academic exchange and collaboration with Tan Trao University, Suan Dusit University, and Rajamagala Universities of Thailand.

In order to display the competence of faculty and pre-service teachers to promote high-quality learning outcomes, the BEEd program has established general objectives for the international linkages and consortia to connect the best practices in terms of MTB-MLE, Cultural Diversity, and Pedagogical knowledge relevant to the teaching-learning process in the ASEAN Education with the following relevant undertakings

1. *Facilitation of the in-country work experience in the Elementary Education Program for the ASEAN Schools.* The facilitation of the in-country work experience for faculty and students to teach in the ASEAN Schools in the best pedagogical and cultural diversity practice in the basic education program.

2. *Joint research and extension activities, lectures, workshops, fora, symposia, and seminars.* The international research and extension activity participated for the elementary education program on pedagogical knowledge, instructional assessment, cultural diversity under the socio-cultural education of the ASEAN Integration.

3. *Exchange of academic materials, scientific publications, and other relevant scholarly information.* The publications along the MTB-MLE and cultural diversity program in support of the UNESCO Heritage City of Vigan and Cultural Diversity program became the relevant academic materials such as ASEAN Integration, Traimit Model.

4. Confucius Classroom/Institute, and UNESCO Heritage Program. Co-operation in basic education program (Kindergarten and Elementary) on the : (1) promotion of staff and student exchanges. (2) the cooperation and collaboration activities in education deemed appropriate mutually beneficial to the foreign schools.

The sustained international linkages and partnerships along with the program outcome and impact of the Bachelor of Elementary Education along with academic collaboration, inter-country facilitation, research, and book publication in the ASEAN countries.

1. **Student Exchange Program from Tan Trao University, May 5-30, 2017 "A Taste of UNP Culture: The Vietnamese Faculty and Students in UNP"**

In partnership with the UNP Center for International Studies, the College of Teacher Education accepted ten students from the Tan Trao University for exposure on May 5-30, 2017. The students were accompanied by their professor. They were exposed to the CTE Best Practices in classroom instruction, co-curriculum activities, extra-curricular activities, extension, and lectures on orthography and culture heritage. The said Vietnamese students underwent a rigid selection process so that the best 10 excellent students were sent to the UNP-CTE to undergo the May 5-30, 2017 exposure.

The College of Teacher Education, the Bachelor of Elementary Education, had strengthened support on the Vietnamese Students' Exchange Program. Through this program, it showcased the many faces of Filipino hospitality and UNP's brand of globally competitive instruction, research, and extension. The Vietnamese Student Exchange Program was implemented with various academic activities in the teacher training which included classroom observations at the Laboratory Schools and the undergraduate courses; field exposures in agricultural and fishing communities; upland communities; program and various activities they were exposed to the rich Ilokano culture and language.

One of the Vietnamese Students wrote in her testimony on the Internship Report of the Student Exchange Program in the College of Teacher Education:

...Then I found out a bit of information about everything I see in the Philippines. Not only being an exchange student but also exchange knowledge and ideas. I think it was good for me when I get to know all things I like and want. Now I know a little bit about the culture of the country and people in the Philippines. I see that the Philippines is actually a beautiful country with all the helpful people and beautiful sights. UNP is a very perfect place to study research and expand my knowledge. And your place City of Vigan is also a worthy place to stay. So many feelings and emotions involved cannot explain through words. The place where I want to spend some more time...

Nguyen Ngoc Quynh (BEEd intern)

Furthermore, the College of Teacher Education (CTE) implemented the Vietnamese Students' Exchange Program with the support of the Center for International Studies with the program outcome in the international linkages to support the supervisory program for the teaching-learning process to enhance the experiential knowledge on cultural diversity and language development. The educational impact of the Vietnamese students' exchange program ensures the continuing support of the university officials of Tan Trao University to give more Vietnamese students and request that the CTE students and faculty would teach English proficiency program. It is also expected to continue giving priority of the student exchange program to be emerged in the CTE as to the best practices on educational administration by sending Vietnamese students' in the Tan Trao University, College of Education those are major in Primary School, Literature Education, and Environment Science to implement the twinning program.

2. The Potent Catalyst of the Emerging Research and International Collaboration with the Tan Trao University, Vietnam

The 1st International Conference at Tan Trao University became the potent Catalyst in the implementation of the academic collaboration and exchange which was started in May 2015 that continued the support of the College of Teacher Education. The international collaboration of Tan Trao University started the signing of Memorandum of Agreement (MOA) Between the University of Northern Philippines and Tan Trao University, Vietnam for Research Collaboration, Academic and Student Exchange Program on May 22, 2015.

The research studies presented in the 1st International Conference with the theme "Assessing Primary Students by Approaching and Evaluating their Competence A Possible Approach to Pedagogic Institutions in Vietnam and same Southeast Asian Countries:" were the following:

1. Implementation of the K to 12 programs in the Laboratory Schools of the College of Teacher Education, University of Northern Philippines

2. The Culture-Based Multidisciplinary Model of the Mother Tongue Based- Multilingual Education (MTB-MLE) of the Primary Schools in the Philippines

3. Interpersonal Conflict Management Style of Future Basic Education Teachers

4. Misconceptions in Astronomy of the Third Year Elementary Education Students, University of Northern Philippines

The program outcome of the 1st conference provided the opportunity to expand the twinning agreement on the teaching-learning process by the faculty and student exchange program that resulted in the crediting of the international linkage points for the application of the Center of Development in the field of teacher education. This was the reason that the evaluators of the CHED panel for the Center of Development consider the sustained international linkages of the College of Teacher Education.

The academic collaboration of Tan Trao University in the Doctor of Education program provided the continuing support of the International research presentations in the area of educational administration the supervision of the teaching-learning process. The Tan Trao University presented the 1st international Conference in Vietnam as an offshoot of the faculty exchange program of Suan Dusit University that supported this activity.

The rationale of the 1st conference adhered to the idea of Holistic Education. The university administration of Tan Trao supported this holistic education which has become a popular teaching and learning approach particularly for primary education in Western countries, but it may appear new to Vietnamese education and perhaps to some Southeast Asian countries. The key characteristics of *Holistic education* are instead of educating students with academic aspects only, the educator should see the student's development as a *'whole'*: hard skills (academic ability); soft skills (presentation, independence, critical thinking…)

The program outcome revolves around the benchmarking of the educational management adopted from the best practices of the Southeast Asian countries particularly the teacher education program that anchored on the policy research of the Blended Education program. The university officials of Tan Trao made mention of the program outcome of the academic collaboration in Vietnam that "Taking account from *Holistic education*, the 1st International Conference at Tan Trao University will raise the issue of whether we should assess students at primary level through exams and marks, or instead, students will be assessed by teachers' comments and evaluations about different skills and abilities at a particular time. The theme of the conference also focuses on the current assessment system of all students in general and primary students in particular in Vietnam and some southeast Asian countries.

This was held in Tuyen Quang, the former temporary capital of Vietnam in the resistance war against the French colony. Tuyen Quang has a complex history in both pre-modern and modern Vietnam which makes it "a place of history". Tan Trao University is also named towards a historical milestone. Tan Trao is a newly founded university, but it has attracted large numbers of young scholars, these staff is expected to be the key people in implementing and renovating what we learn from the conference.

It has shown in the academic collaboration of the Tan Trao University had given the opportunity to provide sustained practices, most especially in the early childhood teaching-learning process. The educational impact of the strong support of the CTE on the ideas and concepts of early childhood education the best practice of the teacher education program emerged the adoption of the twinning program in the student exchange program as deeply rooted by the research collaboration.

3. Student International Internship Program with the Technical Assistance of Romchatra Foundation

The College of Teacher had been supporting the Student International Internship Program through the assistance of the Center for International Studies and Romchatra Foundation by forging an agreement for the Student Exchange Program in Thailand and Vietnam. The Student International Internship Program is designed to expose the Bachelor of Elementary Education (BEEd) interns to foreign schools, particularly in the ASEAN schools.

The BEEd program outcomes and impact had ensured the common sharing of academic resources in the implementation of international conferences and academic collaboration in the student exchange program. The international conferences emerged as the first sustainable academic collaboration that provided the opportunity for Tan Trao University to adopt the best practices in the field of educational administration, teaching process, evaluation and assessment of learning, language proficiency, and implementation of the MTB-MLE. The sustained impact of the twinning agreement defined more on the expertise of the University of Northern Philippines to act as host in the Student Exchange Program for the Vietnamese students with qualitative impact of the experiential learning about cultural diversity, language proficiency, teaching-learning process, and understanding the culture of the Filipinos.

On the other hand, the College of Teacher Education was able to sustain the international linkages particularly in the career development have significant program outcomes in the areas of twinning agreement on research and facilitation of teacher education experiences. The program outcomes of the international linkages have been focused on the best practices of educational administration along with language proficiency, cultural diversity, pedagogical practices, and 21st-century education. These have been the major program outcomes that resulted in the academic partnership with the universities of Thailand.

Specifically, it actively contributed to the sustained academic collaboration on the different themes and features as the impact in advanced education:

a) **Twining Agreement**. The program has contributed to the sharing of best practices along with the educational administration for the faculty and student exchange support program.

b) **Inter-Country Facilitation of Teacher Education Program**. This area provides the educational support of the practice teaching abroad, language proficiency, and sharing the best practices of the educational management including the assistance of faculty development.

4. BEEd Student Academic and Cultural Exchange Collaboration in the International X-Change Camp in Thailand

The Romchatra Foundation and Maritime Silk Road Confucius Institute and SEA -Teacher program supported the faculty and exchange program to strengthen the connection of socio-cultural and academic collaboration of the ASEAN nations through the initiative of the Nakhon Si Thammarat Rajabhat University, Thailand. The cultural and education exposures for the faculty and student exchange program participated by the Bachelor of Elementary Education students and faculty in the international X-Change Camp in Nakhon Si Thammarat Rajabhat University, Thailand, June 24-28, 2019.

The student and faculty exchange program showcases the cultural diversity program in Thailand. The exchange program culminated the learning of Thai Folk Culture by showcasing their cultural dances and watching some presentations, prepared by the NSTRU students and faculty. Furthermore, they had experienced first-hand Thai culture Nang Talung, shadow puppetry in the famous Nang Talung Shadow Puppetry Museum.

Furthermore, the academic and cultural exchange of the International X-Change Camp participated in the challenge to prepare and to cook a Thai traditional dessert called Kanom Ko, known to be sugar dumplings with coconut. Step-by-step, the participants enjoyed preparing and tasting the taste of Thailand. Meanwhile, a Thai traditional dance class was experienced by the participants. Manora, a traditional Thai dance, was taught by Dr. Teerawat Changsan, Asst. Professor on Humanities and Social Science of NSTRU, to the participants, wearing their festive-like costume. Everybody had a great time dancing and learning at the same time.

The environmental and sustainable development program of the university was facilitated for the tree planting activity at the Farm Cum Learning Center; building a dam at Noppitam; short-distance trekking in Krungching; and a hot-spring experience in Onsen. There was also the community immersion in Krungching, where they had a festive lunch with the local people. Delectable and native food was served with the use of coconut shells and bamboos as their bowls and glasses just like what we, Ilocanos do: preserving the traditional doings. Afterward, a tie-dye cloth activity was experienced by the participants.

Further, both universities, UNP and NSTRU, talked about the possible student exchange programs in the future, as to be approved by the concerned parties. Truly, there is a healthy international connection and collaboration between the two universities. The activities and programs held are great manifestations that the University of Northern Philippines – College of Teacher Education can go beyond the expectations.

5. **Academic Collaboration and Blended Education Research in Teacher Education**

The nature of academic collaboration implemented in the blended education considered the area of language proficiency, pre-service education, teacher competence, and pedagogical process as defined and stated in the MOA and MOU in foreign universities in Asia. It must be noted that the career path of the BEEd program initiated by the Center of International Studies has expanded by the academic exchange program in the universities and schools in Thailand.

   a) Rachawanit School (Lecture on ASEAN integration and Research on Blended Education)
   b) Pasinee Kindergarten and Nursery (Pre-school Education)
   c) Mulan Language School Hat Yai (Language Proficiency in English)
   d) Plookpanya School, Thailand(Language Proficiency in English)

e) Apparent Pattansas School (Pre-Service Education)

f) Suan Dusit University (Teacher Competence)

6. **Program Outcome and Impact of the Research Presentation and Collaboration on Teaching and Learning Process Adopted in the Educational Supervision for the International partnership**

The significance of the international linkages and partnerships for the program outcomes has sustained the students and faculty exchange programs with language proficiency training of the Tan Trao University of Vietnam. While the SEA-Teacher sponsored by the SEAMEO was able to strengthen the twinning agreement for the Student Exchange Program in the basic education of Thailand, Indonesia, and Vietnam. The Romchatra Foundation through the support of the Maritime Silk Road Confucius Institute implemented substantial academic activities to pursue better collaboration for the " One Belt One Road Initiative' of the Chinese government.

7. **Technical Assistance on Book Publication Relevant to the Asian Culture, History and Tradition**

The technical assistance on book publication to the Romchatra Foundation has a high level of educational impact in the relevant areas of Asian Culture, History, and Tradition. There were five books published particularly in support of the Maritime Silk Road Confucius Institute disseminated in the ASEAN universities.

The academic exchange provided a greater understanding of Confucian Philosophy, ASEAN Cultural Diversity, Chinese Culture and Tradition, Asian Economic, and Political Development.

a) Enhance the academic relevance in the cultural heritage, history, and tradition in Asian countries.

b) Improve the understanding of the Confucian Philosophy, ASEAN integration, One Belt One Road, Chinese Culture and History, and cultural and educational management practices.

c) Improve academic collaboration and educational assistance in the ASEAN schools in Thailand, Indonesia, and Vietnam.

d) Utilize the book publications as instructional materials in the Asian culture, history, and tradition.

e) Expand the interest of the students and stakeholders in the cultural background of Filipino history and tradition.

8. Academic Visit and Benchmarking in the Advancement of Learning in Higher Education

The College of Teacher Education through the Blended Education program of the Center for International Studies presented the expertise of the faculty to give technical assistance to the Romchatra Foundation in the areas of career development through the Blended Education program including language proficiency which is also a part of the BECEd program The academic visit and benchmarking highlighted the enhancement of the curricular support in the inclusion of higher education lessons on ASEAN integration, cultural and educational exchange, language proficiency program, and other lines of academic interest. This is the integration of the curricular enhancement that the academic visit had given them more opportunities to generate new knowledge on the implementation of the ASEAN Quality Framework as to the ideas of universal adoption of employment requirements for the ASEAN countries.

The significance of the academic visit produced more international linkages and partnership activities along with the cultural exchange program and language proficiency program by the support of Maritime Silk Road Confucius Institutes and Romchatra Foundation.
   a) Sustain the academic commitment of higher education on the generation of knowledge and exchange program in the development of advanced education.
   b) Improve the educational processes as a result of the academic visit and benchmarking
   c) Expand the academic interest of collaboration in the continuing support of the advanced education
   d) Enhance the curricular support in the inclusion of higher education lessons on ASEAN integration, cultural and educational exchange, language proficiency program, and other lines of academic interests.
   e) Generate new knowledge and understanding the contribution of the best practices in the higher education program.

9. ASEAN Partnership on Academic Activities of Teacher Education

The College of Teacher Education was able to sustain the international linkages particularly in the career development of the Bachelor of Elementary program that have significant program outcomes in the areas of twinning agreement on research and facilitation of teacher education experiences. In the case of technical assistance on book publication, the

Romchatra Foundation has a high level of educational impact in the relevant areas of Asian Culture, History and Tradition were five books published particularly in support with the Maritime Silk Road Confucius Institute disseminated in the ASEAN universities.

The academic exchange provided a greater understanding of Confucian Philosophy, ASEAN Cultural Diversity, Chinese Culture and Tradition, Asian Economic, and Political Development. For the academic collaboration, it has the program outcome of the enhancement of academic collaboration by providing complimentary exchange and assistance in the different school activities. These are the research presentation, lecture, and conferences provided by the different partner agencies that have contributed to the understanding of cultural diversity, career development, and ASEAN integration particularly in the area of inclusivity of higher education program .

Finally, the academic visit and benchmarking highlighted the enhancement of the curricular support in the inclusion of higher education lessons on ASEAN integration, cultural and educational exchange, language proficiency program, and other lines of academic interest.

a) Enhance the Cultural Diversity, Heritage Management, History, and Tradition in the ASEAN Community.
b) Expand understanding of ASEAN Culture, History, and Tradition in partnership with the ASEAN universities.
c) Develop awareness in the cultural diversity of the ASEAN Community in support of the Romchatra Foundation
d) Enhance the partnership with the foreign schools in the ASEAN Community to further strengthen the teacher education program.
e) Provide continuing and sustained academic collaboration with the partner

10. **Student International Internship Program through the assistance of Center for International Studies and Romchatra Foundation**

The College of Teacher has been supporting the Student International Internship Program through the assistance of the Center for International Studies and Romchatra Foundation by forging an agreement for the Student Exchange Program in Thailand and Vietnam. The Student International Internship Program is designed to expose interns to foreign schools, particularly in the ASEAN schools. The University of Northern Philippines is an affiliate member of the Maritime Silk Road Confucius Institute with the responsibility to assist and provide academic assistance in the preparation and publications of books relevant to the accomplishments of Romchatra Foundation in the "Belt and Road Initiatives."

The college has been publishing best practices in the teaching and learning process, and social sciences books including coursebooks in general education. Part of the academic package in this area is the training of faculty members and publication of research findings in the Amazon books as part of the e-books needed by the education students. It is expected that the academic publications will further enhance the ability of the students as generalists and specialists in the areas of elementary and secondary education.

11. **The Global Education Development of the 2015 ASEAN Integration: Traimit Model**

The Traimit Model is designed to conduct academic linkages and partnerships in the cultural heritage program relevant to the sustained establishment of the Confucius Classrooms and Institutes. The Romchatra Foundation used the applied educational management theory in the study entitled "Traimit Educational Model for the First Confucius School in Thailand," which was published in the Amazon for its educational management application in the Confucius Classroom in ASEAN countries.

12. **Student International Internship** at Plookpanya School, Nakhon Racatchima, Thailand (January 5-March 5, 2017)

The College of Teacher has been supporting the Student International Internship Program through the assistance of the Center for International Studies and Romchatra Foundation by forging an agreement for the Student Exchange Program in Thailand and Vietnam. The Student International Internship Program is designed to expose the BSEd and BEEd (including the ECEd majors) interns to foreign schools, particularly in the ASEAN schools

Chapter 3
Academic Excellence and International Linkages of the Bachelor of Elementary Education

The Bachelor of Elementary Education (BEEd) is designed to prepare individuals intending to teach in the elementary level for General Education, Early Childhood Education, and Special Needs. It aims to develop highly motivated and competent teachers specializing in the content and pedagogy for elementary education. The BEEd program also draws from various disciplines (allied fields) like social sciences, science, math, technology, languages, and humanities to ensure that the graduates have a multi-disciplinary preparation in content and pedagogy. After successful completion of all academic requirements of the degree/program graduates of BEEd should be able to practice the teaching profession in the elementary level.

I. **Accomplishments on Academic Excellence of the Bachelor of Elementary Education as Center of Development, ISO 9001:2015 Certification and Level IV Phase 2 Accreditation Status (2016-2021)**

The College of Teacher Education (CTE) has been designated as the Center of Development for Teacher Education Program per (CMO No 17, Series of 2016). This recognition has paved the way for the CTE to be a potent catalyst for world class scholarships, best practices, innovative curriculum, research and extension and professional development in the Teacher Education program.

A. AWARDS

1. The College of Teacher Education was designated as **Center of Development** under CHED Memorandum Order No. 17, Series 2016.

2. **ISO- 9001: 2015 Certification Award** granted a Registration Certificate by the AJA Registrars (now SOCOTECH) and registered against the requirements of ISO 9001:2015. The scope of registration includes the provision of tertiary education services in the College of Teacher Education covering the admission and enrollment process of promotion and conferment of degrees. The certification is valid from December5,2018 to December 6, 2021.

3. **"Sustaining Academic Excellence in the Teacher Education Program through Inclusive Education and Sustainable Development** "- Grantee under CMO No. 33, series of 2016 Approved Budget of P 4,000,000.00

This project with the budget of Php 4,000,000.00 would further assist the SUCs and HEIs in the province of Ilocos Sur to implement Teacher Education programs through inclusive education and sustainable development to enhance the basic education program. The general objective of the project is to sustain academic excellence and to cascade the best practices of the Teacher Education program anchored on inclusive education and sustainable development excellence in Teacher Education program in the province of Ilocos Sur.

B. National Topnotcher Awards

1. Jonathan del Castillo, magna cum laude 2018 graduate of the Bachelor of Elementary education, major in Special Education has landed in the illustrious top 10 of the September 2018 Licensure for Licensure Examination for Teachers (BEEd Category) with a rating of 87.60%.

C. National and Regional Award

1. Plaque of Distinction Award for being the **Center of Development in Teacher Education** given by CHED Regional Office last 2016 Regional Higher Education Conference held at Fort Ilocandia, Laoag City last June 8, 2016.

2. SUCTEA Award for the Center of Development

The College of Teacher Education (CTE) has been designated as the Center of Development for Teacher Education Program per (CMO No 17, Series of 2016). This recognition has paved the way for the CTE to be a potent catalyst for world class scholarships, best practices, innovative curriculum, research and extension and professional development in the Teacher Education program.

3. **National Award for Graduate Cultural Education** and **Sentro ng Wika** for the Graduate Diploma for Cultural Education accredited by the Philippine Cultural Education of NCCA.

D. International Awards for Linkages and Collaboration

1. **ASEAN Internship Academy Award** for its invaluable partnership it has forged to implement CHED's Students Internship Abroad Program in Thailand by the ASEAN Internship Academy (October 9,2017)

2. **Student Exchange Tan Trao Award** for the Student Internship Program awarded by the Tan Trao University, Vietnam

In partnership with the UNP Center for International Studies, the College of Teacher Education accepted ten students from the Tan Trao University for exposure on May 5-30, 2017. The students were accompanied by their professor. They were exposed to the CTE Best Practices in classroom instruction, co-curriculum activities, extra-curricular activities, extension and lectures on orthography and culture heritage. The said Vietnamese students underwent a rigid selection process so that the best 10 excellent students were sent to the UNP-CTE to undergo the May 5-30, 2017 exposure

3. **Romchatra Foundation Award for** Traimit Educational Model

The Romchatra Foundation through Phromomankachalan has expanded the international linkages of the UNP to be a partner of the academic publications including cultural exchange activities under Hanban that recognized the effort of the CTE to bring the forefront of scholarly publication through the ASEAN Community. The forging of agreement on Academic and cultural collaboration with the assistance of the Center of International Studies became the Best Practices of International linkages on Academic and Cultural Exchange program through the Confucius Maritime Silk Road of the Romchatra Foundation.

4. SEAMEO -SEA Teacher Award for Student Internship

The University of Northern Philippines implemented the twinning student exchange program for their academic exposures with extra-curricular activities, cultural heritage experiences in the UNESCO Heritage City of Vigan. The participating Foreign Universities for the Pre-service Student Teachers Exchange Program in Southeast Asia

    1. Indonesia University of Education (UPI), Bandung Indonesia
    2. Sebelas Maret University (UNS), Surukarta, Indonesia,
    3. Nakon S. Thammarat Rajabhat (NSTRU), Thammarat,Thailand
    4. Buriram Rajabhat University (BRU), Buriram University

I. Teacher Education Reforms for Academic Excellence in the Bachelor of Elementary Education

The University of Northern Philippines has been granted a Registration Certificate by the AJA Registrars (now SOCOTECH) and registered against the requirements of ISO 9001:2015. The scope of registration includes the provision of tertiary education services in the **College of Teacher Education** covering the admission and enrollment process of promotion and conferment of degrees. The certification is valid from December 5, 2018, to December 6, 2021. The college was also awarded a GRANT of FOUR MILLION PESOS under CMO No. 33, S. 2016 in the K to 12 Transition Program, for the engagement entitled: Sustaining Academic Excellence in the Teacher Education Program through Inclusive Education and Sustainable Development".

Based on the trending analysis of the Licensure Examination of Teachers (LET), the college has been implementing innovative practices and admission policies to ensure the support of the Center of Development. The College of Teacher Education (CTE) has been designated as the Center of Development for Teacher Education Program per (CMO No 17, Series of 2016). This recognition has paved the way for the CTE to be a potent catalyst for world-class scholarships, best practices, innovative curriculum, research and extension, and professional development in the Teacher Education program.

The instructional recognition must be addressed to the current needs to put curricular and policy reform for the learning management to ensure the increasing trend analysis for the Licensure Examination for Teachers (LET). The research findings have been the basis to enhance the academic reforms to support the Center of Development granted in 2016.

These were the considerations for the academic policies based on the empirical result of the previous research on academic performance and the result of the Licensure Examinations since 2016:

1. All of the cum laude graduates (An average of 50 Graduates every year for the last four years from 2016-2019) have successfully passed the Licensure Board Examination for Teachers.

2. Those who passed in the TAT and with high average grades in their professional, major, and general education subjects were the successful graduates who passed the licensure examination.

3. In the College Admission Test (CAT) and Teaching Aptitude Test (TAT) found out to be significantly related in passing the Licensure Examination for Teachers:

4. It can be noted that all the personal profile of the graduates significantly correlates with LET performance. This means that the respondents who obtained higher UNP- CAT rating, TAT result, practicum performance, and those who attended the LET review classes tend to perform better in the LET. This implies that these variables contribute significantly to the success of graduates in taking the LET. This supports the findings of Bañez and Pardo (2016) who found that UNP-CAT score and attendance in LET review classes significantly correlate with LET performance. (Rabanal and Manzano, 2018)

5. The general average in the LET of all the batches of the BEEd graduates shows a passing performance. The passing performance in the LET of the BEEd graduates is an indication of a relatively strong foundation in both the general and professional education courses. This further implies that the faculty who handled these courses were able to impart the essential knowledge and develop the necessary skills among these graduates. (Rabanal and Manzano, 2018)

Based on the conclusions established in the studies of the Licensure Examination for Teachers, the following recommendations are made: (Rabanal and Manzano, 2018)

(1) The university may consider intensifying their admission and retention policies to admit only the most qualified students.

(2) An enhancement and an intensive review program may be undertaken to better prepare graduates for the licensure examination.

(3) The university may consider reviewing the teacher education curriculum to include varied professional development activities as well as the specialization courses to better prepare the graduates for the licensure examination.

Based on the recommendations from the empirical studies of academic performance and results of the Licensure Examination for Teacher implemented the   academic reforms for the admission policies in School Year 2016-2017 to sustain the grant of Center of Development in the Teacher Education:

1.   The admission and retention policies admitted only the most qualified applicants based on the required of 78 percent for College Admission Test and passing of the Teaching Aptitude Tests (TAT)

2.   The LET intensive review program has been a part of the better preparation of the BEEd graduates. The local LET review was conducted by the senior faculty who were national reviewers in CBRC and the national topnotcher of the LET Edmar Paguirigan (8th Placer, 2014). In addition to this local review, the Memorandum of Agreement was signed by the Carl Balita Review Centers (CBRC) to conduct the intensive review for the graduates.

3.   The varied professional activities in the Teacher Education program such as the active participation of the professional organizations of SUCTEA and other teacher education organizations contribution to the enhancement of the pedagogical skills of the faculty members.

4.   The international linkage exposures for the ASEAN countries particularly Romchatra Foundation widened the horizon of educational training of the students. It embarked on the participation of the Student Exchange Programs and Student Internship Abroad in

the foreign universities and SEAMEO has given the opportunity to enhance the content knowledge and experiential learnings of the students.

5. The Center of Development provided the opportunity to get additional funding for the action research capability building and other in-service training of the Fiduciary Funds of the college.

As a result of the substantial accomplishments in the academic activities through the admission policies on College Admission Tests (CAT), Teaching Aptitude Test (TAT), Student Internship Abroad, Student Exchange Program, SEA Teacher, INSET SUCTEA participation, CHED external fund, and Local Review and collaboration with the CBRC, the college achieved the highest licensure examination performance of the elementary education in 2019 with the present administration of President Erwin Cadorna in achieving the **Goal No. 1. Develop ethical leaders through academic excellence** with the strategic direction for the ethical leaders through academic excellence adopted the systems-based approach in teaching and training students to become innovators and ethical leaders for tomorrow.

The continuing academic reforms and policy implementation of quality and excellence the College of Teacher Education has achieved its highest LET rating of 92.38 for first-time takers with the national passing rate of 31.34. Surprisingly, the elementary education graduates surpassed the LET passers of the SUCs offering Teacher Education Program (The Center of Excellence -MMSU, DMMSU, and PSU)

The administration of President Erwin Cadorna immediately achieved the ethical leaders through academic excellence that surpasses the SUCs offering Teacher Education in the whole Region I:

Jonathan del Castillo, magna cum laude 2018 graduate of the Bachelor of Elementary education, major in Special Education has landed in the illustrious top 10 of the September 2018 Licensure for Licensure Examination for Teachers (BEEd Category) with a rating of 87.60%.

The College of Teacher Education submitted the accomplishment report (December 2, 2019) of the Board Licensure Examination for Professional Teachers (BLEPT) conducted last September 2019 for the Bachelor of Elementary Education:

> *The performance of the elementary, secondary, and industrial education to appreciate the academic impact of the innovations and reforms conducted by the college for the last four years (2016-2019) in academic admission, maintain quality and excellence in the Teacher Education program.*

This justifies the existence of the Center of Development for Teacher Education Program per (CMO No 17, Series of 2016) as the potent catalyst for world-class scholarships, best practices, innovative curriculum, research and extension, and professional development in the Teacher Education program. The evidenced-based LET for first-time takers provided the continuing quest to innovate academic programs and policies to support the higher education advocacy on quality and excellence.

II. Accomplishments on International Linkages and Consortia of the Bachelor of Elementary Education (BEEd)

These sustained international linkages and consortia provided the academic excellence in the BEEd program that consequently granted the Center of Development in the College of Teacher Education. The international best practices became a world-class engagement to become a potent catalyst of the professional and academic development in the elementary education program, specifically in the BEEd Program.

It integrates the international linkages and partnerships with the support of the SEAMEO student exchange program, the Cultural Diversity, and Experience of the primary school–future teachers of partner universities were also enhanced. Partnership with different ASEAN Schools such as Romchatra Foundation with the academic exchange program connected with the Maritime Silk Road Confucius Institute. Thus, ASEAN Universities had opened the eyes of one of our students to diversity by academic exchange and collaboration with Tan Trao University, Suan Dusit University, and Rajamagala Universities of Thailand.

In order to display the competence of faculty and pre-service teachers to promote high-quality learning outcomes, the BEEd program has established general objectives for the international linkages and consortia to connect the best practices in terms of MTB-MLE, Cultural Diversity, and Pedagogical knowledge relevant to the teaching-learning process in the ASEAN Education with the following relevant undertakings.

On the other hand, the BEEd program has the following objectives in networking, linkages, and consortia:

(1) connect the teacher education programs with development partners in the academe, national government agencies, and the local government units including those in the international community;

(2) enable education programs on basic education, instructional competence, and others to become responsive to local and national thrusts through linkages in other countries; and

(3) benchmark standards (local and international) for integration in the education programs.

(4) Facilitate of the in-country work experience in the Elementary Education Program for the ASEAN Schools.

(5) Collaborate the joint research and extension activities, lectures, workshops, fora, symposia, and seminars.

(6) Exchange of academic materials, scientific publications, and other relevant scholarly information.

The BEEd program made sure that its program outcomes were fully realized by supporting culture-based education. The sustained international linkages and partnerships along with the program outcome and impact of the Bachelor of Elementary Education along with academic collaboration, inter-country facilitation, research, and book publication in the ASEAN countries.

(1) The foundation of the MTB-MLE provides the support of the and academic collaboration of the SEAMEO for the young children (Kindergarten to Grade 3 of the K to 12 enhanced curricula) with the foreign universities in the ASEAN region.

(2) The facilitation of the in-country work experience for faculty and students to teach in the ASEAN Schools in the best pedagogical and cultural diversity practice in the basic education program.

(3) The international research and extension activity participated for the elementary education program on pedagogical knowledge, instructional assessment, cultural diversity under the socio-cultural education of the ASEAN Integration.

(4) The publications along the MTB-MLE and cultural diversity program in support of the UNESCO Heritage City of Vigan and Cultural Diversity program became the relevant academic materials such as ASEAN Integration, Traimit Model, Confucius Classroom/Institute, and UNESCO Heritage Program.

(5) Co-operation in basic education program (Kindergarten and Elementary) on the promotion of staff and student exchanges.

(6) Other cooperation and collaboration activities in education deemed appropriate mutually beneficial to the foreign schools.

A. **Tan Trao Student Exchange Program from Tan Trao University (May 5-30, 2017)**
"A Taste of UNP Culture: The Vietnamese Faculty and Students in UNP"

In partnership with the UNP Center for International Studies, the College of Teacher Education accepted ten students from the Tan Trao University for exposure on May 5-30, 2017. The students were accompanied by their professor. They were exposed to the CTE Best Practices in classroom instruction, co-curriculum activities, extra-curricular activities, extension and lectures on orthography and culture heritage. The said Vietnamese students underwent a rigid selection process so that the best 10 excellent students were sent to the UNP-CTE to undergo the May 5-30, 2017 exposure.

The College of Teacher Education ,the Bachelor of Elementary Education, had strengthened support on the Vietnamese Students' Exchange Program. Through this program, it showcased the many faces of Filipino hospitality and UNP's brand of globally competitive instruction, research, and extension. The Vietnamese Student Exchange Program was implemented with various academic activities in the teacher training which included classroom observations at the Laboratory Schools and the undergraduate courses; field exposures in agricultural and fishing communities; upland communities; program and various activities they were exposed to the rich Ilokano culture and language.

Figure 2: After a month exposure of the Vietnamese students, they posed together with the faculty and selected students of the College of Teacher Education during their send-off program

Specifically, there were four (4) out of the ten Vietnamese students, who were also taking up Bachelor in Elementary Education major in Early Childhood Education who were accepted for exposure to the CTE were:

1. Tran Thi Nghia - **Primary School**

2. Linh Huru Khurong - Land and Environment Science

3. Tran Hien Quang - Land and Environment Science

4. Phung Tien Thong - Literature   Education

5. Hoang Thi Trang - Language Education

6. Nguyen Thi Lan Anh - Land and Environment Science

7. Nguyen Ngoc Quynh - **Primary School**

8. Nguyen Thi Phrong Thao- **Primary School**

9. Nguyen Thu Uyen - **Primary School**

10. Tran Van Bac - Physical and Environment Science

Figure 3. A Vietnamese student belts out a song while the other delegates prepare for their respective parts during the send-off program tendered by the College of Teacher Education.

*Figure 4. Vietnamese students' snapshot of observation in the UNP Laboratory
School*

One of the Vietnamese Students wrote in her testimony on the
Internship Report of the Student Exchange Program in the College of
Teacher Education:

*...Then I found out a bit of information about everything I
see in the Philippines. Not only being an exchange student
but also exchange knowledge and ideas. I think it was good
for me when I get to know all things I like and want.
Now I know a little bit about the culture of the
country and people in the Philippines. I see that the
Philippines is actually a beautiful country with all the
helpful people and beautiful sight. UNP is a very
perfect place to study research and expand my
knowledge. And your place City of Vigan is also a
worthy place to stay. So many feelings and emotions
involved cannot explain through words. The place where
I want to spend some more time...*

Nguyen Ngoc Quynh   (BEEd intern)

Furthermore, the College of Teacher Education (CTE) implemented the Vietnamese Students' Exchange Program with the support of the Center for International Studies with the program outcome in the international linkages to support the supervisory program for the teaching-learning process to enhance the experiential knowledge on cultural diversity and language development. The educational impact of the Vietnamese students' exchange program ensures the continuing support of the university officials of Tan Trao University to give more Vietnamese students and request that the CTE students and faculty would teach English proficiency program. It is also expected to continue giving priority of the student exchange program to be emerged in the CTE as to the best practices on educational administration by sending Vietnamese students' in the Tan Trao University, College of Education those are major in Primary School, Literature Education, and Environment Science to implement the twinning program.

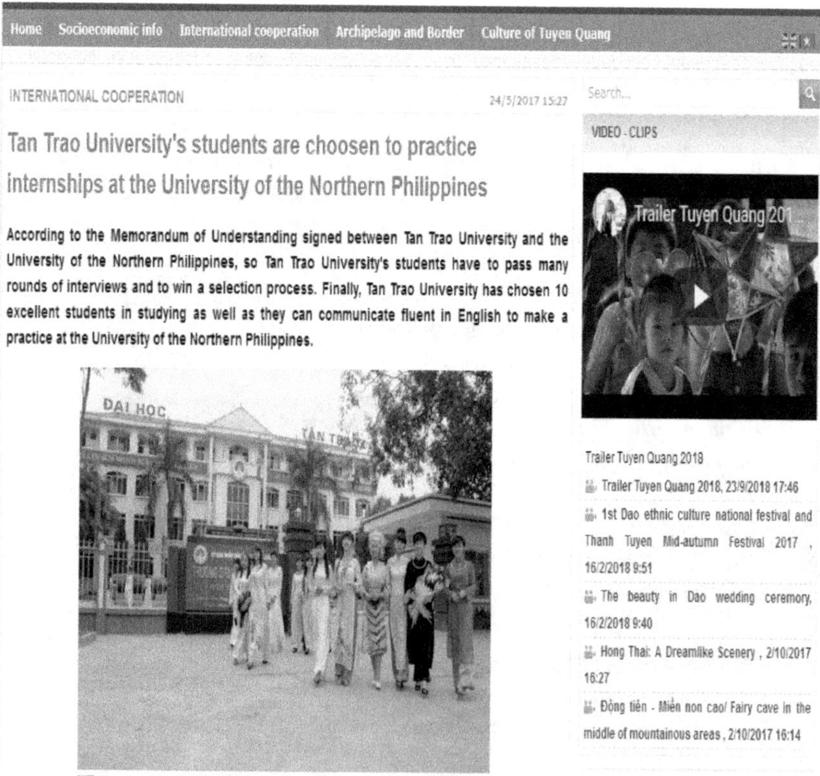

Figure 5. UNP in the Official Website of the Tan Trao University

The Potent Catalyst of the Emerging Research and International Collaboration in Vietnam

The 1st International Conference at Tan Trao University became the potent Catalyst in the implementation of the academic collaboration and exchange which was started in May 2015 that continued the support of the College of Teacher Education. The international collaboration of Tan Trao University started the signing of Memorandum of Agreement (MOA) Between the University of Northern Philippines and Tan Trao University, Vietnam for Research Collaboration, Academic and Student Exchange Program on May 22, 2015.

MEMORANDUM OF AGREEMENT

BETWEEN

TAN TRAO UNIVERSITY (VIETNAM) and UNIVERSITY OF NORTHERN PHILIPPINES (PHILIPPINES)

KNOW ALL MEN BY THESE PRESENTS:

This Memorandum of Agreement made and entered into by and between:

TAN TRAO UNIVERSITY (TTrU), with office address at **Trung Mon Commune, Yen Son District, Tuyen Quang Province, Vietnam**, represented by, **DR. NGUYEN BA DUC** his capacity as **President**, referred to as **"THE FIRST PARTY"**; and

UNIVERSITY OF NORTHERN PHILIPPINES with business and postal address at **Tamag, Vigan City, Ilocos Sur, Philippines**, represented by **DR. GILBERT R. ARCE**, in his capacity as **University President**, hereafter referred to as **"THE SECOND PARTY"**.

WITNESSETH:

WHEREAS, the both parties manifest the willingness to enter into academic and non-academic ventures that will redound to their mutual benefits;

WHEREAS, the both parties agree to pursue collaboration in research and extension programs; cultural and scientific interests; faculty, staff and student exchanges; and other activities for the advancement of global excellence in education, governance, business, technology and health;

WHEREAS, the First Party, in its desire to satisfy growing demand for global higher education in Vietnam, would like to tap the expertise of the Second Party along its mature academic programs and as a party in future innovative academic programs, subject to existing laws and legal orders of the government of Vietnam;

WHEREAS, the Second Party, as a mature institution of learning in the Philippines, commits itself to assist the First Party, while at the same time implores its assistance to enhance further the latter's existing programs to meet global students, subject to existing laws and legal orders of the Republic of the Philippines;

NOW THEREFORE, for and in consideration of the foregoing premises, parties agree that:

OBLIGATIONS

The University shall:

1. Provide and deploy qualified student teachers in English, Science and Mathematics;
2. Conduct supervisory visit by the Center for International Studies during the stay of the student teachers in Tan Trao University;
3. Gather feedback from Tan Trao University regarding the Student-Teachers' performance as basis in improving the program;
4. Take responsibility on the expenses of the Students for one airfare, pre-departure and arrival expenses; and entire duration of practice teaching;
5. Arrange and provide temporary entrance visas for deployed student teachers.

The Tan Trao University shall:

1. Accept and provide opportunities for student teachers to apply real world teaching experiences;
2. Provide the student teachers with best mentors to enhance their teaching competencies;
3. Provide necessary compliments by securing the safety of student teachers during their stay in Tan Trao University;
4. Allow the practice teachers to have access to information related to the school needed for the training;
5. Determine the number of student teachers to be deployed at Tan Trao University in any given time;
6. Provide one way airfare, transport, accommodation and subsistence daily allowance (no less than 2.500.000 Dong per month) to the student teachers during their stay in Tan Trao University;
7. Submit student teachers performance evaluation to the University of Northern Philippines;
8. Arrange and provide extended visas for deployed student teachers as required.

Figure 6: Mr. Albert R. Tejero (8th from left), Vice President for Finance and Administration   with CTE faculty and Tan Trao University representatives after the Signing of Memorandum of Agreement (MOA) Between the University of Northern Philippines and Tan Trao University, Vietnam for Research Collaboration, Academic and Student Exchange Program on May 22, 2016.

Figure 7. In the CTE faculty and Tan Trao University representatives after the Signing of Memorandum of Agreement (MOA) Between the University of Northern Philippines and Tan Trao University, Vietnam for Research Collaboration, Academic and Student Exchange Programon May 22, 2015.

The research studies presented in the 1st International Conference with the theme "Assessing Primary Students by Approaching and Evaluating their Competence A Possible Approach to Pedagogic Institutions in Vietnam and same Southeast Asian Countries:" were the following:

1. Implementation of the K to 12 programs in the Laboratory Schools of the College of Teacher Education, University of Northern Philippines
2. The Culture-Based Multidisciplinary Model of the Mother Tongue Based- Multilingual Education (MTB-MLE) of the Primary Schools in the Philippines
3. Interpersonal Conflict Management Style of Future Basic Education Teachers (Including the BECEd students)
4. Misconceptions in Astronomy of the Third Year Elementary Education Students, University of Northern Philippines

The program outcome of the 1st conference provided the opportunity to expand the twinning agreement on the teaching-learning process by the faculty and student exchange program that resulted in the crediting of the international linkage points for the application of the Center of Development in the field of teacher education. This was the reason that the evaluators of the CHED panel for Center of Development to consider the sustained international linkages of the College of Teacher Education.

International Collaboration and Research Presentations . A number of CTE faculty attended the International Conference held at Tan Trao University, Vietnam on May 22, 2015. Five researches were presented by CTE researchers during the conference.

Assessing Primary Students by Approaching and Evaluating their Competence A Possible Approach to Pedagogic Institutions in Vietnam and same Southeast Asian Countries (May 22, 2015)

- Implementation of the K to 12 program in the Laboratory Schools of the College of Teacher Education, University of Northern Philippines - Dr. Gilbert Arce

- The Culture-Based Multidisciplinary Model of the Mother Tongue Based- Multilingual Education (MTB-MLE) of the Primary Schools in the Philippines – Dr. Christopher Bueno and Eden A. Bueno

- Correlation Analysis of Licensure Examination for Teacher and Academic Performance of BEEd Students – Dr. Jose P. Pichay

- Interpersonal   Conflict Management Style of Future Basic Education Teachers – Dr. Luzviminda P. Relon

- Misconceptions in Astronomy of the Third Year Elementary Education Students, University of Northern Philippines- Dr. Corazon G. Pardo

Student International Internship Program

The College of Teacher had been supporting the Student International Internship Program through the assistance of Center for International Studies and Romchatra Foundation by forging an agreement for Student Exchange Program in Thailand and in Vietnam. The Student International Internship Program is designed to expose the BSEd, BECEd and BEEd interns to the foreign schools, particularly in the ASEAN schools.

*Figure 7: During the awarding of Certificate of Completion on March 4, 2017 to the 2 student interns, **Rowena Perinion, BEEd (BECEd) IV** and Cherry Mae Rol, BEEd IV with the School Director, Teacher Paty*

The Demonstration Teaching

Figure 8: During the Demonstration Teaching of Cherry Mae Rol in her Elementary Class (January- March, 2017)

Table 1. Sustained International Linkage and Partnership with Tan Trao University in line with the BEED Program

Nature of Assistance	Number of Activities	Program Outcomes and Impact
International Conference	3	Presentation of best practices in educational management, teaching-learning process, language proficiency, MTB-MLE
Twinning Agreement on Research for Teaching competence	4	Sharing of best practices in educational assessment
Academic Visit and Benchmarking	3	Faculty and Students exchange activities
Academic Partnership	4	International conference and research collaboration

The BEEd program outcomes and impact had ensured the common sharing of academic resources in the implementation of international conferences and academic collaboration in the student exchange program. The international conferences emerged the first sustainable academic collaboration that provided the opportunity of Tan Trao University to adopt the best practices in the field of educational administration, teaching process, evaluation and assessment of learning, language proficiency, and implementation of the MTB-MLE. The sustained impact of the twinning agreement defined more on the expertise of the University of Northern Philippines to act as host in the Student Exchange Program for the Vietnamese students with qualitative impact of the experiential learning about cultural diversity, language proficiency, teaching-learning process, and understanding the culture of the Filipinos.

On the other hand, the College of Teacher Education was able to sustain the international linkages particularly in the career development have significant program outcomes in the areas of twinning agreement on research and facilitation of teacher education experiences. The program outcomes of the international linkages have been focused on the best practices of educational administration along with language proficiency, cultural diversity, pedagogical practices, and 21st-century education. These have been the major program outcomes that resulted in the academic partnership with the universities of Thailand.

Specifically, it actively contributed to the sustained academic collaboration on the different themes and features as the impact in advanced education:

1. **Twining Agreement**. The program has contributed to the sharing of best practices along with the educational administration for the faculty and student exchange support program.

2. **Inter-Country Facilitation of Teacher Education Program**. This area provides the educational support of the practice teaching abroad, language proficiency, and sharing the best practices of the educational management including the assistance of faculty development.

BEEd Student Academic and Cultural Exchange Collaboration in the International X-Change Camp in Thailand

To strengthen the connection of ASEAN nations as well as their respective universities, selected students and faculty from the University of Northern Philippines-College of Teacher Education (UNP-CTE) attended the international X-Change Camp in Nakhon Si Thammarat Rajabhat University, Thailand, June 24-28, 2019.

The participants from the University of Northern Philippines - College of Teacher Education during the Campus Tour at Nakhon Si Thammarat Rajabhat University, June 24, 2019.

READY TO COOK. (From left to right) Jhon Paul Ric Corpuz, Dr. Luzviminda Relon and John Bernard Degracia, before they experience the Thai cooking class.

On their first day, an opening program was held at their university hall. Each university presented some of its programs and activities, in which, Dr. Relon, the faculty designate internship abroad program stood for UNP. A campus tour was facilitated afterwards, allowing all the participants to visit the university's best features and to learn their culture as well.

The learning of Thai Folk Culture was held on their second day showcasing their cultural dances and watching some presentations, prepared by the NSTRU students and faculty. Furthermore, they had experienced first-hand Thai culture Nang Talung, a shadow puppetry in the famous Nang Talung Shadow Puppetry Museum.

The partcipants from University of Northern Philippines before the tree-planting activity, June 27, 2019.

Participants had also the chance to experience Thai cooking class on the third day. They were challenged to prepare and to cook a Thai traditional dessert called Kanom Ko, known to be sugar dumplings with

DISTRIBUTION OF CERTIFICATES. The students of both UNP and NSTRU, receiving their certificates of participation in the X-Change Camp, together with Dr. Kanata Thattong, the university president.

coconut. Step-by-step, the participants enjoyed preparing and tasting the taste of Thailand. Meanwhile, a Thai traditional dance class was experienced by the participants, too. Manora, a traditional Thai dance, was taught by Dr. Teerawat Changsan, Asst. Professor for Humanities and Social Science of NSTRU, to the participants, wearing their festive-like costume. Everybody had a great time dancing and learning at the same time.

The participants from Univercity of Northern Philippines experiencing the Onsen hot spring, June 27, 2019.

The partcipants from University of Northern Philippines during the Thai dance class under Dr. Teerawat Changsan, June 26, 2019. Meanwhile, John Bernard Degracia, wearing a festive-like costume is with the dance instructor, Dr. Changsan.

On their fourth day, activities outside the university were facilitated. They had a tree planting activity at the Farm Cum Learning Center; building a dam at Noppitam; short-distance trekking in Krungching; and a hot-spring experience in Onsen. Meanwhile, they were immersed with the community in Krungching, where they had a festive lunch with the local people. Delectable and native food were served with the use of coconut shells and bamboos as their bowls and glasses just like what we, Ilocanos do: preserving the traditional doings. Afterwards, a tie-dye cloth activity was experienced by the participants.

On their last day, a closing program was held at the NSTRU's conference room in which Dr. Kanata Thatthong, the university president of NSTRU had a thorough discussion with the participants. During the ceremony, Dr. Jeanina Batin delivered a message representing the faculty of UNP, and Mr. John Bernard D. Degracia (a BEEd student), shared his experience and impression in behalf of the students of UNP.

Further, both universities, UNP and NSTRU, talked about the possible student exchange programs in the future, as to be approved by the concerned parties.

Truly, there is a healthy international connection and collaboration between the two universities. The activities and programs held are great manifestations that University of Northern Philippines – College of Teacher Education can go beyond the expectations.

Table 2. Academic Collaboration and Blended Education Research in Teacher Education

Foreign School	Number of Activities	Beneficiaries	Nature of Academic Collaboration in Blended Education Research
Rachawanit	3	40	Lecture on ASEAN integration and Research on Blended Education
Pasinee Kindergarten and Nursery, Thailand	1	40	Pre-school Education
Mulan Language School Hat Yai, Thailand	1	60	Language Proficiency in English
Plookpanya School, Thailand	2	40	Language Proficiency in English
Apparent Pattansas School, Thailand	1	35	Pre-Service Education
Bannmaechan School, Thailand	1	50	Confucius School Program
Suan Dusit University, Thailand	3	25	Teacher Competence

The nature of academic collaboration implemented in the blended education considered the area of language proficiency, pre-service education, teacher competence and pedagogical process as defined and stated in the MOA and MOU in foreign universities in Asia. It must be noted that the career path of the BEEd program initiated by the Center of International Studies has expanded by the academic exchange program in the universities and schools in Thailand.

1 OF 4 PAGES

MEMORANDUM OF AGREEMENT

BETWEEN
MULAN LANGUAGE SCHOOL HAT YAI (THAILAND)
and

UNIVERSITY OF NORTHERN PHILIPPINES (PHILIPPINES)

KNOW ALL MEN BY THESE PRESENTS:

This Memorandum of Agreement made and entered into by and between:

MULAN LANGUAGE SCHOOL HAT YAI, with office address at 3 304-306 ChockChai4 rd., Lat Phrao Bangkok Thailand 10230, represented by MS. WAKOTCHAKORN RAKKAMNERD, in her capacity as School Director, referred to as "THE SCHOOL"; and

UNIVERSITY OF NORTHERN PHILIPPINES with business and postal address at Tamag, Vigan City, Ilocos Sur, Philippines, represented by DR. GILBERT R. ARCE, in his capacity as University President, hereafter referred to as "THE UNIVERSITY".

WITNESSETH:

WHEREAS, the both parties manifest the willingness to enter into academic and non-academic ventures that will redound to their mutual benefits;

WHEREAS, the both parties agree to pursue faculty, staff and student exchanges; and other activities for the advancement of global excellence in education;

WHEREAS, the SCHOOL, in its desire to satisfy growing demand for global education in Thailand, would like to tap the expertise of the UNIVERSITY along its Teacher Education programs and as a party in future innovative academic programs, subject to existing laws and legal orders of the government of Thailand;

WHEREAS, the UNIVERSITY, as a mature institution of learning in the Philippines, commits itself to assist the SCHOOL, while at the same time implores

Figure 9. MOA to the different educational institutions in Thailand

MEMORANDUM OF AGREEMENT

BETWEEN

ROMCHATRA FOUNDATION (THAILAND)

and

UNIVERSITY OF NORTHERN PHILIPPINES (PHILIPPINES)

KNOW ALL MEN BY THESE PRESENTS:

This Memorandum of Agreement made and entered into by and between:

UNIVERSITY OF NORTHERN PHILIPPINES with business and postal address at Tamag, Vigan City, Ilocos Sur, Philippines, represented by DR. GILBERT R. ARCE, in his capacity as University President, hereinafter called the "UNIVERSITY" and

ROMCHATRA FOUNDATION with office address at Charoenkrung Road, Samphantawong District, BKK, Thailand represented by PHRAPROMMANGKALACHAN in his capacity as Chairman of the Board, referred hereinafter called the "FOUNDATION".

WITNESSETH:

WHEREAS, the both parties manifest the willingness to enter into academic and non-academic ventures that will redound to their mutual benefits;

WHEREAS, the UNIVERSITY is an institution of higher learning offering various programs in accordance with its mandate;

WHEREAS, one of the objectives of the UNIVERSITY is to maintain international linkages with foreign universities and entities in pursuance with the government's globalization program;

WHEREAS, the FOUNDATION is a duly recognized entity in THAILAND that oversees the operations of Confucius Classroom at Traimitwittayalai Public High School and Confucius Institute of Maritime Silk Road;

WHEREAS, the parties mutually agreed to help each other to attain their objectives in accordance with applicable laws and regulations;

NOW, THEREFORE, the UNIVERSITY and the FOUNDATION mutually agreed to the following terms and conditions:

Page 1 of 4

MEMORANDUM OF UNDERSTANDING

BETWEEN
PASINEE KINDERGARTEN AND NURSERY (THAILAND)
and
UNIVERSITY OF NORTHERN PHILIPPINES (PHILIPPINES)

The **OWNER** of PASINEE KINDERGARTEN AND NUSERY, with office address at Samut Prakan Thailand 10540 and the **PRESIDENT** of UNIVERSITY OF NORTHERN UNIVERSITY (UNP), Tamag, Vigan City, Ilocos Sur 2700 Philippines desire to promote their mutual interest in promoting academic cooperation and exchange between their institutions and in pursuant to the prevailing laws and regulations in their respective countries, as well as the policies and procedures of PASINEE KINDERGARTEN AND NURSERY and UNIVERSITY OF NORTHERN PHILIPPINES concerning academic cooperation and collaboration; have reached the following scope and details of the Memorandum of Understanding:

1. The two institutions agree to encourage and promote cooperation on the following academic activities:
   a. Faculty and Staff Exchange;
   b. Student Exchange;
   c. Facilitation of in-country work experience for students in relevant field of studies;
   d. Joint research and extension activities, lectures, workshops, fora, symposia and seminars;
   e. Exchange of academic materials, scientific publications and other relevant scholarly information; and
   f. Other cooperation and collaboration activities in education, governance, business, technology and health deemed appropriate mutually.
2. Specific activities to be carried out under this Memorandum of Understanding shall be negotiated, consulted and agreed upon through a Memorandum of Agreement as its implementing guidelines. The Memorandum of Agreement within general framework of the Memorandum of Understanding shall detail all the financial arrangements and other requirements prior to the commencement of activities.
3. Only the English version of this Memorandum of Understanding and the subsequent Memorandum of Agreement have binding effect.
4. Modifications and/or amendments to this Memorandum of Understanding shall be instigated through mutual consent.
5. Any disputes arising from the execution of this Memorandum of Understanding, both institutions on the basis of mutual trust and benefit, shall be resolved through friendly consultation.

The significance of the international linkages and partnerships for the program outcomes has sustained the students and faculty exchange programs with language proficiency training of the Tan Trao University of Vietnam. While the SEA-Teacher sponsored by the SEAMEO was able to strengthen the twinning-agreement for the Student Exchange Program in the basic education of Thailand, Indonesia, and Vietnam. The Romchatra Foundation through the support of the Maritime Silk Road Confucius Institute implemented substantial academic activities to pursue better collaboration for the " One Belt One Road Initiative' of the Chinese government.

Figure 10. Maritime Silk Road Confucius Institute Learning Resource Center located in 4th Floor CTE Academic Building

A. Program Outcome and Impact of the Research Presentation and Collaboration on Teaching and Learning Process Adopted in the Educational Supervision for the International partnership with Tan Trao University.

The academic collaboration of Tan Trao University in the Doctor of Education program provides the continuing support of the International research presentations in the area of educational administration the supervision of the teaching-learning process. The Tan Trao University presented the 1st international Conference in Vietnam as an offshoot of the faculty exchange program of Suan Dusit University that supported this activity.

The rationale of the 1st conference adhered to the idea of Holistic Education. The university administration of Tan Trao supported this holistic education which has become a popular teaching and learning approach particularly for primary education in Western countries, but it may appear new to Vietnamese education and perhaps to some Southeast Asian countries. The key characteristics of *Holistic education* are instead of educating students with academic aspects only, the educator should see the student's development as a *'whole'*: hard skills (academic ability); soft skills (presentation, independence, critical thinking…).

The program outcome revolves around the benchmarking of the educational management adopted from the best practices of the Southeast Asian countries particularly the teacher education program that anchored on the policy research of the Blended Education program. The university officials of Tan Trao made mention of the program outcome of the academic collaboration in Vietnam that "Taking account from *Holistic education*, the 1st International Conference at Tan Trao University will raise the issue of whether we should assess students at primary level through exams and marks, or instead, students will be assessed by teachers' comments and evaluations about different skills and abilities at a particular time. The theme of the conference also focuses on the current assessment system of all students in general and primary students in particular in Vietnam and some southeast Asian countries.

This was held in Tuyen Quang, the former temporary capital of Vietnam in the resistance war against the French colony. Tuyen Quang has a complex history in both pre-modern and modern Vietnam which makes it "a place of history". Tan Trao University is also named towards a historical milestone. Tan Trao is a newly founded university, but it has attracted large numbers of young scholars, these staff is expected to be the key people in implementing and renovating what we learn from the conference.

It has shown in the academic collaboration of the Tan Trao University had allowed providing sustained practices, most especially in the early childhood teaching-learning process. The educational impact of the strong support of the CTE on the ideas and concepts of early childhood education the best practice of the teacher education program emerged the adoption of the twinning program in the student exchange program as deeply rooted by the research collaboration.

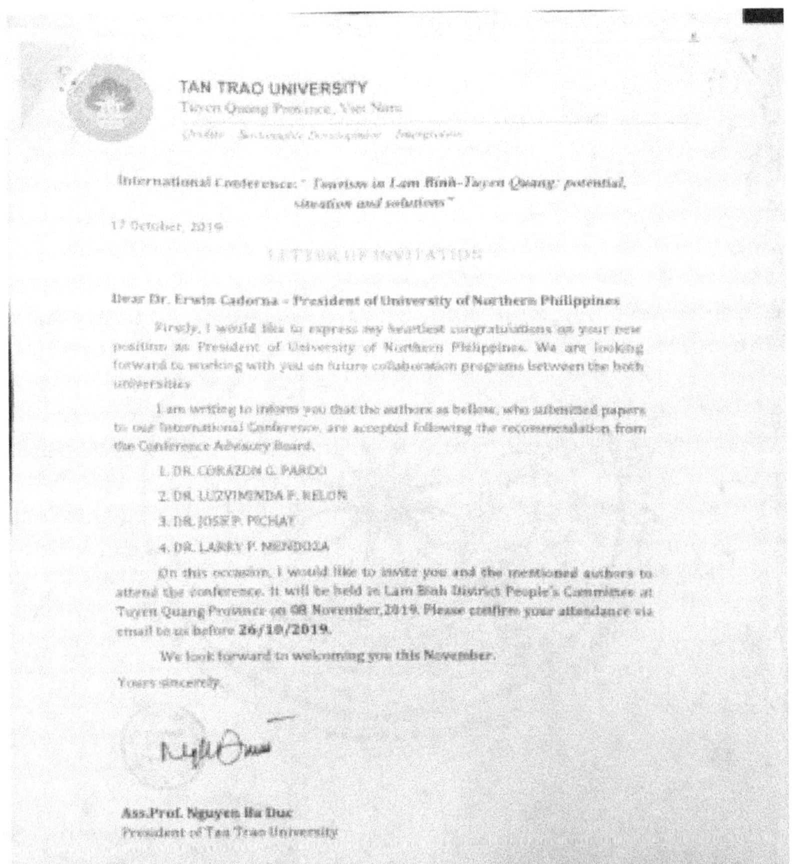

Figure 1. Letter of Invitation of Tan Trao University to the University of Northern Philippines

Figure 1. Some BECEd Faculty who attended the 1ˢᵗ international Conference in Vietnam

C. Technical Assistance on Book Publication Relevant to the Asian Culture, History and Tradition

The technical assistance on book publication to the Romchatra Foundation has a high level of educational impact in the relevant areas of Asian Culture, History, and Tradition. There were five books published particularly in support of the Maritime Silk Road Confucius Institute disseminated in the ASEAN universities. The academic exchange provided a greater understanding of Confucian Philosophy, ASEAN Cultural Diversity, Chinese Culture and Tradition, Asian Economic, and Political Development.

Table 3. Program Impact of the Technical Assistance on Book Publication Relevant to the Asian Culture, History and Tradition

Description	X	DR
1. Enhance the academic relevance in the cultural heritage, history, and tradition in Asian countries.	4.73	VH
2. Improve the understanding of the Confucian Philosophy, ASEAN integration, One Belt One Road, Chinese Culture and History, and cultural and educational management practices.	4.82	VH
3. Improve academic collaboration and educational assistance in the ASEAN schools in Thailand, Indonesia, and Vietnam.	4.79	VH
4. Utilize the book publications as instructional materials in the Asian culture, history, and tradition.	4.90	VH
5. Expand the interest of the students and stakeholders in the cultural background of Filipino history and tradition.	4.78	VH
Average Mean	4.78	VH

Note :

Statistical Range	*Descriptive Range*
4.21 – 5.00	Very High(VH)
3. 41- 4.20	High (H)
2.61 – 3.40	Fair (F)
1.81 – 2.60	Low (L)
1.00 – 1.80	Very Low (VL)

Part of the BECEd curriculum is inclusive education in the early childhood which also covers multi-cultural education. In order to attain this, there were publications published in relation to this. Based on the result of the study, the utilization of book publications (X-4.90) as instructional materials in the Asian culture, history, and tradition was given the recognition of the Romchatra officials as to the program impact of the project. The Romchatra Foundation was able to publish the One Belt One Road initiative of the Chinese government in support of the Maritime Silk Road Initiative. The Maritime Silk Road which is the basis of the "One Belt One Road," evolves as a good model of political and economic life in which the Asian nations respected the ideas of wholesome development of the society where independence and freedom existed vis-à-vis to technological innovations (see figure 10).

Figure 10. A copy of the Global Intervention Lecture on "One Belt, One Road" by the 21ˢᵗ Century Maritime Silk Road

Table 4. Academic Visit and Benchmarking in the Advancement of Learning in Higher Education

Description	X	DR
1. Sustain the academic commitment of higher education on the generation of knowledge and exchange program in the development of advanced education.	4.58	VH
2. Improve the educational processes as a result of the academic visit and benchmarking.	4.62	VH
3. Expand the academic interest of collaboration in the continuing support of the advanced education	4.64	VH
4. Enhance the curricular support in the inclusion of higher education lessons on ASEAN integration, cultural and educational exchange, language proficiency program, and other lines of academic interests.	4.80	VH
5. Generate new knowledge and understanding the contribution of the best practices in the higher education program.	4.71	VH
Average Mean	4.67	VH

The academic visit and benchmarking highlighted the enhancement of the curricular support in the inclusion of higher education lessons on ASEAN integration, cultural and educational exchange, language proficiency program, and other lines of academic interest. (X-4.80) Based on this finding, the respondents were able to integrate the curricular enhancement that the academic visit had given them more opportunities to generate new knowledge on the implementation of the ASEAN Quality Framework as to the ideas of universal adoption of employment requirements for the ASEAN countries. The significance of the academic visit produced more international linkages and partnership activities along with the cultural exchange program and language proficiency program by the support of Maritime Silk Road Confucius Institutes and Romchatra Foundation.

Furthermore, this finding revealed that this generated new knowledge and understanding of the best practices in the higher education program. The College of Teacher Education through the Blended Education program of the Center for International Studies presented the expertise of the faculty to give technical assistance to the Romchatra Foundation in the areas of career development through the Blended Education program including language proficiency which is also a part of the BECEd program.

Figure 11. UNP *President,* **Dr. Edwin F. Cadorna,** *assisted by Dr. Generoso Gudelio Pajarillo, Director of the Public and International Affairs Office who initiated the collaboration, displaying the signed MOU in the presence of Atty. Jonalyn Almachar, UNP Board Secretary (left), and the 2nd highest Rank Buddhist Monk of Thailand,* **Somdetphramaharatchamongkhonlumani,** *Chairman of the Board of Romchatra Foundation showing the signed MOU (right).*

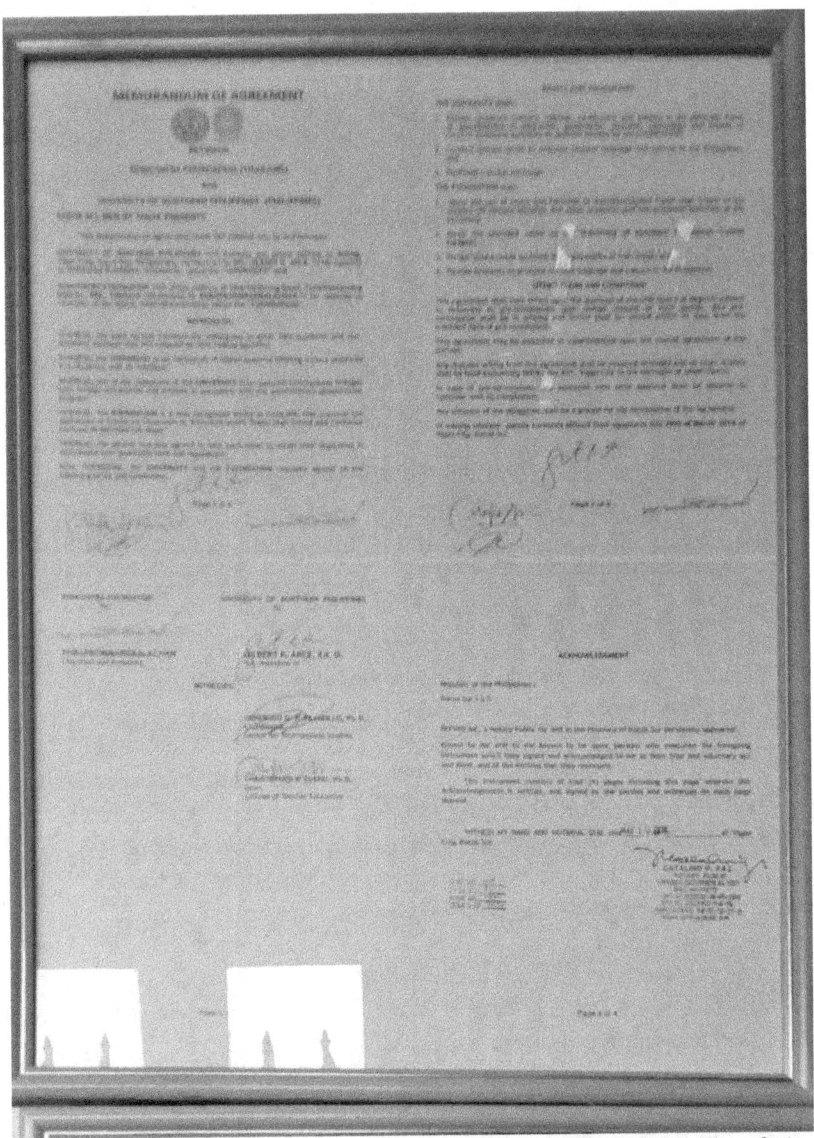

Figure 12. Original copy of the MOU between Romchatra Foundation (Thailand) and University of Northern Philippines located in the Maritime Silk Road 4th floor CTE academic building

Table 5. ASEAN Partnership on Academic Activities of Teacher Education

Description	X	DR
1. Enhance the Cultural Diversity, Heritage Management, History, and Tradition in the ASEAN Community.	4.97	VH
1. Expand understanding of ASEAN Culture, History, and Tradition in partnership with the ASEAN universities.	4.96	VH
2. Develop awareness in the cultural diversity of the ASEAN Community in support with the Rom	4.92	VH
3. Enhance the partnership with the foreign schools in the ASEAN Community to further strengthen the teacher education program	4.73	VH
4. Provide continuing and sustained academic collaboration with the partner schools in the ASEAN countries	4.86	VH

The effectiveness of the ASEAN partnerships with universities of Thailand, Vietnam, and Indonesia has been the enhancement of Cultural Diversity, Heritage Management, History, and Tradition. (4.97) The educational impact can be attributed to the sustained technical assistance provided to the Romchatra Foundation in support of the Maritime Silk Road Confucius Institute for the academic dissemination of the " One Belt and One Road Initiative" in the ASEAN countries. The College of Teacher Education-Graduate Studies ensures the complementary support for the cultural heritage program of the UNESCO Heritage City of Vigan.

This was the reason for the full support of the Confucius Institutes of the Romchatra Foundation to sustain the implementation of cultural diversity and a greater understanding of the ASEAN culture, tradition, and history. Furthermore, the respondents have agreed that the ASEAN partnership strengthens the academic collaboration in teacher education will have a better opportunity to expand the understanding of the totality of the ASEAN culture.

The College of Teacher Education was able to sustain the international linkages particularly in the career development of BECEd program that have significant program outcomes in the areas of twinning agreement on research and facilitation of teacher education experiences.

In the case of technical assistance on book publication, the Romchatra Foundation has a high level of educational impact in the relevant areas of Asian Culture, History and Tradition were five books published particularly in support with the Maritime Silk Road Confucius Institute disseminated in the ASEAN universities. The academic exchange provided a greater understanding of Confucian Philosophy, ASEAN Cultural Diversity, Chinese Culture and Tradition, Asian Economic, and Political Development.

For the academic collaboration, it has the program outcome of the enhancement of academic collaboration by providing complimentary exchange and assistance in the different school activities. These are the research presentation, lecture, and conferences provided by the different partner agencies that have contributed to the understanding of the cultural diversity, career development and ASEAN integration particularly in the area of inclusivity of higher education program Finally, the academic visit and benchmarking highlighted the enhancement of the curricular support in the inclusion of higher education lesson on ASEAN integration, cultural and educational exchange, language proficiency program and other lines of academic interest.

Figure 12. Student International Internship at Plookpanya School, Nakhon Racatchima, Thailand (January 5-March 5, 2017)

The College of Teacher has been supporting the Student International Internship Program through the assistance of Center for International Studies and Romchatra Foundation by forging an agreement for Student Exchange Program in Thailand and Vietnam. The Student International Internship Program is designed to expose interns to the foreign schools, particularly in the ASEAN schools.

WELCOME!
FACULTY and STUDENTS
TAN TRAO UNIVERSITY
TUYEN QUANG CITY, VIETNAM

Figure 13. UNP showcases the many faces of Filipino hospitality and UNP's brand of globally competitive instruction, research and extension

The University of Northern Philippines is an affiliate member of the Maritime Silk Road Confucius Institute with the responsibility to assist and provide academic assistance in the preparation and publications of books relevant to the accomplishments of Romchatra Foundation in the "Belt and Road Initiatives."

The college has been publishing best practices in teaching and learning process, and social sciences books including coursebooks in general education. Part of the academic package in this area is the training of faculty members and publication of research findings in the Amazon books as part of the e-books needed by the education students. It is expected that the academic publications will further enhance the ability of the students as generalists and specialists in the areas of elementary and secondary education.

The Global Education Development of the 2015 ASEAN Integration: **Traimit** Model

The Traimit Model is designed to conduct academic linkages and partnerships in the cultural heritage program relevant to the sustained establishment of the Confucius Classrooms and Institutes. The Romchatra Foundation used the applied educational management theory in the study entitled "Traimit Educational Model for the First Confucius School in Thailand," which was published in the Amazon for its educational management application in the Confucius Classroom in ASEAN countries.

Student International Internship at Plookpanya School, Nakhon Racatchima, Thailand (January 5-March 5, 2017)

The College of Teacher has been supporting the Student International Internship Program through the assistance of Center for International Studies and Romchatra Foundation by forging an agreement for Student Exchange Program in Thailand and Vietnam. The Student International Internship Program is designed to expose the BSEd and BEEd (including the ECEd majors) interns to the foreign schools, particularly in the ASEAN schools

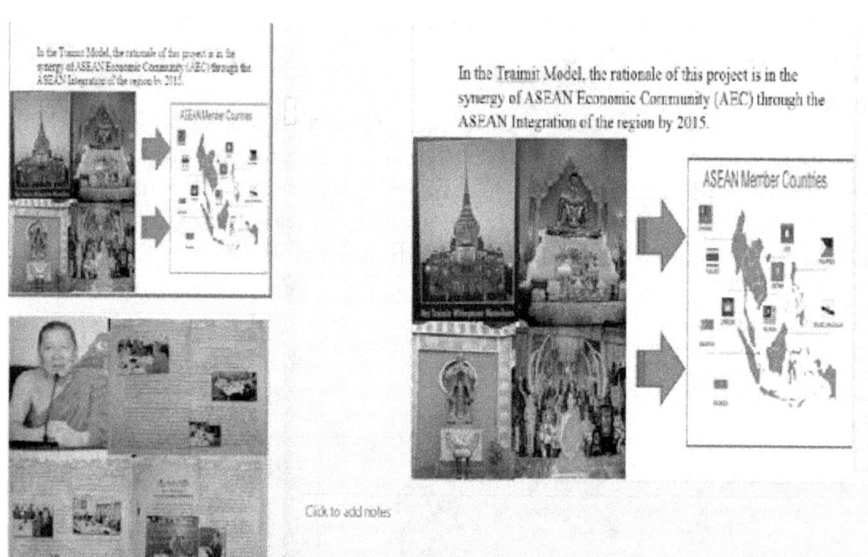

In connection with this, teaching competencies in other countries were benchmarked and compared as a way of improving its international linkages:

- **Teaching Competency Standards in the Philippines.** The Philippines defines a competent teacher as one of the most significant elements of the country's education system. The Philippine teaching competency standards known as the NCBTS comprises seven major strands of social regard for learning; learning environment; diversity of learners; curriculum; planning, assessing, and reporting; community linkages; and personal growth and professional development.

- **Teaching Competency Standards in Indonesia.** Indonesia defines a competent teacher as one who meets the components of the four major competencies defined by the country's Teacher Law. Indonesia's teaching competency standards are grouped into four major strands pedagogical, personal, professional, and social.

- **Teaching Competency Standards in Vietnam.** Vietnam defines a competent teacher as one who possesses both the knowledge and skills required to teach students well. Teachers should have specialized knowledge in their respective subjects as well as general knowledge to answer all kinds of questions that their students may ask. They should have the necessary pedagogical, communication, presentation, and classroom management skills to successfully perform their roles as classroom managers, facilitators, organizers, and resource persons.

Chapter 3
Overview of the International Linkages and Consortia of the College of Teacher Education, University of Northern Philippines

I. Introduction

The effectiveness of the ASEAN partnerships with universities of Thailand, Vietnam, and Indonesia has been the enhancement of Cultural Diversity, Heritage Management, History, and Tradition. (4.97) The educational impact can be attributed to the sustained technical assistance provided to the Romchatra Foundation in support of the Maritime Silk Road Confucius Institute for the academic dissemination of the " One Belt and One Road Initiative" in the ASEAN countries. The College of Teacher Education-Graduate Studies ensures the complementary support for the cultural heritage program of the UNESCO Heritage City of Vigan.

This was the reason for the full support of the Confucius Institutes of the Romchatra Foundation to sustain the implementation of cultural diversity and a greater understanding of the ASEAN culture, tradition, and history. Furthermore, the respondents have agreed that the ASEAN partnership strengthens the academic collaboration in teacher education will have a better opportunity to expand the understanding of the totality of the ASEAN culture.

The College of Teacher Education was able to sustain the international linkages particularly in the career development of the BECEd program that have significant program outcomes in the areas of twinning agreement on research and facilitation of teacher education experiences.

In the case of technical assistance on book publication, the Romchatra Foundation has a high level of educational impact in the relevant areas of Asian Culture, History and Tradition were five books published particularly in support with the Maritime Silk Road Confucius Institute disseminated in the ASEAN universities. The academic exchange provided a greater understanding of Confucian Philosophy, ASEAN Cultural Diversity, Chinese Culture and Tradition, Asian Economic, and Political Development.

The university mainly supports the education programs through the Center for International Studies in the Blended Education System for Foreign Students as approved by the UNP Board Resolution No. 19, s.2012. This is CHED compliant advanced education program with customized EdD programs for foreign students who hold high positions in the national and local government agencies as well as private entities. The complementation process of the Blended Education System integrates the international linkages and partnerships with the support of the Romchatra Foundation with the academic exchange program connected with the Maritime Silk Road Confucius Institute through the ASEAN Universities. These have been the continuing academic exchange such as Tan Trao University, Suan Dusit University, and Rajamagala Universities of Thailand.

Furthermore, the implementation of the international linkages and partnership revolved in the presentation of the technical papers relevant to the cultural heritage and ASEAN Integration. The internationalization efforts of the education program provided the research utilization of the strategic opportunity of the location of the university to share the academic experience is the engineering structural conservation management of the UNESCO Heritage City of Vigan. It also presented an overview of the ASEAN Integration and Technology.

The College of Teacher Education has the following objectives in networking, linkages, and consortia:

(1) connect the graduate education program with a development partner in the academe, national government agencies, and the local government units in the international community ;
(2) enable education programs on basic education, instructional competence, educational management and supervision, and others to become responsive to local and national thrusts through linkages in foreign countries;
(3) benchmark standards (local and international) for integration in the education programs in advanced higher education; and
(4) transfer educational models through the product of research and linkages for the enhancement of the education program.

The international linkages in the education programs are implemented by the Center for International Studies for the Graduate Studies for Education and the undergraduate programs of the College of Teacher Education reflected by the holistic framework of the university on the following development undertakings:

1. *Facilitation of in-country work experience for faculty and students in a relevant field of study.* The in-country work experience provides the academic collaboration of the faculty and students in the student internship abroad, student exchange on cultural diversity program, the socio-cultural blueprint of the ASEAN Integration, cultural heritage management and pedagogical implementation of contextualized curricula such as MTB-MLE, career development including the on-job-training of the CTE students to work in ASEAN universities.

2. *Joint research and extension activities, lectures, workshops, fora, symposia, and seminars.* The international research and extension activity participated by the core and affiliate faculty in the graduate and undergraduate programs such as international research collaboration, research journal publications, academic participation of socio-cultural blueprint of the ASEAN Integration, Cultural Heritage Collaboration, English Proficiency Training, Career Advancement, Technical Education, and Sports Development Programs.

3. *Exchange of academic materials, scientific publications, and other relevant scholarly information.* The institutional participation in the book publication of the education program in providing relevant academic materials such as ASEAN Integration, Traimit Model, Confucius Classroom/Institute, UNESCO Heritage Program, and Career Development Program.

4. Co-operation in education and training, including curriculum development, specialized training courses, staff development, and the promotion of staff and student exchanges.

5. Other cooperation and collaboration activities in education are deemed appropriate mutually.

The globalization efforts of the Graduate Studies of the University started after the approval of the Blended Education System for Foreign Students (BESFS) Program by the University Board of Regents under Board Resolution No.19, Series 2012. The Blended Education System for Foreign Student Students complies with CHED programs and standards which is a customized special program specifically for foreign students who hold high positions in the national and local government agencies as well as private entitics. Its implementing guidelines were approved by the UNP Board of Regents (BOR No. 74, s.2013). The three (3) doctorate programs offered are the Doctor of Education, Doctor of Public Administration, and Doctor of Administration. As an offshoot of the implementation of this program, The Graduate School Center for International Studies was established and created to be responsible for the operation of the Blended Education System for Foreign Students.

The Center for International Studies (now Public and International Affairs) was created under Special Order No. GRA45, Series of 2013 designating Dr. Generoso Gudelio P. Pajarillo, as the program coordinator attached under the Office of the President as Special project to coordinate and spearhead academic-related development programs for the University including the Graduate Studies for Education about its internationalization efforts along with the implementation of the blended education system. Furthermore, the center provides strategic support to explore, initiate, and negotiate international linkages, partnerships, cooperation, and collaboration with schools, universities institutions, and centers.

These are the implemented international linkages in the College of Teacher Education with the strategic support of the Center for International Studies with an excellent outcome in the development programs along with basic education; career development; academic lecture; cultural heritage advocacy; and research projects that produced technical and research papers in the international community. Furthermore, the international linkages in the academe and international institutions/organizations forged Memorandum of Understanding (MOU) and Memorandum of Agreement (MOA) in the promotion and cooperation of development programs in the education sector. The college has been publishing best practices in the teaching and learning process, and social sciences books including coursebooks in general education. Part of the academic package in this area is the training of faculty members and publication of research findings in the Amazon books as part of the e-books needed by the education students. It is expected that the academic publications will further enhance the ability of the students as generalists and specialists in the areas of elementary and secondary education.

The Global Education Development of the 2015 ASEAN Integration: Traimit Model

The Traimit Model is designed to conduct academic linkages and partnerships in the cultural heritage program relevant to the sustained establishment of the Confucius Classrooms and Institutes. The Romchatra Foundation used the applied educational management theory in the study entitled "Traimit Educational Model for the First Confucius School in Thailand," which was published in the Amazon for its educational management application in the Confucius Classroom in ASEAN countries. and conferences provided by the different partner agencies that have contributed to the understanding of the cultural diversity, career development and ASEAN integration particularly in the area of inclusivity of higher education program Finally, the academic visit and benchmarking highlighted the enhancement of the curricular support in the inclusion of higher education lesson on ASEAN integration, cultural and educational exchange, language proficiency program and other lines of academic interest.

II. Objectives

The specific objectives of the International Linkages and Consortia of the College of Teacher Education along with academic collaboration, inter-country facilitation, research, and book publication in the ASEAN countries are the following:

a) Sustain the Academic Collaboration and Assistance on Research, Lecture, and Conferences of the Teacher Education Program.
b) Enhance the Academic Visit and Benchmarking in the Advancement of Learning in Higher Education.
c) Sustain the implementation of the Blended Education Program for Career Development with Support of ASEAN Integration, Cultural and Educational Exchange Program.
d) Sustain the sustained International Linkages in the Graduate Studies for Education and undergraduate programs along with Academic Exchange and Collaboration, Research and Extension Development Programs.
E. Strengthen the conduct of the facilitation of Faculty Exchange Exposure and enhance the ASEAN Partnership on Academic Activities of Teacher Education.

III. Scope of the International Linkages and Consortia in the College of Teacher Education (2016-2021)

The College of Teacher Education has been responding to the international linkages and consortia through the presentation of the documentary and key informant responses on the descriptive analysis on the assessment of the international linkages and partnership with the ASEAN countries. The documentary evidences were taken from the Memorandum of Agreement (MOA) and Memorandum of Understanding (MOU) in the previous institutional engagement with foreign universities in Thailand, Vietnam, China, and Indonesia. The program outcomes and impacts of the graduate and undergraduate degree programs were taken from the accomplishments in the documents of ISO: 9001:2015 and Center of Development (COD).

Primarily, the sustained international linkage of Romchatra Foundation through the Maritime Silk Road Confucius Institute that given the opportunity for the College of Teacher Education to extend technical assistance in varied forms such as book publications, career development, academic exchange and collaboration, language proficiency, and understanding of the ASEAN culture, history, and tradition. This is in response to the strategic location of the College of Teacher Education, University of Northern Philippines in the UNESCO Heritage City of Vigan.

Vigan City is the best-preserved example of a planned Spanish colonial town in Asia. Its architectural design reflects the coming together of cultural elements from elsewhere in the Philippines, from China and from Europe, resulting in a culture and townscape that have no parallel anywhere in East and South-East Asia. This was considered under the Criterion (ii): Vigan represents a unique fusion of Asian building design and construction with European colonial architecture and planning. Criterion (iv): Vigan is an exceptionally intact and well preserved example of a European trading town in East and South-East Asia. The strategic vision of the Historic City of Vigan has fulfilled for its revitalization as the best practice in World Heritage Property management and one of the seven wonder cities of the world for the contemporary time. The next phase of the development to sustain its tangible path in the knowledge-based society is to document and publish the best practices for the cultural management as part of the good governance practice that may be adopted to the local government units in the Philippines.

https://www.researchgate.net/publication/279671836_Local_Governance_Practice_of_the_UNESCO_Heritage_City_of_Vigan_The_Seven_Wonder_City_of_the_World

The scope of documentary and qualitative analysis includes academic activities accomplished in the Memorandum of Agreement (MOA) and Memorandum of Understanding (MUO) along with career development, inter-country facilitation, academic collaboration, and faculty-student exchange program which evaluated the program outcomes of the College of Teacher Education who were actively involved in the implementation of the Blended Education Program who were enrolled in the undergraduate and graduate studies (30 percent), international linkages with the support of the Romchatra Foundation 35 percent), and other stakeholders of the ASEAN universities who were directly involved in the implementation of the academic exchange program (35 percent).

The highlights of the research findings were studied based on its effectiveness of the program outcomes along strengthening the partnership collaboration in improving the educational management process, pedagogical competence, promotion of current designation, publication of books relevant to the implementation of the Maritime Silk Road Confucius Institute, and language competence of the stakeholders.

A. Scope of the Memorandum of Understanding (MOU) and Memorandum of Agreement (MOA) in the Socio-Cultural Blueprint of the ASEAN Integration

The College of Teacher Education was able to sustain the international linkages and consortia particularly in the significant program outcomes in the areas of twinning agreement on research and facilitation of teacher education experiences. The CTE research studies have been focused on the best practices of academic collaboration along with language proficiency, cultural diversity, pedagogical practices, and 21st-century education. These have been the major program outcomes that resulted in the academic partnership with the universities of Thailand, Vietnam, Indonesia and China.

1. MOU and MOA Features and Themes Relevant to the Research and Academic Collaboration of the Higher and Advanced Education in the ASEAN universities

Specifically, it actively contributed to the sustained academic collaboration on the different themes and features as the impact in the undergraduate and advanced education program. Furthermore, the academic collaboration has the program outcome of the enhancement of academic collaboration by providing complimentary exchange and assistance in the different school activities . These are the research presentation, lectures, and conferences provided by the different partner agencies that have contributed to the understanding of cultural diversity, career development, and ASEAN integration particularly in the area of inclusivity of higher education programs. The program outcomes were able to sustain the research productivity, culture, economic enterprise, educational management, and administration.

1.1 Twining Agreement.

The program has contributed to the sharing of best practices along with the educational administration by the faculty support in enrolling the Blended Education for Advanced Education. These are the continuing support of academic collaboration to the Foreign Universities for the expanded course offerings for the higher and advanced education programs in support of the Socio-Cultural Blueprint of the ASEAN Integration. The twinning agreement provides the inclusivity to address the strategic position of the College of Teacher Education to contribute significant scholarly works in the field of the teacher education programs, culture-based education, socio-cultural education, and continuing professional education of the ASEAN professionals for undergraduate and advanced education.

1.2 Inter-Country Facilitation of Teacher Education Program

This area provides the educational support of the practice teaching abroad, language proficiency, and sharing the best practices of the educational management including the assistance of faculty development through the support of their enrolment in the Blended Education program. The student internship abroad, student exchange program, and SEA Teacher have contributed so much to the professional development and global exposures of the teacher education students . The experiential learning for the inter-country facilitation has given so much opportunity for the CTE students to be exposed to foreign universities. The UNESCO Heritage City of Vigan provides the same inter-country facilitation to support culture-based education, cultural diversity, heritage management, and supporting socio-cultural blueprint in the ASEAN countries.

1.3 Research Productivity

These are the sharing experiences and best practices in the teacher education program as to the research studies on educational and economic enterprises in the Blended Education program that contributed to the career promotion and development of the stakeholders. The knowledge generation can be attributed to the actual practices in the field of educational management and business administration which contributed to the paradigm shift of management activities by the stakeholders.

1.3 Culture, History, and Tradition

The academic collaboration reflected from the result of the continuing technical assistance of the Maritime Silk Road Confucius Institutes of Romchatra Foundation for the academic engagement with Rajamagala Universities of Thailand, Suan Dusit University including Traimit Wittayalai High School of Thailand, Tan Trao University of Vietnam and other Universities connected with the SEAMEO project on SEA Teachers. 3. **Educational and Economic Enterprise**. The research studies were relevant to the implementation of quality education in the field of teacher education. It also provides the academic support of finding out the best practices in the advanced education program including the areas of language proficiency, cultural diversity, economic development, and career promotion.

1.4 Educational Management and Administration

This reflects the research studies on the themes of ASEAN Integration, Career Development, Pedagogical Approaches, and cultural exchange programs to support the holistic development in advanced education. The educational management programs are also provided in the support of career and promotion of graduate and undergraduate students in the Blended Education System.

1.5 Cultural Diversity, Culture-Based Education and Heritage Management and Development of the UNESCO Heritage City of Vigan

The strategic location of the UNESCO Heritage City of Vigan becomes the masterpiece of global competitiveness in the academic exchange program and international research collaboration within the area of Cultural Diversity, Cultural Heritage Management, Pedagogical Support of Culture-based Education (including MTB-MLE) and the Socio-Cultural Blueprint of the ASEAN Integration.

The College of Teacher Education , University of Northern Philippines ensures the full support of the UNESCO Heritage City of Vigan in the global window for the academic and research collaborations in the Philippines. Thus, the international linkages and consortia of the College of Teacher Education extensively advocated the socio-cultural blueprint of the ASEAN Integration including culture-based education, cultural heritage management and administration, and pedagogical enhancement on MTB-MLE and other cultural diversity programs.

It is only the College of Teacher Education in this location to promote and assist the UNESCO Heritage City of Vigan in the Philippines in the right position to value the international linkages for the development of the socio-cultural blueprint in the ASEAN Integration . The foreign universities are collaborating and assisting the college to promote the diplomatic position for the cultural heritage and diversity in quest of international linkages and consortia to support the UNESCO advocacy on cultural heritage preservation in the world.

Chapter 4
The Global Sustainability of the Teacher Education Program in the University of Northern Philippines for the Cultural Inscription of the Historic Centre of Vigan under the UNESCO World Heritage Property

The operational guidelines for the implementation of the World Heritage Convention, UNESCO Intergovernmental Committee for 2008 aims to facilitate the implementation of the convention concerning the protection of the world cultural and natural heritage. The World Heritage Committee decides on the inscription of a site on the basis of a nomination made by the Government of the country where is the site is located. The site is judged on its merits, in accordance to sets of criteria as provided in the Article 77 the guidelines of the Committee considers a property as having outstanding universal value.

Historically, the concern of the cultural and natural heritage and eventually the formation of the UNESCO World Heritage had adopted in the General Conference of the United Nations Educational, Scientific and Cultural Organization meeting in Paris from 17 October to 21 November 1972, at its seventeenth session,

Noting that the cultural heritage and the natural heritage are increasingly threatened with destruction not only by the traditional causes of decay, but also by changing social and economic conditions which aggravate the situation with even more formidable phenomena of damage or destruction,

Considering that deterioration or disappearance of any item of the cultural or natural heritage constitutes a harmful impoverishment of the heritage of all the nations of the world,

Considering that protection of this heritage at the national level often remains incomplete because of the scale of the resources which it requires and of the insufficient economic, scientific, and technological resources of the country where the property to be protected is situated,

Recalling that the Constitution of the Organization provides that it will maintain, increase, and diffuse knowledge by assuring the conservation and protection of the world's heritage, and recommending to the nations concerned the necessary international conventions,

Considering that the existing international conventions, recommendations and resolutions concerning cultural and natural property demonstrate the importance, for all the peoples of the world, of safeguarding this unique and irreplaceable property, to whatever people it may belong,

Considering that parts of the cultural or natural heritage are of outstanding interest and therefore need to be preserved as part of the world heritage of mankind as a whole,

Considering that, in view of the magnitude and gravity of the new dangers threatening them, it is incumbent on the international community as a whole to participate in the protection of the cultural and natural heritage of outstanding universal value, by the granting of collective assistance which, although not taking the place of action by the State concerned, will serve as an efficient complement thereto,

Considering that it is essential for this purpose to adopt new provisions in the form of a convention establishing an effective system of collective protection of the cultural and natural heritage of outstanding universal value, organized on a permanent basis and in accordance with modern scientific methods,

In this study, the inscription of Vigan City is presented in Article 1 of the guideline the definition of "cultural heritage" which has considered monuments, group buildings and sites. These are the three considered groupings of cultural heritage:

1. Monuments. The architectural works, works of monumental sculpture and painting, elements or structures of an archaeological nature, inscriptions, cave dwellings and combinations of features, which are of outstanding universal value from the point of view of history, art or science;

2. Groups of Buildings These are the groups of separate or connected buildings which, because of their architecture, their homogeneity or their place in the landscape, are of outstanding universal value from the point of view of history, art or science;

3. Sites. These are works of man or the combined works of nature and of man, and areas including archaeological sites which are of outstanding universal value from the historical, aesthetic, ethnological or anthropological points of view.

For Cultural Property on UNESCO Heritage Convention a nominated cultural property must meet at least one of the following criteria, before it is inscribed in the World Heritage List:

(i) represent a masterpiece of human creative genius;

(ii) exhibit an important interchange of human values, over a span of time or within a cultural area of the world, on developments in architecture or technology, monumental arts, town-planning or landscape design;

(iii) bear a unique or at least exceptional testimony to a cultural tradition or to a civilization which is living or which has disappeared;

(iv) be an outstanding example of a type of building, architectural or technological ensemble or landscape which illustrates (a) significant stage(s) in human history;

(v) be an outstanding example of a traditional human settlement, land-use, or sea-use which is representative of a culture (or cultures), or human interaction with the environment especially when it has become vulnerable under the impact of irreversible change;

(vi) be directly or tangibly associated with events or living traditions, with ideas, or with beliefs, with artistic and literary works of outstanding universal significance.

The justification for the inscription was established in the 16th century, Vigan is the best-preserved example of a planned Spanish colonial town in Asia. Its architectural design reflects the coming together of cultural elements from elsewhere in the Philippines, from China and from Europe, resulting in a culture and townscape that have no parallel anywhere in East and South-East Asia. This was considered under the Criterion (ii): Vigan represents a unique fusion of Asian building design and construction with European colonial architecture and planning. Criterion (iv): Vigan is an exceptionally intact and well preserved example of a European trading town in East and South-East Asia.

The World Heritage Committee has identified and defined several specific types of cultural and natural properties and has adopted specific guidelines to facilitate the evaluation of such properties when nominated for inscription on the World Heritage List. To date, these cover the following categories, although it is likely that others may be added in due course: (a) Cultural Landscapes; (b) Historic Towns and Town Centres;(c) Heritage Canals; and (d) Heritage Routes.

The inscription of Vigan City is considered under the specific guideline on Historic Towns and Town Centres. There are three main categories on the groups of urban buildings eligible for inscription on the World Heritage List:

(i) towns which are **no longer inhabited** but which provide unchanged archaeological evidence of the past; these generally satisfy the criterion of authenticity and their state of conservation can be relatively easily controlled;

(ii) **historic towns which are still inhabited** and which, by their very nature, have developed and will continue to develop under the influence of socio-economic and cultural change, a situation that renders the assessment of their authenticity more difficult and any conservation policy more problematical;

(iii) **new towns of the twentieth century** which paradoxically have something in common with both the aforementioned categories: while their original urban organization is clearly recognizable and their authenticity is undeniable, their future is unclear because their development is largely uncontrollable.

The significance of Historic Towns and Town Centres which Vigan City was considered in this area is on (ii) **Inhabited historic towns:**

In the case of inhabited historic towns the difficulties are numerous, largely owing to the fragility of their urban fabric (which has in many cases been seriously disrupted since the advent of the industrial era) and the runaway speed with which their surroundings have been urbanized. To qualify for inscription, towns should compel recognition because of their architectural interest and should not be considered only on the intellectual grounds of the role they may have played in the past or their value as historical symbols under criterion (vi) for the inscription of cultural properties on the World Heritage List .

In the operational guidelines on Paragraph 77 (vi) "To be eligible for inscription in the List, the spatial organization, structure, materials, forms and, where possible, functions of a group of buildings should essentially reflect the civilization or succession of civilizations which have prompted the nomination of the property. Four categories can be distinguished:

a) Towns which are typical of a specific period or culture, which have been almost wholly preserved and which have remained largely unaffected by subsequent developments. Here the property to be listed is the entire town together with its surroundings, which must also be protected;

b) Towns that have evolved along characteristic lines and have preserved, sometimes in the midst of exceptional natural surroundings, spatial arrangements and structures that are typical of the successive stages in their history. Here the clearly defined historic part takes precedence over the contemporary environment;

c) "Historic centres" that cover exactly the same area as ancient towns and are now enclosed within modern cities. Here it is necessary to determine the precise limits of the property in its widest historical dimensions and to make appropriate provision for its immediate surroundings;

d) Sectors, areas or isolated units which, even in the residual state in which they have survived, provide coherent evidence of the character of a historic town which has disappeared. In such cases surviving areas and buildings should bear sufficient testimony to the former whole.

Historic centres and historic areas should be listed only where they contain a large number of ancient buildings of monumental importance which provide a direct indication of the characteristic features of a town of exceptional interest. Nominations of several isolated and unrelated buildings which allegedly represent, in themselves, a town whose urban fabric has ceased to be discernible, should not be encouraged.

However, nominations could be made regarding properties that occupy a limited space but have had a major influence on the history of town planning. In such cases, the nomination should make it clear that it is the monumental group that is to be listed and that the town is mentioned only incidentally as the place where the property is located. Similarly, if a building of clearly outstanding universal value is located in severely degraded or insufficiently representative urban surroundings, it should, of course, be listed without any special reference to the town.

There is a good reason to preserve the historic centres and towns just like Vigan City. The Philippine government through the Department of Tourism and City Government of Vigan City was able to implement inscription of the Historic Center of Vigan. In the operational guidelines for the inscription of a cultural heritage site must fully consider that: "While fully respecting the sovereignty of the States on whose territory the cultural and natural heritage is situated, States Parties to the *Convention* recognize the collective interest of the international community to cooperate in the protection of this heritage." States Parties to the *World Heritage Convention*, have the responsibility to: (Article 6(1) of the *World Heritage Convention*).:

a) ensure the identification, nomination, protection, conservation, presentation, and transmission to future generations of the cultural and natural heritage found within their territory, and give help in these tasks to other States Parties that request it; (Article 4 and 6(2) of the *World Heritage Convention*)

b) adopt general policies to give the heritage a function in the life of the community;(Article 5 of the *World Heritage Convention Operational Guidelines for the Implementation of the World Heritage Convention*

c) integrate heritage protection into comprehensive planning programmes;

d) establish services for the protection, conservation and presentation of the heritage;

e) develop scientific and technical studies to identify actions that would counteract the dangers that threaten the heritage;

f) take appropriate legal, scientific, technical, administrative and financial measures to protect the heritage;

g) foster the establishment or development of national or regional centres for training in the protection, conservation and presentation of the heritage and encourage scientific research in these fields;

h) not take any deliberate measures that directly or indirectly damage their heritage or that of another State Party to the *Convention*; (Article 6(3) of the *World Heritage Convention)*

i) submit to the World Heritage Committee an inventory of properties suitable for inscription on the World Heritage List (referred to as a Tentative List); (Article 11(1) of the *World Heritage Convention.)*

j) make regular contributions to the World Heritage Fund, the amount of which is determined by the General Assembly of States Parties to the *Convention*; (Article 16(1) of the *World Heritage Convention)*

k) consider and encourage the establishment of national, public and private foundations or associations to facilitate donations for the protection of World Heritage; (Article 17 of the *World Heritage Convention)*

l) give assistance to international fund-raising campaigns organized for the World Heritage Fund; (Article 18 of the *World Heritage Convention)*

m) use educational and information programmes to strengthen appreciation and respect by their peoples of the cultural and natural heritage defined in Articles 1 and 2 of the *Convention*, and to keep the public informed of the dangers threatening this heritage;(Article 27 of the *World Heritage Convention.)*

(n) provide information to the World Heritage Committee on the implementation of the *World Heritage Convention* and state of conservation of properties; (and   Article 29 of the *World Heritage Convention* Resolution adopted by the 11th General Assembly of States Parties (1997) *Operational Guidelines for the Implementation o 4 f the World Heritage Convention*

The historic city of Vigan was inscribed in the UNESCO World Heritage in December 2, 1999.The basis on its inscription was under the criterion (ii) *"exhibit an important interchange of human values, over a span of time or within a cultural area of the world, on developments in architecture or technology, monumental arts or town planning and landscape design"..* Likewise in criterion (iv) *"be an outstanding example of a type of building or architectural or technological ensemble, or landscape which illustrates a significant stage or significant stages in human history.* The UNESCO World Heritage List of Cultural Properties has acknowledged the Vigan Ancestral Houses as a historic buildings and monuments that was constructed during the reign of European power and adopted from the participation of the Chinese on its economic trade and cultural relations of the Ilocanos. The native artisans were given an opportunity to redefine the architectural legacy of the European and behind the support of the East Asian influence.

The World Heritage Centre officially cites *"Vigan represents a unique fusion of Asian building design and construction with European colonial architecture and planning"*. Furthermore , *"Vigan is an exceptionally intact and well preserved example of a European trading town in East and East Asia."*

In the applicability of "Historic Towns and Town Centres" in Vigan can be traced from the Spanish colonial period. As a town centre, it conformed with Ley de las Indias (the Law of the Indies) that regulated on its spatial form which was similar with the European structure. The urban planning has street patterns that radiated form a central park.

The historic town was transformed as a bustling city called "Ciudad Fernandina de Vigan" that had complete administrative and religious buildings to show the complementary structure for the church and state which was located in central plaza (Plaza Salcedo). These were the Casa Real, Capitolio , Municipio, Colegio de Ninas, Cathedral, and the other Spanish structures.

In October 25, 2012, the UNESCO Spanish Heritage City of Vigan was recognized in the UNESCO Best Practice in World Heritage Site Management :This is the UNESCO website article as to its inscription and recognition :

The Historic Town of Vigan (Philippines), inscribed on the World Heritage List in 1999, has been recognized as a model of best practices in World Heritage site management, at the occasion of the 40th anniversary of the World Heritage Convention. The distinction will be officially announced and a certificate presented to the Mayor of Vigan, Ms Eva Marie S. Medina, during the closing event of the celebrations of the 40th anniversary of the World Heritage Convention in Kyoto, Japan, on 8 November.

Vigan's successful and sustainable management has been achieved with relatively limited resources, which should make it adaptable to sites in all countries; the local community is well integrated into many aspects of the sustainable conservation and management of the property; and a multi-faceted approach to the protection of the site has been developed.

Recognizing and rewarding best practice in World Heritage site management on the occasion of the 40th Anniversary of the World Heritage Convention was called for by the World Heritage Committee at its 35th session in Paris, France in 2011. Twenty-three countries participated by sending in proposals for 28 World Heritage sites, both cultural and natural. Submissions were reviewed by a selection committee mandated by the UNESCO World Heritage Centre.

In social science research, this is a break through to decode the meaning of the value-life experiences on the social and cultural reality of the colonial diplomacy of Spain about the continuing historical events of Ciudad Fernandina de Vigan which originally created by the Royal Decrees of September 7,1757 issued by Fernando VI, King of Spain . In the contemporary time, it regained this Spanish grandeur of colonial diplomacy as the Philippine state recognized its creation by Republic Act No. 8988 approved on December 27,2000 .The legislative intent on the approval of the Philippine State distinctly viewed on its historical perspective as " *An Act Validating and Recognizing the Creation of the City of Vigan by the Royal Decree of September 7,1757 issued by Fernando VI, King of Spain.*" After more than two and half centuries from its recognition in Spain as Ciudad Fernandina de Vigan, now becomes the famous Spanish heritage city with Outstanding Universal Value as listed in the UNESO World Heritage site of the Historic City of Vigan.

The UNESCO World Heritage Committee defined its path as Worl Heritage Property by the Historical Perspective deeply rotted by the colonial diplomacy of Spain in the Asia-Pacific:

Established in the 16th century, Vigan is the best-preserved example of a planned Spanish colonial town in Asia. Its architecture reflects the coming together of cultural elements from elsewhere in the Philippines, from China and from Europe, resulting in a culture and townscape that have no parallel anywhere in East and South-East Asia.

Established in the 16th century, Vigan is the best-preserved example of a planned Spanish colonial town in Asia. Its architecture reflects the coming together of cultural elements from elsewhere in the Philippines, from China and from Europe, resulting in a culture and townscape that have no parallel anywhere in East and South-East Asia.

In the social science international perspective of colonial diplomacy of Spain, the tangible proof of the sociological diffusion, amalgamation and integration of Spanish life in the Asia-Pacific as defined by its architectural structure in Ciudad Fernandina de Vigan. The distinct cultural elements are totally different from its neighbouring Southeast Asia states as the Philippines is the only Asian country that around 80 percent of the population are Roman Catholic entangled by the Spanish culture and history. It is not only its religion and people with Spanish blood but the uniqueness of the famous place called the Historic City of Vigan.

The Advisory Body Evaluation of the UNESCO World Heritage site approved by its inscription as the Historic Town of Vigan with the Justification :

> *Criterion (ii): Vigan represents a unique fusion of Asian building design and construction with European colonial architecture and planning. Criterion (iv): Vigan is an exceptionally intact and well preserved example of a European trading town in East and South-East Asia.*

The UNESCO World Heritage Committee justified this Hsitoric Town of Vigan on this long description from its origin as the European trading town in East and South-East Asia as to the emergence and fusion of the Asian building design and construction with European colonial architecture :

> *The town is located in the delta of the Abra River, off the coastal plain of the China Sea, close to the north-east tip of the island of Luzon. The present-day municipality divided into nine urban districts and thirty rural villages. Almost half the total area is still in use for agriculture. The Historic Core Zone is defined on two sides by the Govantes and Mestizo rivers.*

> *Before the arrival of the Spanish, there was a small indigenous settlement on what was at that time an island, consisting of wooden or bamboo houses on stilts. In 1572 the conquistador Juan de Salcedo founded a new town, which he named Villa Ferdinandina, and made it his capital when appointed Lieutenant Governor (Encomendero) of the entire Ilocos region. Intended as a trading centre rather than a fortress, it was the northernmost city established in the Philippines by the Spanish. At the end of the 17th century a new form of architecture evolved, which combined traditional construction with the techniques of building in stone and wood*

introduced by the Spanish. Brick was introduced by the Augustinians for their churches and other buildings. In 1778, as a result of its expansion, it was renamed Ciudad Ferdinandina. The Mestizo River was central to the development of the town in the 16th-19th centuries: large sea-going vessels could berth in the delta and small craft communicated with the interior. It is no longer navigable owing to silting, and so the town is no longer an island. As the major commercial centre for the region, Vigan traded directly with China. As a stage in the Manila-Acapulco galleon trade in the Spanish colonial period, it supplied goods for shipping to Mexico, and thence onwards to Europe. This trade resulted in constant exchanges of peoples and cultures between the Ilocanos, Filipinos, Chinese, Spanish, and (in the 20th century) North Americans.

The traditional Spanish chequerboard street plan opens up into a main plaza, in two parts. The Plaza Salcedo is the longer arm of an L-shaped open space, with the Plaza Burgos as the shorter. The former is dominated by the Municipal Hall and the Provincial Capitol and the latter by the cathedral. The urban plan of the town closely conforms to the Renaissance grid plan specified in the Ley de las Indias for all 149 new towns in the Spanish Empire. There is, however, a noticeable difference between Vigan and contemporary Spanish colonial towns in Latin America in the Historic Core (known as the Mestizo district), where the Latin tradition is tempered by strong Chinese, Ilocano and Filipino influences.

The building materials used in Vigan are terracotta, wood, shells, stone and lime, all obtained from the surrounding area. The architecture of the typical Vigan house is derived from the traditional Filipino dwelling, the bahay kubo, a small one-room hut built from light woven materials (wood, bamboo, thatch), raised on stilts for ventilation and as protection against monsoon flooding. Such structures are no longer to be found in Vigan, but their influence is discernible in the much larger bahay na bato (stone house), a much more solid structure, with a stone-built lower storey surmounted by a timber-framed upper storey, and with a steeply pitched tiled roof (reminiscent of traditional Chinese architecture). The exterior walls of the upper storey are enclosed by window panels of kapis shells framed in wood which can be slid back for better ventilation. The Chinese merchants and traders conducted their business from offices and warehouses on the ground floors of their houses, with the living quarters above. This is characteristic of Chinese society. Vigan also possesses a number of significant public buildings, which also show multi-cultural influences. These include the Cathedral of St Paul, the Archbishop's Palace, St Paul's College, the Catholic Cemetery Chapel, and the neoclassical early 20th-century provincial Capitol.

Furthermore, the multi-disciplinary approach of cultural management provides important insights as to the development of the UNESCO World Heritage site in its Universal Outstanding Value on the following:

1. The human society on its social and cultural facts based on historical antecedents provides the strategic opportunity to revive the concept of cultural management and the development of cultural tourism to transform the town or municipality as a tourists' hubs for local economic growth and development.

2. The international recognition of the historic town or city as supported by the UNESCO World Heritage Committee based on their evaluation of its Outstanding Universal Value provides the historical and cultural awakening of the human society for its cultural tourism development of a given site.

3. The local government officials and the concerned stakeholders are the keys in the sustainable development of the UNESCO World Heritage site as their innovative strategy to promote historical and cultural tourism ensure the right path for the local economic growth and development.

The UNESCO World Heritage site of the Historic City of Vigan is a exemplar case of good governance and committed leadership of the local government officials to transform the old town by its strategic opportunity to redefine its Outstanding Universal Values by the revival of the famous historic city called *Ciudad Fernandina de Vigan* originally created by the Royal Decrees of September 7,1757 issued by Fernando VI, King of Spain.

Chapter 5
Program Outcomes and Academic Impacts of the International Linkages and Consortia of the College of Teacher Education, University of Northern Philippines

These are the research studies conducted with Program Outcomes and Academic Impacts of the International Linkages and Consortia in the College of Teacher Education, University of Northern Philippines, UNESCO Heritage City of Vigan:

A. Sustaining the Cultural and Academic Exchange Program of the Romchatra Foundation with the Confucius Institute of Maritime Silk Road : An Impact Study on the International Linkages of the Blended Education Program in the ASEAN Countries

The Romchatra Foundation through Phromomankachalan has expanded the international linkages of the University of Northern Philippines (UNP) to be a partner of the academic publications including cultural exchange activities under Hanban that recognized the effort of the College of Teacher Education to bring the forefront of scholarly publication through the ASEAN Community. The forging of agreement on Academic and cultural collaboration with the assistance of the Center of International Studies became the Best Practices of International linkages on Academic and Cultural Exchange program through the Confucius Maritime Silk Road of the Romchatra Foundation.

1. Academic Cooperation through the Confucius Institute of Maritime Silk Road with Foreign Universities and Schools in Thailand

The foreign universities and schools in the ASEAN countries forged agreement with the University of Northern Philippines to promote academic cooperation and exchange through facilitation of in-country work experience for student and faculty; joint research activities including book publications and other scholarly information:

2 Romchatra Foundation Initiative in Book Publications on "Belt and Road Initiatives" for the ASEAN Community

The University of Northern Philippines is an affiliate member of the Maritime Silk Road Confucius Institute with the responsibility to assist and provide academic assistance in the preparation and publications of books relevant to the accomplishments of Romchatra Foundation in the "Belt and

Road Initiatives."

The college has been publishing best practices in teaching and learning process, and social sciences books including coursebooks in general education. Part of the academic package in this area is the training of faculty members and publication of research findings in the Amazon books as part of the e-books needed by the education students. It is expected that the academic publications will further enhance the ability of the students as generalists and specialists in the areas of elementary and secondary education.

3 Romchatra Foundation with the Confucius Institute of Maritime Silk Road

The cultural and academic exchange program for the Teacher Education has been sustained in the ASEAN community to fulfill the vision of global university anchored on excellence through the technical assistance in book publication given to the Romchatra Foundation. As a global university in the teacher education program, the scholarly books of the Belt and Road Initiative became the academic flagship project of the Confucius Institute of Maritime Silk Road.

The Romchatra Foundation through Phromomankachalan expand the international linkages of the UNP to be a partner of the academic publications including cultural exchange activities under Hanban that recognized the effort of the CTE to bring the forefront of scholarly publication through the ASEAN Community. The forging of agreement on Academic and cultural collaboration with the assistance of the Center of International Studies became the Best Practices of International linkages on Academic and Cultural Exchange program through the Confucius Maritime Silk Road of the Romchatra Foundation.

The foreign universities and schools in the ASEAN countries forged agreement with the University of Northern Philippines to promote academic cooperation and exchange through facilitation of in-country work experience for student and faculty; joint research activities including book publications and other scholarly information:

4 Romchatra Foundation Initiative in Book Publications on "Belt and Road Initiatives" for the ASEAN Community

The University of Northern Philippines is an affiliate member of the Maritime Silk Road Confucius Institute with the responsibility to assist and provide academic assistance in the preparation and publications of books relevant to the accomplishments of Romchatra Foundation in the "Belt and Road Initiatives."

The college has been publishing best practices in teaching and learning process, and social sciences books including coursebooks in the general education. As part of the academic package in this area is the training of faculty members and publication of research findings in the Amazon books as part of the e-books needed by the education students. It is expected that the academic publications will further enhance the intellectual ability of the students as generalists and specialists in the areas of elementary and secondary education

5. The Global Education Development of the ASEAN Integration: Traimit Model

The Traimit Model is designed to conduct academic linkages and partnerships in the cultural heritage program relevant to the sustained establishment of the Confucius Classrooms and Institutes. The Doctor of Education Program has been very supportive of the outcome-based research particularly in the Dissertation which the Romchatra Foundation used the applied educational management theory in the study entitled "Traimit Educational Model for the First Confucius School in Thailand." This was published in the Amazon for its educational management application in the Confucius Classroom in ASEAN countries.

B. Academic Exchange and Research Collaboration in the Teacher Education Program of the University of Northern Philippines and Tan Trao University

The academic collaboration of the College Teacher Education with Tan Trao University has the educational impact in the areas of educational administration, cultural diversity, language proficiency, pedagogical assessment and teaching-learning process. It has shared the faculty expertise in the field of educational administration with the actual exposures of the visiting professors of Tan Trao University to bring Vietnamese students to learn and experience the culture, history and tradition of the Ilocanos. Furthermore, the academic exchange has achieved greater access to student and faculty exchange program through language proficiency training, cultural diversity and pedagogical assessment participation of the stakeholders.

1. Program Outcome and Impact of the Research Presentation and Collaboration on Teaching and Learning Process Adopted in the Educational Supervision for the International partnership with Tan Trao University.

The academic collaboration of Tan Trao University in the teacher education program provides the continuing support of the international research presentations in the area of educational administration and the supervision of the teaching- learning process. The Tan Trao University presented the 1st International Conference in Vietnam as an offshoot of the faculty exchange program of Suan Dusit University that supported this activity.

The rationale of the 1st conference adhered to the idea of holistic education. The university administration of Tan Trao supported this holistic education which has become a popular teaching and learning approach particularly for primary education in Western countries, but it may appear new to Vietnamese education and perhaps to some South East Asian countries. The key characteristics of *Holistic education* are instead of educating students with academic aspects only, educator should see the student's development as a *'whole'*: hard skills (academic ability); soft skills (presentation, independence, critical thinking…

The program outcome revolves from the benchmarking of the educational management adopted from the best practices of the Southeast Asian countries particularly the teacher education program that anchored on the policy research of the Blended Education program. The university officials of Tan Trao made mention of the program outcome of the academic collaboration in Vietnam that "Taking account from *Holistic education*, the 1st International Conference at Tan Trao University will raise the issue of whether we should assess students at primary level through exams and marks, or instead, students will be assessed by teachers' comments and evaluations about different skills and abilities at a particular period. The theme of the conference also focuses on the current assessment system of all students in general and primary students in particular in Vietnam and some Southeast Asian countries.

This was held in Tuyen Quang, the former temporary capital of Vietnam in the resistance war against the French colony. Tuyen Quang has a complex history in both pre-modern and modern Vietnam which makes it "a place of history". Tan Trao University is also named towards a historical milestone. Tan Trao is a newly founded university, but it has attracted large numbers of young scholars, these staffs are expected to be the key people in implementing and renovating what we learn from the conference.

It has shown in the academic collaboration of the Tan Trao University had given an opportunity to provide sustained support in the educational management practices and the teaching-learning process. The educational impact of the strong support of the Graduate School on the ideas and concepts of Educational Administration the best practice of the teacher education program emerged the adoption of the twinning program in the student exchange program as deeply rooted by the research collaboration.

2. The Potent Catalyst of the Emerging Research and International Collaboration in Vietnam by the Graduate Studies for Education

The 1st International Conference at Tan Trao University became the potent Catalyst in the implementation of the academic collaboration and exchange which was started in May 2015 that continued the support of the College of Teacher Education in the University of Northern Philippines. The international collaboration of Tan Trao University started the signing of Memorandum of Agreement (MOA) Between the University of Northern Philippines and Tan Trao University, Vietnam for Research Collaboration, Academic and Student Exchange Program on May 22, 2015.

The research studies presented in the 1st International Conference with the theme "Assessing Primary Students by Approaching and Evaluating their Competence A Possible Approach to Pedagogic Institutions in Vietnam and same Southeast Asian Countries:" were the following:

1. Implementation of the K to 12 program in the Laboratory Schools of the College of Teacher Education, University of Northern Philippines.

2. The Culture-Based Multidisciplinary Model of the Mother Tongue Based- Multilingual Education (MTB-MLE) of the Primary Schools in the Philippines

3. Correlation Analysis of Licensure Examination for Teacher and Academic Performance of BEEd Students

4. Interpersonal Conflict Management Style of Future Basic Education Teachers

5. Misconceptions in Astronomy of the Third Year Elementary Education Students, University of Northern Philippines

The program outcome of the 1st conference provided the opportunity to expand the twinning agreement on the teaching-learning process by the faculty and student exchange program that resulted to the crediting of the international linkage points for the application of Center of Development in the field of teacher education. This was the reason that the evaluators of the CHED panel for Center of Development to consider the sustained international linkages of the College of Teacher Education.

3. Academic Exchange Program on Cultural Diversity and Language Development Program

The continuing academic collaboration with Tan Trao University improved the technical assistance on the Student Exchange Program with the exposure of the Vietnamese students on the Cultural Diversity and Language Development program last May 2017. The partnership title of the student exchange program was "A Taste of UNP Culture: The Vietnamese Faculty and Students in UNP- The CTE Exchange Program in Partnership with the Center for International Studies."

In partnership with the UNP Center for International Studies through the Blended program of the College of Teacher Education accepted ten students from the Tan Trao University for exposure on May 5-30, 2017. The students were accompanied by their professors. They were exposed to the CTE Best Practices in classroom instruction, co-curriculum activities, extra-curricular activities, extension and lectures on orthography and culture heritage. The said Vietnamese students underwent a rigid selection process so that the best 10 excellent students were sent to the UNP-CTE to undergo the May 5-30, 2017 exposure.

The ten Vietnamese students who were accepted for exposure to the College of Teacher Education, University of Northern Philippines:

1. Tran Thi Nghia - Primary School
2. Linh Huru Khurong - Land and Environment Science
3. Tran Hien Quang - Land and Environment Science
4. Phung Tien Thong - Literature   Education
5. Hoang Thi Trang - Language Education
6. Nguyen Thi Lan Anh - Land and Environment Science
7. Nguyen Ngoc Quynh - Primary School
 8. Nguyen Thi Phrong Thao- Primary School
 9. Nguyen Thu Uyen - Primary School
10. Tran Van Bac - Physical and Environment Science

The College of Teacher Education on the Vietnamese Students' Exchange Program showcases the many faces of Filipino hospitality and UNP's brand of globally competitive instruction, research and extension.

The Vietnamese Student Exchange Program was implemented with various academic activities in the teacher training which included classroom observations at the Laboratory Schools and at the undergraduate courses; field exposures in agricultural and fishing communities; upland communities; program and various activities they were exposed to the Ilokano culture and language.

One of the Vietnamese Students wrote in his testimony on the Internship Report of the Student Exchange Program in the College of Teacher Education:

…Then I found out a bit information about everything I see in the Philippines. Not only being exchange student but also exchange knowledge and ideas. I think it was good for me when I get to know all things I like and want. Now I know a little bit about the culture of the country and people in the Philippines. I see that Philippines is actually a beautiful country with all helpful people and beautiful sight. UNP is a very perfect place to study research and expand my knowledge. And your place City of Vigan is also a worthy place to stay. So many feelings and emotions involved cannot explain through words. The place where I want to spend some more time…

Nguyen Ngoc Quynh

The College of Teacher Education (CTE) implemented the Vietnamese Students' Exchange Program with the support of the Center for International Studies with the program outcome of the insights in the international linkages to support the supervisory program for the teaching-learning process to enhance the experiential knowledge on cultural diversity and language development. The educational impact of the Vietnamese Students' Exchange program ensures the continuing support of the university officials of Tan Trao University to give more Vietnamese students and request that the CTE students and faculty would teach English proficiency program.

It is also expected to continue giving priority of the student exchange program to be emerged in the CTE as to the best practices on educational administration by sending Vietnamese students' in the Tan Trao University, College of Education those are major in Primary School, Literature Education, and Environment Science to implement the twinning program.

4. Student Exchange Program on Practice Teaching Abroad

The College of Teacher Education has established a Student Exchange Program through the Memorandum of Agreement (MOA) between Tan Trao University and University of Northern Philippines issued last March 6, 2015 . The MOA manifested the Higher Education collaboration in research and extension programs, cultural and scientific , interests, faculty, staff and student exchanges and other activities for the advancement of global excellence in education, governance, business, technology and health.

This was properly endorsed by the Commission on Higher Education in compliance with the provisions of CMO No. 22, S. 2013 entitled " Revised Policies, Standards and Guidelines on Student Internship Abroad Program (SIAP). The Chairperson of CHED approved the International Internship/Training for two months. The international internship was justified by its outcome-based initiative for the practice teaching at Tan Trao University with this expected program outcome:

To fully realize the vision and mission of the University, the College of Teacher Education, a newly designated Center of Development along teacher education in the region, collaborated with other higher education institutions in the ASEAN region to become partners in transforming and molding the faculty and the future educators with the values, ideals and aspirations of the ASEAN community. Thus, the exposure of these future teachers through their Practice Teaching Internship in ASEAN countries like Vietnam will definitely equip them with the necessary capabilities to responded to the needs and demands of the ASEAN and global community.

The language competence of the Filipino students was given opportunity to be deployed in the Practice Teaching Abroad in Tan Trao University, Tuyen Quang Province, Vietnam on July 15-November 2016. During the four-month internship, they taught in English classes, proof read English documents and final teaching demonstration. " First I have learned to adjust where people speak alien language and to the students with their level of competency. I have learned to realize that English is not just learned out of necessity but it is a lifelong skill which they can never take away from you." quipped Racachot when asked about the things she learned during the said intern.

In the publication of The Rabii (August-December 2016) through the article "CTE goes Global," the International Internship was implemented by the four month journey of the two student-teachers included tasks namely ; conducting English classes inside and outside the university; assisting in the development of teading materials and activities related to English language and proof read-reading English documents for the University. They also conducted the final demonstration in the said university.

In the practice teaching abroad, the host university provided one way airfare, transport, accommodation and subsistence daily allowance (no less than 2,500,000 Dong per month) to the student teachers.

5. Partnering Cultural Diversity of Tan Trao University of the Vietnamese Internship for the Student Exchange Program

The sustained international linkages with Tan Trao University was implemented last March 2018 with the Student Exchange theme " On Heart , One Soul, One Family: Partnering Cultural Diversity." There were 8 delegates who participated in the 2018 Student Exchange Program as part of the twinning agreement on cultural immersion between Tan Trao University and University of Northern Philippines.

1. Lam Lai Dang
2. Ma Thi Huong

3. Dang Bich Ngoc
4. Do Thi Ha Thrang
5. Tran Thi Thuy Tien
6. Hoang Phuong Thao
7. Kita Bounkhampha
8. Dam Xuan Quynh

The enriching cultural immersion in the student exchange program implemented the experiential learning on the Ilocano culture and tradition, the festivals in the UNESCO Heritage City of Vigan as the Seven Wonder Cities of the World, the pedagogical exposures in the basic education through their academic exposures in the CTE Laboratory Schools and the cultural engagement with the Filipino Society. The experiential learning had given opportunity to enhance their insights in the pre-service education with cultural exposures in the UNESCO Heritage city of Vigan.

B. Program Outcome and Impact of Pre-Service Student Teacher Exchange in Southeast Asia (SEA-Teacher) of the Southeast Asian Ministers of Education Organization (SEAMEO)

The College of Teacher Education was able to sustain the international linkages with significant program outcomes and impact in the area Pre-Service Student Teacher Exchange Program facilitates the promotion of the Best Practices of Pre-Service Education along language proficiency, cultural diversity, experiential learning, pedagogical practices and 21st century education. The program outcomes in the vertical articulation of the graduate and undergraduate programs in the teacher education resulted to the award of the Center of Development and paradigm shift of documentation process under the ISO 9001: 2015.

C. Academic and Research Collaboration of Suan Dusit Rajabhat University and University of Northern Philippines

The College of Teacher Education has sustained its linkages with Suan Dusit Rajabhat University (SDRU) in the areas of Academics/Instruction and Research. The said collaboration was effected by virtue of a Memorandum of Understanding (MOU) which was signed at SDRU, Sukhothai Rd, Dusit Bangkok, Thailand on May 28, 2014. The SDRU is a Thailand government institution of higher learning.

An ongoing research collaboration is the study entitled, **"The**

Comparative Study and Development of Teaching Competency Standards in Higher Education Level Between Faculty Members and Senior Students among 5 ASEAN Universities."

This research endeavour is participated by Dongkhamxang College (Laos), Universitas Negeril Jakarta (Indonesia), Tan Trao University (Vietnam), from the Philippines – University of Northern Philippines in Vigan, Ilocos Sur and University of Southeastern Philippines, Davao City, and the lead university Suan Dusit Rajabhat University of Bangkok, Thailand.

Objectives of this study are:

a) Study and survey the needs of participants from 5 universities of ASEAN countries in developing the teaching competency standards in Higher Education,

b) Analyze and compare the survey data in 4 attributes that relate to

1. Pedagogical skills of teachers,

2. Teacher performance assessment skills,

3. Classroom management skills, and

4. Professional development skills. and

5. Develop the teaching competency standards in Higher Education level among 5 ASEAN countries.

The SDRU research team led by Dr. Prakit Bhulapatna (left photo), Dean of Graduate School was able to gather data by sending the questionnaires to each respondent university which were brought back to Thailand by the university representatives from the 5 countries who also attended the Focus Group Discussion conducted in January 12-17, 2015.

USEP was represented by Dr. Edna H. Jalotjot, Teacher Training Center Director and Prof. Marivic N. Neri, Language Faculty of the College of Education. Other participants include Dr. Vila Sengsavang and Dr. Bounchanh Xaivouth (Laos), Dr. Muchlas Suseno, Dr. Ekka Yunita and Dr. Asep Supeno (Indonesia), Dr. Duc ba Ngugen, Prof. Linh Thi Troung and Ms. Trang Thi Kieu Pham (Vietnam), Dr. Adelina Rapanut, Dr. Tirso Tactay and Dr. Christopher Bueno (UNP-Phils) and the research team of SDRU.

Chapter 5
Program Outcome and Impact of International Linkages and Partnerships of the College of Teacher Education in the University of Northern Philippines

Abstract

The College of Teacher Education was able to sustain the international linkages particularly in the career development of Doctor of Education (Ed.D.) that have significant program outcomes in the areas of twinning agreement on research and facilitation of teacher education experiences. It has a significant educational impact on the stakeholders' adoption of the best practices of educational administration along with language proficiency, cultural diversity, pedagogical practices, and 21st-century education. The program outcomes in the vertical articulation of the graduate and undergraduate programs in the teacher education resulted in the award of the Center of Development and paradigm shift of documentation process under the ISO 9001: 2015.

It must be noted that the career path of the Doctor of Education program initiated by the Center of International Studies has expanded by the academic exchange program in the universities and schools in Thailand. The Blended Education Program through the support of the Center for International Studies has supported the Thai Executives Officials in their career path to finish the degree program on Doctor of Education and Doctor of Business Administration.

In the case of technical assistance on book publication, the Romchatra Foundation has a high level of educational impact in the relevant areas of Asian Culture, History and Tradition were five books published particularly in support with the Maritime Silk Road Confucius Institute disseminated in the ASEAN universities. The academic exchange provided a greater understanding of Confucian Philosophy, ASEAN Cultural Diversity, Chinese Culture and Tradition, Asian Economic, and Political Development. For the academic collaboration, it has the program outcome of the enhancement of academic collaboration by providing complimentary exchange and assistance in the different school activities.

These are the research presentation, lecture and conferences provided by the different partner agencies that have contributed to the understanding of the cultural diversity, career development and ASEAN integration particularly in the area of inclusivity of higher education program Finally, the academic visit and benchmarking highlighted the enhancement of the curricular support in the inclusion of higher education lesson on ASEAN integration, cultural and educational exchange, language proficiency program and another line of academic interest.

I. Introduction

The College of Teacher Education has been designated as the Center of Development for Teacher Education Program (CMO No 17, Series of 2016). This serves as a potent catalyst for world-class scholarships, best practices, innovative curriculum, research and extension, and professional development in the Teacher Education program. Furthermore, it is only this HEI that has a Center of Development (COD) in the province of Ilocos Sur that can avail of the financial grant in institutional innovation to sustain and respond to the advocacy for academic excellence in the Teacher Education program.

The university mainly supports the education programs through the Center for International Studies in the Blended Education System for Foreign Students as approved by the UNP Board Resolution No. 19, s.2012. This is CHED compliant advanced education program with customized EdD programs for foreign students who hold high positions in the national and local government agencies as well as private entities. The complementation process of the Blended Education System integrates the international linkages and partnerships with the support of the Romchatra Foundation with the academic exchange program connected with the Maritime Silk Road Confucius Institute through the ASEAN Universities. These have been the continuing academic exchange such as Tan Trao University, Suan Dusit University, and Rajamagala Universities of Thailand.

Furthermore, the implementation of the international linkages and partnership revolved in the presentation of the technical papers relevant to the cultural heritage and ASEAN Integration. The internationalization efforts of the education program provided the research utilization of the strategic opportunity of the location of the university to share the academic experience is the engineering structural conservation management of the UNESCO Heritage City of Vigan. It also presented an overview of the ASEAN Integration and Technology.

The College of Teacher Education) has the following objectives in networking, linkages and consortia: (1) connect the graduate education program with a development partner in the academe, national government agencies, and the local government units in the international community ; (2) enable education programs on basic education, instructional competence, educational management and supervision, and others to become responsive to local and national thrusts through linkages in foreign countries; (3) benchmark standards (local and international) for integration in the education programs in advanced higher education; and (5) transfer educational models through the product of research and linkages for the enhancement of the education program.

The international linkages in the education programs implemented by the Center for International Studies for the Graduate Studies for Education and the undergraduate programs of the College of Teacher Education reflected by the holistic framework of the university on the following development undertakings:

1. *Facilitation of in-country work experience for faculty and students in a relevant field of study.* The in-country work experience provides the academic lectures of the faculty in ASEAN Integration, Career Path, and cultural heritage program including the on-job-training of the CTE students to work at Senior High Schools in Thailand.

2. *Joint research and extension activities, lectures, workshops, fora, symposia, and seminars.* The international research and extension activity participated by the core and affiliate faculty and graduate students about the ASEAN Integration, Cultural Heritage, English Proficiency Training, Career Advancement, Technical Education, and Sports Development Programs.

3. *Exchange of academic materials, scientific publications, and other relevant scholarly information.* The institutional participation of the education program (through the Graduate Studies for Education) in providing relevant academic materials such as ASEAN Integration, Traimit Model, Confucius Classroom/Institute, UNESCO Heritage Program, and Career Development Program.

4. Co-operation in education and training, including curriculum development, specialized training courses, staff development, and the promotion of staff and student exchanges.

5. Other cooperation and collaboration activities in education deemed appropriate mutually.

The globalization efforts of the Graduate Studies of the University started after the approval of the Blended Education System for Foreign Students (BESFS) Program by the University Board of Regents under Board Resolution No.19, Series 2012. The Blended Education System for Foreign Student Students is in compliance with CHED programs and standards which is a customized special program specifically for foreign students who hold high positions in the national and local government agencies as well as private entities. Its implementing guidelines were approved by the UNP Board of Regents (BOR No. 74, s.2013). The three (3) doctorate programs offered are the Doctor of Education, Doctor of Public Administration, and Doctor of Administration. As an offshoot of the implementation of this program, The Graduate School Center for International Studies was established and created to be responsible in the operation of the Blended Education System for Foreign Students.

The Center for International Studies was created under the Special Order No. GRA45, Series of 2013 designating Dr. Generoso Gudelio P. Pajarillo, as the program coordinator attached under the Office of the President as Special project to coordinate and spearhead academic-related development programs for the University including the Graduate Studies for Education in relation to its internationalization efforts along with the implementation of the blended education system. Furthermore, the center provides strategic support to explore, initiate, and negotiate international linkages, partnerships, cooperation, and collaboration with schools, universities institutions, and centers.

These are the implemented international linkages in the Graduate Studies for Education with the strategic support of the Center for International Studies with an excellent outcome in the development programs along with basic education; career development; academic lecture; cultural heritage advocacy; and research projects that produced technical and research papers in the international community. Furthermore, the international linkages in the academe and international institutions/organizations forged Memorandum of Understanding (MOU) and Memorandum of Agreement (MOA) in the promotion and cooperation of development programs in the education sector.

II. Objectives

Generally, the research study identifies the sustained international linkages and partnerships along with the program outcome and impact of the Doctor of Education along with academic collaboration, inter-country facilitation, research and book publication in the ASEAN countries

The specific objectives of the study are the following:

1. Sustain the Academic Collaboration and Assistance on Research, Lecture, and Conferences
    of the Teacher Education Program
2. Enhance the Academic Visit and Benchmarking in the Advancement of Learning in Higher Education
3. Sustain the implementation of the Blended Education Program for Career Development with Support of ASEAN Integration, Cultural and Educational Exchange Program
4. Identify the sustained International Linkages in the Graduate Studies for Education along with Academic Exchange and Collaboration, Research and Extension Development Programs
5. Strengthen the conduct of the facilitation of Faculty Exchange Exposure and enhance the ASEAN Partnership on Academic Activities of Teacher Education

III. Methodology

The study utilized the documentary and descriptive analysis of international linkages and partnerships with the ASEAN countries. The documentary evidence was taken from the Memorandum of Agreement (MOA) and Memorandum of Understanding (MOU) in the previous institutional engagement with foreign universities in Thailand, Vietnam, and Indonesia. The program outcomes and impacts of the graduate and undergraduate degree programs were taken from the accomplishments in the documents of ISO: 9001:2015 and the Center of Development (COD).

Primarily, the sustained international linkage of Romchatra Foundation through the Maritime Silk Road Confucius Institute that given the opportunity for the College of Teacher Education- Graduate Studies to extend technical assistance in varied forms such as book publications, career development, academic exchange and collaboration, language proficiency and understanding of the ASEAN culture, history and tradition.

The scope of documentary and qualitative analysis includes academic activities accomplished in the Memorandum of Agreement (MOA) and Memorandum of Understanding (MUO) along with career development, inter-country facilitation, academic collaboration, and faculty-student exchange program. 84 respondents evaluated the program outcomes of the Doctor of Education who were actively involved in the implementation of the Blended Education Program who were enrolled in the Doctor of Education (30 percent), international linkages with the support of the Romchatra Foundation (35 percent) and other stakeholders of the ASEAN universities who were directly involved in the implementation of the academic exchange program (35 percent).

The norm of interpretation includes the effectiveness of the implementation of the academic exchange, career development through blended education, inter-country facilitation, language proficiency, and other relevant undertakings in the higher education program.

Statistical Range	*Descriptive Range*
4.21 – 5.00	Very High(VH)
3. 41- 4.20	High (H)
2.61 – 3.40	Fair (F)
1.81 – 2.60	Low (L)
1.00 – 1.80	Very Low (VL)

The highlights of the research findings were studied based on its effectiveness of the program outcomes along strengthening the partnership collaboration in improving the educational management process, pedagogical competence, promotion of current designation, the publication of books relevant to the implementation of the Maritime Silk Road Confucius Institute, and language competence of the stakeholders.

IV. Results and Discussions

This section provides the interpretation of the findings of the study along with the sustained international linkages and partnerships along with the program outcome and impact of the Doctor of Education along with academic collaboration, inter-country facilitation, research and book publication in the ASEAN countries

Table 1

Sustained International Linkage and Partnership in Teacher Education program of the University of Northern Philippines

Nature of Assistance	Number of Activities	Program Outcomes and Impact
International Conference	3	Presentation of best practices in educational management, teaching-learning process, language proficiency, MTB-MLE
English Language Proficiency and Sharing of history, tradition, and culture	5	Student Exchange
Twinning Agreement on Research for Teaching competence	8	Sharing of best-practices in educational assessment
Academic Visit and Benchmarking	3	Faculty and Students exchange activities
Blended Education Program	10	Doctor of Education program under the Blended Education on International Studies
Facilitation of Teacher Education Experiences	8	Sharing of experiences in the pedagogical practices in the 21st-century learning
Faculty Exchange Exposure	2	Involvement of the teaching practice and language proficiency
Academic Partnership	4	Institutional arrangement of

Table 2
Academic Collaboration and Blended Education Research in
Teacher Education

Foreign School	Number of Activities	Beneficiaries	Nature of Academic Collaboration in Blended Education Research
Rachawanit	3	40	Lecture on ASEAN integration and Research on Blended Education
Pasinee Kindergarten and Nursery, Thailand	1	40	Pre-school Education
Mulan Language School Hat Yai, Thailand	1	60	Language Proficiency in English
Plookpanya School, Thailand	2	40	Language Proficiency in English
Apparent Pattansas School, Thailand	1	35	Pre-Service Education
Bannmaechan School, Thailand	1	50	Confucius School Program
Suan Dusit University, Thailand	3	25	Teacher Competence
University of Sebellas, Indonesia	1	30	SEA- Teacher
University of Pendidikan, Indonesia	2	30	SEA-Teacher
Buriram Rajabbhat, Indonesia	1	30	SEA-Teacher
Nakhon SI Thammarat Rajabbhat University	1	30	SEA-Teacher
Tan Trao University	4	30	SEA-Teacher

The College of Teacher Education was able to sustain the international linkages that have significant program outcomes in the areas of twinning agreement on research and facilitation of teacher education experiences. The research studies have been focused on the best practices of educational administration along with language proficiency, cultural diversity, pedagogical practices, and 21st-century education. These have been the major program outcomes that resulted in the academic partnership with the universities of Thailand.

Specifically, the Teacher Education program actively contributed to the sustained academic collaboration on the different themes and features as the impact in advanced education:

1. **Twining Agreement**. The program has contributed to the sharing of best practices along with the educational administration by the faculty support in enrolling the Blended Education for Doctor of Education.

2. **Inter-Country Facilitation of Teacher Education Program**. This area provides the educational support of the practice teaching abroad, language proficiency, and sharing the best practices of the educational management including the assistance of faculty development through the support of their enrolment in the Blended Education program.

The nature of academic collaboration implemented in the blended education considered the area of language proficiency, pre-service education, teacher competence and pedagogical process as defined and stated in the MOA and MOU in foreign universities in Asia. It must be noted that the career path of the Doctor of Education program initiated by the Center of International Studies has expanded by the academic exchange program in the universities and schools in Thailand.

The significance of the international linkages and partnerships for the program outcomes has sustained the students and faculty exchange programs with language proficiency training of the Tan Trao University of Vietnam. While the SEA-Teacher sponsored by the SEAMEO was able to strengthen the twinning-agreement for the Student Exchange Program in the basic education of Thailand, Indonesia, and Vietnam. The Romchatra Foundation through the support of the Maritime Silk Road Confucius Institute implemented substantial academic activities to pursue better collaboration for the " One Belt One Road Initiative' of the Chinese government.

Table 3

Technical Assistance on Book Publication Relevant to the Asian Culture, History and Tradition

Description	X	DR
1. Enhance the academic relevance in the cultural heritage, history, and tradition in Asian countries.	4.73	VH
2. Improve the understanding of the Confucian Philosophy, ASEAN integration, One Belt One Road, Chinese Culture and History, and cultural and educational management practices.	4.82	VH
3. Improve academic collaboration and educational assistance in the ASEAN schools in Thailand, Indonesia, and Vietnam.	4.79	VH
4. Utilize the book publications as instructional materials in the Asian culture, history, and tradition.	4.90	VH
5. Expand the interest of the students and stakeholders in the cultural background of Filipino history and tradition.	4.78	VH
Average Mean	4.78	VH

Note :

Statistical Range	Descriptive Range
4.21 – 5.00	Very High(VH)
3. 41- 4.20	High (H)
2.61 – 3.40	Fair (F)
1.81 – 2.60	Low (L)
1.00 – 1.80	Very Low (VL)

The technical assistance on book publication to the Romchatra Foundation has a high level of educational impact (X-4.78) in the relevant areas of Asian Culture, History, and Tradition. There were five books published particularly in support of the Maritime Silk Road Confucius Institute disseminated in the ASEAN universities. The academic exchange provided a greater understanding of Confucian Philosophy, ASEAN Cultural Diversity, Chinese Culture and Tradition, Asian Economic, and Political Development.

Based on the result of the study, the utilization of book publications (X-4.90) as instructional materials in the Asian culture, history, and tradition was given the recognition of the Romchatra officials as to the program impact of the project. The Romchatra Foundation was able to publish the One Belt One Road initiative of the Chinese government in support of the Maritime Silk Road Initiative. The Maritime Silk Road which is the basis of the "One Belt One Road," evolves as a good model of political and economic life in which the Asian nations respected the ideas of wholesome development of the society where independence and freedom existed vis-à-vis to technological innovations.

The sovereign states transformed into dynamic and vibrant economic order with good diplomatic ties among Asian nations. In contemporary times, this has been achieved by the industrialized states of Asia. However, the political and economic philosophy may be different from the western nations but the genuine principles are still reflective in its underlying principles of the quality of life in the Asian region. The idea of world peace must always bring the principles of peaceful co-existence within the ambit of amity and comity through the interdependence of the sovereign states.

The implementation of "One Belt One Road" can be extracted from the principles of the paradigm shift for World Peace and Development in the ideas of the President Xi Jinping that discusses the features of the change, innovation, idealism, and freedom. The diplomacy strategy is to apply the regional cooperation for bilateral and multilateral agreements among the countries of the world. Likewise, the realignment of the development agenda and thrusts of the sovereign nations are anchored on the quality of life that can be articulated in employment generation, poverty reduction, universal education, cultural diversity, technological and infrastructure economic support, and other means to enhance the productivity in the macro-level that be cascaded in the masses.

Table 4

Academic Collaboration and Assistance on Research, Lecture, and Conferences of the Teacher Education Program

Description	X	DR
1. Sustain the research productivity that contributes in the areas of language proficiency, culture, history, economic enterprise, educational management, and administration.	4.92	VH
2. Enhance academic collaboration by providing complimentary exchange and assistance in the different school activities	4.97	VH
3. Develop the academic commitment to collaborating the varied expertise in the lecture, research, and conference.	4.83	VH
4. Expand the academic interest and assistance in doing research in the areas of basic education and advanced education	4.86	VH
5. Generate relevant academic information to enhance the teaching and learning in the advanced education program	4.75	VH
Average Mean	4.87	VH

The academic collaboration has the program outcome of the enhancement of academic collaboration by providing complimentary exchange and assistance in the different school activities (X-4.97). These are the research presentation, lectures, and conferences provided by the different partner agencies that have contributed to the understanding of cultural diversity, career development, and ASEAN integration particularly in the area of inclusivity of higher education programs. Furthermore, the program outcomes were able to sustain research productivity, culture, economic enterprise, educational management, and administration.

Basically, the program outcomes have the following features and themes relevant to the advance education in the ASEAN universities:

1. **Research Productivity** - These are the sharing experiences and best practices in the teacher education program as to the research studies on educational and economic enterprises in the Blended Education program that contributed to the career promotion and development of the stakeholders. The knowledge generation can be attributed to the actual practices in the field of educational management and business administration which contributed to the paradigm shift of management activities by the stakeholders.

2. **Culture, History, and Tradition** - The academic collaboration reflected from the result of the continuing technical assistance of the Maritime Silk Road Confucius Institutes of Romchatra Foundation for the academic engagement with Rajamagala Universities of Thailand, Suan Dusit University including Traimit Wittayalai High School of Thailand, Tan Trao University of Vietnam and other Universities connected with the SEAMEO project on SEA Teachers.

3. **Educational and Economic Enterprise**. The research studies were relevant to the implementation of quality education in the field of teacher education. It also provides the academic support of finding out the best practices in the advanced education program including the areas of language proficiency, cultural diversity, economic development, and career promotion.

4. **Educational Management and Administration**. This reflects the research studies on the themes of ASEAN Integration, Career Development, Pedagogical Approaches, and cultural exchange programs to support holistic development in advanced education. The educational management programs are also provided in the support of career and promotion of graduate students in the Blended Education System.

Table 5
Academic Visit and Benchmarking in the Advancement of Learning in Higher Education

Description	X	DR
1. Sustain the academic commitment of higher education on the generation of knowledge and exchange program in the development of advanced education.	4.58	VH
2. Improve the educational processes as a result of the academic visit and benchmarking.	4.62	VH
3. Expand the academic interest of collaboration in the continuing support of the advanced education	4.64	VH
4. Enhance the curricular support in the inclusion of higher education lessons on ASEAN integration, cultural and educational exchange, language proficiency program, and other lines of academic interests.	4.80	VH
5. Generate new knowledge and understanding the contribution of the best practices in the higher education program.	4.71	VH
Average Mean	4.67	VH

The academic visit and benchmarking highlighted the enhancement of the curricular support in the inclusion of higher education lessons on ASEAN integration, cultural and educational exchange, language proficiency program, and other lines of academic interest. (X-4.80) Based on this finding, the respondents were able to integrate the curricular enhancement that the academic visit had given them more opportunities to generate new knowledge on the implementation of the ASEAN Quality Framework as to the ideas of universal adoption of employment requirements for the ASEAN countries. The significance of the academic visit produced more international linkages and partnership activities along with the cultural exchange program and language proficiency program by the support of Maritime Silk Road Confucius Institutes and Romchatra Foundation.

Furthermore, this finding revealed that this generated new knowledge and understanding of the best practices in the higher education program. The College of Teacher Education through the Blended Education program of the Center for International Studies presented the expertise of the faculty to give technical assistance to the Romchatra Foundation in the areas of career development through the Blended Education program including language proficiency.

Table 6

Blended Education Program for Career Development with Support of ASEAN Integration, Cultural and Educational Exchange Program

Description	X	DR
1. Continue the implementation of research-based curricula for the advanced education program.	4.65	VH
2. Enhance the career opportunities of the graduate students to link with the other ASEAN partners.	4.80	VH
3. Sustain academic competence in the areas of language proficiency, knowledge enhancement, and career development.	4.85	VH
4. Sustain the international linkage with the ASEAN partners in the areas of Asian culture, language proficiency, career development, and academic exchange.	4.90	VH
5. Expand the ASEAN partnership with the support of the Romchatra Foundation and other universities in Asia.	4.89	VH
Average Mean	4.82	VH

The Blended Education Program through the support of the Center for International Studies has supported the Thai Executives Officials in their career path to finish the degree program on Doctor of Education and Doctor of Business Administration. The program outcome for career development (X-4.90) has resulted in the sustained international linkages with the ASEAN partners in the areas of Asian Culture, language proficiency, career development, and academic exchange.

Based on the findings of the study as to the program outcomes of the career development of the Doctor of Education program, it implemented the academic partnership primarily with the Romchatra Foundation which instituted the student exchange and academic collaboration with the Confucius Institutes in the Universities of Thailand. There were spill-over international partnerships to sustain the academic collaboration in ASEAN countries that supported the SEA- Teacher program of SEAMEO.

These are the specific Blended Education Program implemented by the College of Teacher Education in partnership with the Center for International studies particularly in the degree program on Doctor of Education

Table 8
Inter-Country Facilitation of Teacher Education Experiences

Description	X	DR
1. Generate international linkages and partnership with universities connected with the SEA-Teacher	4.94	VH
2. Sustain the academic support of faculty and student exchange programs in teacher education.	4.93	VH
3. Enhance the academic activities of other universities in Asia relevant to cultural development, language proficiency, career development	4.89	VH
4. Generate new knowledge in the field of teacher education that will have spillover of the best practices in the ASEAN Universities	4.92	VH
5. Enhance academic excellence as a result of the continuing initiative for international linkages in teacher education.	4.71	VH

The inter-country facilitation emphasizes the educational impact that generates international linkages and partnerships with universities connected with the SEA-Teacher of the SEAMEO. (X-4.94) which is expected to provide the academic support on the student and faculty exchange program. It must be noted that the inter-country facilitation has been successful in the implementation of academic collaboration by generating new knowledge in the field of teacher education (X-4.92) and enhancing the academic activities of other universities in Asia relevant to cultural development, language proficiency, career development. (X- 4.89)

Table 8

Faculty Exchange Exposure in the ASEAN Teacher Education Program

Description	X	DR
1. Improve the experiential learning of faculty to engage in the various international activities for the teacher education	4.78	VH
2. Enhance the international linkages with the ASEAN universities that would support career development, cultural diversity, language proficiency, and academic advocacy in higher education.	4.96	VH
3. Generate a greater understanding of the best practices of the ASEAN universities relating to the pedagogical and career development in teacher education.	4.92	VH
4. Sustain the international linkages by providing more support on the research-based outputs in the teacher education	4.90	VH
5. Improve the faculty competence as a result of the academic exchange in the teacher education	4.56	VH

As shown in Table 8, it has a significant contribution to the faculty exchange exposure in enhancing the international linkages with the ASEAN universities that would support career development, cultural diversity, language proficiency, and academic advocacy in higher education. (X-4.96). it also generates a greater understanding of the best practices of the ASEAN universities relating to the pedagogical and career development in teacher education (X- 4.92). It holds true with the support of the research-based outputs in the teacher education program (X-4.90). The faculty exposures have improved the knowledge and understanding of the ASEAN culture, history, education, and tradition.

Table 9
ASEAN Partnership on Academic Activities of Teacher Education

Description	X	DR
1. Enhance the Cultural Diversity, Heritage Management, History, and Tradition in the ASEAN Community.	4.97	VH
2. Expand understanding of ASEAN Culture, History, and Tradition in partnership with the ASEAN universities.	4.96	VH
3. Develop awareness in the cultural diversity of the ASEAN Community in support with the Rom	4.92	VH
4. Enhance the partnership with the foreign schools in the ASEAN Community to further strengthen the teacher education program	4.73	VH
5. Provide continuing and sustained academic collaboration with the partner schools in the ASEAN countries	4.86	VH

The effectiveness of the ASEAN partnerships with universities of Thailand, Vietnam, and Indonesia has been the enhancement of the Cultural Diversity, Heritage Management, History, and Tradition. ((4.97) The educational impact can be attributed to the sustained technical assistance provided to the Romchatra Foundation in support of the Maritime Silk Road Confucius Institute for the academic dissemination of the " One Belt and One Road Initiative" in the ASEAN countries. The College of Teacher Education-Graduate Studies ensures the complementary support for the cultural heritage program of the UNESCO Heritage City of Vigan. This was the reason for the full support of the Confucius Institutes of the Romchatra Foundation to sustain the implementation of cultural diversity and a greater understanding of the ASEAN culture, tradition, and history. Furthermore, the respondents have agreed that the ASEAN partnership strengthens the academic collaboration in teacher education will have a better opportunity to expand the understanding of the totality of the ASEAN culture.

Conclusion

The College of Teacher Education was able to sustain the international linkages have significant program outcomes in the areas of twinning agreement on research and facilitation of teacher education experiences. The research studies have been focused on the best practices of educational administration along with language proficiency, cultural diversity, pedagogical practices, and 21st-century education. These have been the major program outcomes that resulted in the academic partnership with the universities of Thailand.

In the case of technical assistance on book publication, the Romchatra Foundation has a high level of educational impact in the relevant areas of Asian Culture, History and Tradition were five books published particularly in support with the Maritime Silk Road Confucius Institute disseminated in the ASEAN universities. The academic exchange provided a greater understanding of Confucian Philosophy, ASEAN Cultural Diversity, Chinese Culture and Tradition, Asian Economic, and Political Development. For the academic collaboration, it has the program outcome of the enhancement of academic collaboration by providing complimentary exchange and assistance in the different school activities. These are the research presentation, lecture and conferences provided by the different partner agencies that have contributed to the understanding of the cultural diversity, career development and ASEAN integration particularly in the area of inclusivity of higher education program Finally, the academic visit and benchmarking highlighted the enhancement of the curricular support in the inclusion of higher education lesson on ASEAN integration, cultural and educational exchange, language proficiency program and other lines of academic interest.

Chapter 6
Sustaining the Cultural and Academic Exchange Program of the Romchatra Foundation with the Confucius Institute of Maritime Silk Road : An Impact Study on the International Linkages of the Blended Education Program in the ASEAN Countries

The Romchatra Foundation through Phromomankachalan has expanded the international linkages of the University of Northern Philippines (UNP) to be a partner of the academic publications including cultural exchange activities under Hanban that recognized the effort of the College of Teacher Education to bring the forefront of scholarly publication through the ASEAN Community. The forging of agreement on Academic and cultural collaboration with the assistance of the Center of International Studies became the Best Practices of International linkages on Academic and Cultural Exchange program through the Confucius Maritime Silk Road of the Romchatra Foundation.

A. Academic Cooperation through the Confucius Institute of Maritime Silk Road with Foreign Universities and Schools in Thailand

The foreign universities and schools in the ASEAN countries forged agreement with the University of Northern Philippines to promote academic cooperation and exchange through facilitation of in-country work experience for student and faculty; joint research activities including book publications and other scholarly information:

1. 1st RMUTP-UNP Joint International Engineering Research Dissemination and Collaboration on August 21, 2014, Wongsawang Bangsue North Bangkok 108000 Thailand

2. Memorandum of Understanding (MOU) Between the University of Northern Philippines and Rachawinit School, Nakhon Rachasima Road, Dusit Bangkok, 10300 Thailand May 28, 2014 (Student Exchange Program).

3. Memorandum of Understanding Between the University of Northern Philippines and Ramkhamhaeng University, Ramkamhaeng Road, Bangkapi, Bangkok, 10240 Thailand, May 28, 2014

B. Romchatra Foundation Initiative in Book Publications on "Belt and Road Initiatives" for the ASEAN Community

The University of Northern Philippines is an affiliate member of the Maritime Silk Road Confucius Institute with the responsibility to assist and provide academic assistance in the preparation and publications of books relevant to the accomplishments of Romchatra Foundation in the "Belt and Road Initiatives."

The college has been publishing best practices in teaching and learning process, and social sciences books including coursebooks in general education. Part of the academic package in this area is the training of faculty members and publication of research findings in the Amazon books as part of the e-books needed by the education students. It is expected that the academic publications will further enhance the ability of the students as generalists and specialists in the areas of elementary and secondary education.

Cultural and Academic Exchange Program with Romchatra Foundation Through the Maritime Silk Road Confucius Institute of Thailand

Romchatra Foundation with the Confucius Institute of Maritime Silk Road

The cultural and academic exchange program for the Teacher Education has been sustained in the ASEAN community to fulfill the vision of global university anchored on excellence through the technical assistance in book publication given to the Romchatra Foundation. As a global university in the teacher education program, the scholarly books of the Belt and Road Initiative became the academic flagship project of the Confucius Institute of Maritime Silk Road.

The Romchatra Foundation through Phromomankachalan expand the international linkages of the UNP to be a partner of the academic publications including cultural exchange activities under Hanban that recognized the effort of the CTE to bring the forefront of scholarly publication through the ASEAN Community. The forging of agreement on Academic and cultural collaboration with the assistance of the Center of International Studies became the Best Practices of International linkages on Academic and Cultural Exchange program through the Confucius Maritime Silk Road of the Romchatra Foundation.

The foreign universities and schools in the ASEAN countries forged agreement with the University of Northern Philippines to promote academic cooperation and exchange through facilitation of in-country work experience for student and faculty; joint research activities including book publications and other scholarly information:

1st RMUTP-UNP Joint International Engineering Research Dissemination and Collaboration on August 21, 2014, Wongsawang Bangsue North Bangkok 108000 Thailand

Memorandum of Understanding Between the University of Northern Philippines and Rachawinit School, Nakhon Rachasima Road, Dusit Bangkok, 10300 Thailand
May 28, 2014

Memorandum of Understanding Between the University of Northern Philippines and Ramkhamhaeng University, Ramkamhaeng Road, Bangkapi, Bangkok, 10240 Thailand
May 28, 2014

The signing of other Memorandum of Understanding in the Foreign Universities and Schools in Thailand :

Romchatra Foundation Initiative in Book Publications on " Belt and Road Initiatives" for the ASEAN Community

The University of Northern Philippines is an affiliate member of the Maritime Silk Road Confucius Institute with the responsibility to assist and provide academic assistance in the preparation and publications of books relevant to the accomplishments of Romchatra Foundation in the "Belt and Road Initiatives."

The college has been publishing best practices In teaching and learning process, and social sciences books including coursebooks in the general education. As part of the academic package in this area is

the training of faculty members and publication of research findings in the Amazon books as part of the e-books needed by the education students. It is expected that the academic publications will further enhance the intellectual ability of the students as generalists and specialists in the areas of elementary and secondary education.

The Global Education Development of the 2015 ASEAN Integration: Traimit Model

The Traimit Model is designed to conduct academic linkages and partnerships in the cultural heritage program relevant to the sustained establishment of the Confucius Classrooms and Institutes. The Doctor of Education Program has been very supportive of the outcome-based research particularly in the Dissertation which the Romchatra Foundation used the applied educational management theory in the study entitled "Traimit Educational Model for the First Confucius School in Thailand." This was published in the Amazon for its educational management application in the Confucius Classroom in ASEAN countries.

Student International Internship at Plookpanya School, Nakhon Racatchima, Thailand (January 5-March 5, 2017)

The College of Teacher has been supporting the Student International Internship Program through the assistance of Center for International Studies and Romchatra Foundation forging agreement for Student Exchange Program in Thailand and Vietnam. The Student International Internship Program is designed to train and expose the BSEd and BEEd interns to the foreign schools in the academic instruction of the 21st Century Skills in the ASEAN Community.

During the awarding of Certificate of Completion on March 4, 2017 to the 2 student interns, Rowena Perinion, BEEd IV-ECE and Cherry Mae Rol, BEEd IV-Gen Education with the School Director, Teacher Paty The Demonstration Teaching

Cherry Mae Rol with her pupils Rowena Perinion ,BEEd IV-ECE major with her pre- school pupils during her Demonstration Teaching

Student Exchange Program on International Leadership Development Youth Camp in Thailand

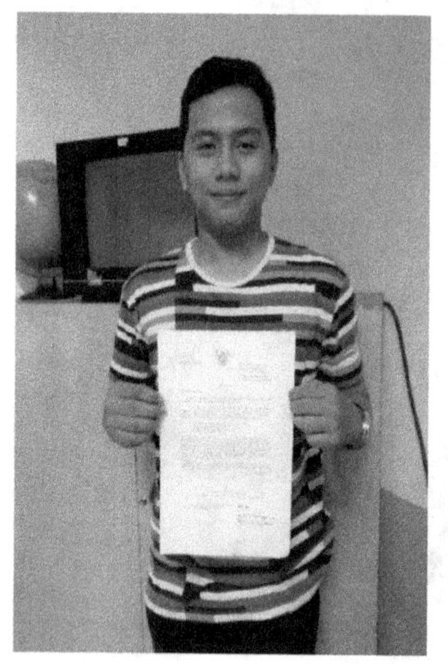

The Rajamangala University of Technology Rattanakosim (96 M.3 Phutamonthon, Nakhopathom 73170) has been working with the University of Northern Philippines through the Center for International Studies as implemented by the College of Teacher Education in working out the sustained student exchange program for Thailand. The college implemented this student exchange program with the participation of the Student Council President, Tessie Ann Reyes in the Youth Camp last December 2016.

This sustained program has been part of the best practices of Student Exchange Program for Leadership Development. The college has been recipient on this program and the Rajamangala University of Technology Rattanakosin provides the participants' accommodation, meals, transportation and program expenses at the camp. This Student Exchange Program has been a part of the leadership training among the ASEAN Universities to share their academic and cultural experiences to provide the harmonious relationships of the ASEAN youth. This further provides the sharing of ideas in the educational systems of the ASEAN particularly the operation of Higher Education Institutions in Asia.

Table 10

Program Outcomes and Sustained International Linkage and Partnership with Romchatra Foundation through the Maritime Silkroad Confucius Institute

Nature of Assistance	Number of Activities	Program Outcomes and Impact
Technical Assistance on Book Publication, Research, Lecture and Conferences	5	Distribution of 5 books on Confucius Institutes on ASEAN Silk Road Initiatives
Academic Collaboration		Cultural Heritage Management on ASEAN Integration
Academic Visit and Benchmarking	3	Confucius Institute
Blended Education Program	1	Doctor of Education program under the Blended Education on International Studies
Facilitation of Teacher Education Experiences	13	Thailand Schools on Basic Education
Faculty Exchange Exposure	2	
Thailand Partnership on Academic Activities	12	

Chapter 7
Academic Outcome and Impact of the Research Collaboration of Suan Dusit Rajabhat University and University of Northern Philippines

The College of Teacher Education has sustained its linkages with Suan Dusit Rajabhat University (SDRU) in the areas of Academics/Instruction and Research. The said collaboration was effected by virtue of a Memorandum of Understanding (MOU) which was signed at SDRU, Sukhothai Rd, Dusit Bangkok, Thailand on May 28, 2014. The SDRU is a Thailand government institution of higher learning.

The Memorandum of Understanding between the University of Northern Philippines and Suan Dusit Rajabhat University (SDRU) aimed to develop cooperation in education and make contributions to the development of friendship and mutual understanding between the people of Philippines and the people of Kingdom of Thailand.

The international cooperation and partnership considered in the MUO are the following:
1. Strengthening mutual understanding of culture and language;
2. Exchange of scientific officer, management officers, specialists and students;
3. Organizing common scientific research activities;
4. Training and standardizing officers;
5. Organizing conference, seminar workshops and other similar activities; and
6. Co-publishing educational and scientific publications.

The Suan Dusit Rajabhat University is a Thailand government university and has been in pursuit of quality education in the university level. The researchers then based this study on the demand of stakeholders that universities invest in teacher development the way business leaders invest in their employees.

The University of Northern Philippines started the international cooperation by joining the Suan Dusit Rajabhat University the ASEAN research project entitled, "The Comparative Study and Development of Teaching Competency Standards in Higher Education Level Between Faculty Members and Senior Students among 5 ASEAN Universities." This research endeavour is participated by Dongkhamxang College (Laos), Universitas Negeril Jakarta (Indonesia), Tan Trao University (Vietnam), from the Philippines – University of Northern Philippines in Vigan, Ilocos Sur and University of Southeastern Philippines, Davao City, and the lead university Suan Dusit Rajabhat University of Bangkok, Thailand.

The rationale of the study reflected from the collective vision of the ASEAN participation as a "Green and Happy Society", where ASEAN people are endowed with morality – based Knowledge and resilience against the adverse impacts of globalization. Southeast Asian countries have actively participated in the global agenda is pursuit of international development goals. But in the last few years, concern for harmonization of international standards appears to have grown significantly, which the potential to facilitate regional educational development goals and systems improvement in the region

In this regard, eleven member' countries of the Southeast Asian Minister of Education Organization (SEAMEO) were invited to take stock of their teaching competency standards, policies, capacity building programs, implementation and monitoring and evaluation activities. The study explores commonalities is teaching competency standards across the region that will support and vigorous regional complementation of capacity building, teacher exchange and lifelong learning. Coming back to the eleven Southeast Asian member countries of SEAMEO (Southeast Asian Ministers of Education Organization) pursue the goals of the Dakar Framework on Education for All aimed at increasing the quality of teaching and learning for better educational outcomes.

So, the development of teaching standards has been a growing feature of the global education agenda since the inception of the Dakar Framework during the World Education Forum held in Dakar, Senegal, on 26 – 28 April 2000 to provide quality education that will give learners the opportunities for effective participation in the societies and economics of the twenty – first century.

The results of the Teaching Competency Survey used in the "Teaching Competency Standards in Southeast Asian Countries", remarked that the competency framework for Southeast Asian Teacher of the 21ˢᵗ Century should be "set of common core teacher competency standards for eleven countries."

The general area competencies of Southeast Asian teachers in above mentioned, identified by a term of Southeast Asian experts through a Modified DACUM Workshop process are as follows conclusion:

1. Facilitating the development of learner's life and career skills.
2. Creating a conductive learning environment.
3. Facilitating learning.
4. Preparing appropriate lesson plans in line with the school vision and mission.
5. Developing higher order thinking skills.
6. Developing and utilizing teaching and learning resources.
7. Enhancing ethical and moral value.
8. Assessing and evaluation learner performance.
9. Engaging in professional development.
10. Networking with stakeholders especially with parents.
11. Managing student's welfare and other tasks.

Even from the above mentioned, it seemed to be ASIAN's education concentrate is prompting the fundamental education on level only, but in contrary it also promote another levels of Education too, such as the higher education. The higher education is one of the major levels of Education in Southeast Asian Countries, and then it was believed that, this type of education promoted or developed the citizens of ASEAN countries in perfection.

Initially aimed at literacy and higher education level, higher education services have expanded significantly into career path for life -long learning. This reason in each country, a central ministry of education sets schooling structures and curriculum requirement, from the primary level until the higher level, which some responsibilities for school supervision, curriculum, and financial management often delegated to provincial and local education authorities.

The problems which almost Southeast Asian University continue to face relate to maintain educational quality, reducing university dropout, providing enough buildings and other educational inputs, and enhancing the qualifications of teachers to serve for the quality of university students.

The Suan Dusit Rajabhat University is a governmental University under higher commission organization of the Ministry of Education that provided the education in higher level in Bachelor degree, Master degree and Doctoral degree, and then participated and joined with another countries in Southeast Asian, such as the Philippines, Indonesia, Lao and etc. in Educational Cooperative working, management and then needs the progressive of cooperation in advanced. The researchers believe that in the pursuit of quality education for University level, much more work needs to be done. More parents are demanding that their children be taught by well – prepared, competent and qualified teacher. More business leaders in all section of society are demanding that Universities invest in teacher development, just as they invest in their own employee. More educational policymakers are making quality teaching and the recruitment of well – prepared teachers their number one education priority.

So, this research looked into the major characteristics that define a "competent teacher" in cooperative between 6 universities in 5 countries in Southeast Asia is four attributes related to: 1) pedagogical skills of teachers, 2) teacher performance assessment skills, 3) classroom management skills, and 4) professional development skills and then develop the Teaching Competency Standards in Higher Education level for 6 universities.

These were the research activities participated by the university of Northern Philippines in the conduct of the International Research in the ASEAN region:

1. The Suan Dusit Rajabhat University included the University of Northern Philippines in the research collaboration with among 5 ASEAN Universities under MOU and Plus one (China).

2. The implementation of the research collaboration with the ASEAN countries through the Memorandum of Understanding signed between Suan Dusit Rajabhat University (Thailand) and University

of Northern Philippines (Philippines) at Likit room, Suan Dusit Place, Bangkok, Thailand.

3. The academic visit and research collaboration of Suan Dusit Rajabhat University in University Northern Philippines last October 21,2014.

These were the delegates of the Faculty members of Graduate School, Suan Dusit Rajabhat University:

Dr. Thawatchai Kanchanathaweekul- ResearchLeader
Dr. Prakit Bhulaphatna- Dean, Graduate School
Dr. Thawatchai Kanchanathaweeku

Research Coordinator
Mrs. Ong-Orn Singuanyat –Lecturer
Mrs. Jongkorn Boonchart -Researcher
Mrs. Samram Soisirisuntorn-Secretary

Furthermore, the implementation of the international linkages and partnership revolved in the presentation of the technical papers relevant to the cultural heritage and ASEAN Integration. The internationalization efforts of the education program provided the research utilization of the strategic opportunity of the location of the university to share the academic experience is the engineering structural conservation management of the UNESCO Heritage City of Vigan. It also presented the overview of the ASEAN Integration and Technology.

It was participated by universities in ASEAN-member nations namely: Dongkhamxang College (Laos), Universitas Negeril Jakarta (Indonesia), Tan Trao University (Vietnam), from the Philippines – University of Northern Philippines in Vigan, Ilocos Sur and University of Southeastern Philippines, Davao City, and the lead university Suan Dusit Rajabhat University of Bangkok, Thailand

International Research Collaboration With Suan Dusit Rajabhat University

The research entitled *"The Comparative Study and Development of Teaching Competency Standards in Higher Education Level Between Faculty Members and Senior Students among 5 ASEAN Universities"* *with following* objectives:

a) Study and survey the needs of participants from 5 universities of ASEAN countries in developing the teaching competency standards in Higher Education,

b) Analyse and compare the survey data in 4 attributes that relate to
    1. Pedagogical skills of teachers,
    2. Teacher performance assessment skills,
    3. Classroom management skills, and
    4. Professional development skills. and
    5. develop the teaching competency standards in Higher Education level among 5 ASEAN countries.

The SDRU research team led by Dr. Prakit Bhulapatna, Dean of Graduate School was able to gather data by sending the questionnaires to each respondent university which were brought back to Thailand by the university representatives from the 5 countries who also attended the Focus Group Discussion conducted in January 12-17, 2015.

USEP was represented by Dr. Edna H. Jalotjot, Teacher Training Center Director and Prof. Marivic N. Neri, Language Faculty of the College of Education. Other participants include Dr. Vila Sengsavang and Dr. Bounchanh Xaivouth (Laos), Dr. Muchlas Suseno, Dr. Ekka Yunita and Dr. Asep Supeno (Indonesia), Dr. Duc ba Ngugen, Prof. Linh Thi Troung and Ms. Trang Thi Kieu Pham (Vietnam), Dr. Adelina Rapanut, Dr. Tirso Tactay and Dr. Christopher Bueno (UNP-Phils) and the research team of SDRU.

A. Research Inputs in the Comparative Study and Development of Teaching Competency Standards in Higher Education Level : Teaching Competency Standards in Southeast Asian Countries

The inputs on existing Frameworks for Teaching Competency Standards in Southeast Asian Countries, such as the Philippines, Indonesia, Vietnam, Lao and Thailand are as follows :

A. Teaching Competency Standards in Philippines

The Philippines defines a competent teacher as one of the most significant elements of the country's education system. The Philippine teaching competency standards known as the NCBTS comprises seven major strands social regard for learning; learning environment; diversity of learners; curriculum; planning, assessing, and reporting; community linkages; and personal growth and professional development.

B. Teaching Competency Standards in Indonesia

Indonesia defines a competent teacher as one who meets the components of the four major competencies defined by the country's Teacher Law. Indonesia's teaching competency standards are grouped into four major strands pedagogical, personal, professional, and social.

4. Teaching Competency Standards in Vietnam

Vietnam defines a competent teacher as one who possesses both the knowledge and skills required to teach students well. Teachers should have specialized knowledge in their respective subjects as well as general knowledge to answer all kinds of questions that their students may ask. They should have the necessary pedagogical, communication, presentation, and classroom management skills to successfully perform their roles as classroom managers, facilitators, organizers, and resource persons.

5. Teaching Competency Standards in Lao

Lao defines a competent teacher as one who satisfies the required skills and competencies mandated in the country's NCTC. Lao's teaching competency standards are grouped into three major strands characteristics and professional ethics, knowledge of children, and subject knowledge and practical teaching wisdom.

A. Academic Outcome and Impact of the Research Collaboration of Suan Dusit Rajabhat University and University of Northern Philippines

Abstract

The College of Teacher Education has sustained its linkages with Suan Dusit Rajabhat University (SDRU) in the areas of Academics/Instruction and Research. The said collaboration was effected by virtue of a Memorandum of Understanding (MOU) which was signed at SDRU, Sukhothai Rd, Dusit Bangkok, Thailand on May 28, 2014. The SDRU is a Thailand government institution of higher learning. The higher educational impact of the research collaboration of Suan Dusit Rajabhat University (SDRU) provided the development of twinning agreement between the University of Northern Philippines and Tan Trao University.

Introduction

The research collaboration was entitled, "The Comparative Study and Development of Teaching Competency Standards in Higher Education Level Between Faculty Members and Senior Students among 5 ASEAN Universities." This research endeavour is participated by Dongkhamxang College (Laos), Universitas Negeril Jakarta (Indonesia), Tan Trao University (Vietnam), from the Philippines – University of Northern Philippines in Vigan, Ilocos Sur and University of Southeastern Philippines, Davao City, and the lead university Suan Dusit Rajabhat University of Bangkok, Thailand.

The second round of research collaboration was the development of training course that adopted the pedagogical competence, capacity and ability to promote the business service in ASEAN countries. This was participated by the Suan Dusit University-Thailand as main benefactor of the research in the ASEAN countries on training course competence for business service with the participation of University of Southeastern Philippines, University of Northern Philippines, Tan Trao University-Vietnam, Dong Kham Chang Teacher College- Lao and Universistas Negeri Jakarta-Indonesia. The training competence of the ASEAN framework investigated this study the development of competency standards relevant to the need of the professional in the ASEAN countries.

The objectives of the study are to show the research findings along the teaching competence along: (1) Pedagogical skills of teachers; (2) Teacher performance assessment skills; (3) Classroom management skills; and (4) Professional development skills; and (5) Develop the teaching competency standards in Higher Education level among 5 ASEAN countries.

Methodology

The study utilized a descriptive form of research for the institutional survey for the courses on Accounting and Management, Tourism, Information Technology, and Teacher Education of the University of Northern Philippines to conform with the results of "The Comparative Study and Development of teaching Competency Standards in Higher Education level between Faculty members and Senior Students among 5 ASEAN Universities under MOU and Plus one (China)."

The questionnaire of the study is designed for collecting the data to develop the Teaching Competency for higher education in South East Asian Country. It was divided into 2 parts as A) the general information or demographics of the participant and B) the teaching competency into 4 aspects on the level of importance of the composition of pedagogical skills of lecturers. The rating key for activities are evaluated by the following: 5 = Very Important, 4 = Important, 3 = moderately Important, 2 = Slightly Important, 1 = Not Important.

Table 1

Demographic Profile in Accountancy and Management; Tourism, Information Technology, and Teacher Education
of the University of Northern Philipines

Variables	f	%
Gender		
Female	77	62.1
Male	47	37.9
Total	124	100
Age		
23 and above	4	3.2
21 - 22	12	9.7
19 -20	96	77.4
17 - 18	12	9.7
Total	124	100.0
Field of Learning		
Management	48	38.7
SocSci	6	4.8
Education	32	25.8
Sci n tech	38	30.6
Total	124	100
Country		
Philippines	124	100
Total	124	100

This section provides the table presentation of the research study conducted in the College of Teacher Education, University of Northern Philippines, Vigan City to identify the teaching competency standards in higher education. Based on the findings of the study in the University it has similar results as to the teaching competency standards in higher education for Accountancy and Management; Tourism, Information Technology, and Teacher Education.

Results and Discussions

The research collaboration is entitled, "The Comparative Study and Development of Teaching Competency Standards in Higher Education Level Between Faculty Members and Senior Students among 5 ASEAN Universities." This research endeavour is participated by Dongkhamxang College (Laos), Universitas Negeril Jakarta (Indonesia), Tan Trao University (Vietnam), from the Philippines – University of Northern Philippines in Vigan, Ilocos Sur and University of Southeastern Philippines, Davao City, and the lead university Suan Dusit Rajabhat University of Bangkok, Thailand.

Objectives of this study are: a) Study and survey the needs of participants from 5 universities of ASEAN countries in developing the teaching competency standards in Higher Education, b) Analyze and compare the survey data in 4 attributes that relate to 1. Pedagogical skills of teachers, 2. Teacher performance assessment skills, 3. Classroom management skills, and 4. Professional development skills. and 5. Develop the teaching competency standards in Higher Education level among 5 ASEAN countries.

Teaching Competency Standards of the ASEAN Countries

The level of importance in the teaching competency standards have the following significant findings similar with the results of other ASEAN universities :

On Pedagogical Skills of Lecture

In Management, the important pedagogical skills is focused on helping students develop a reflective attitude and critical thinking. (X-4.80) this is followed by continuously updating his or her (lecturer) knowledge (4.78) and being competent within his/her subject area. (X-4.76). Other relevant is having good curriculum knowledge with understanding. (X-4.74)

Table 2

Level of Importance in the Pedagogical Skills of Lecturer as Assessed by the College of Teacher Education, Laboratory Schools

No.	Description	M	SS	E	ST	W
1.	Skillful listening reasonably and patiently to his or her students.	4.70	4.50	4.76	4.60	4.64
2.	Being competent within his/her subject area.	4.76	4.50	4.62	4.43	4.58
3.	Being awareness of general goals, policies, and regulations of higher education.	4.65	4.50	4.72	4.51	4.60
4.	Having good curriculum knowledge with understanding.	4.74	4.50	4.79	4.66	4.67
5.	Letting student participation on the discussion of learning goals and framework.	4.72	5.00	4.69	4.63	4.76
6.	Lecturer self-informing about the other parts of the course or programme.	4.41	3.50	4.34	4.37	4.16
7.	Explaining to his or her students how the course at hand relates to their educations as a whole.	4.72	5.00	4.48	4.69	4.72
8.	Coordination attainment between different course sections and lecturers.	4.46	3.50	4.62	4.49	4.27
9.	Developing course and teaching activities.	4.46	4.50	4.83	4.54	4.58
10.	Being an appreciated leader of pedagogical activities.	4.57	3.50	4.62	4.57	4.31
11.	Connection drawing between the content of the field and that of related fields.	4.35	4.00	4.38	4.37	4.27
12.	Contribution abilities to the development and improvement of the programme.	4.61	4.50	4.62	4.40	4.53
13.	Personal developing adjustment according to the policy of the programme.	4.37	4.00	4.52	4.43	4.33
14.	Adaptabilities when circumstances change and can apply alternative approaches.	4.37	4.00	4.48	4.40	4.31
15.	Keeping abreast of developments in the field.	4.48	4.00	4.48	4.46	4.35
16.	Having students as the starting point when planning teaching.	4.52	4.00	4.55	4.60	4.42
17.	Helping students develop a reflective	4.80	4.50	4.79	4.63	4.93

	attitude and critical thinking.					
18.	Having good knowledge about teaching.	4.67	4.00	4.83	4.57	4.52
19.	Continuously updating his or her (lecturer) knowledge	4.78	4.00	4.69	4.66	4.53
20.	Providing an overview of course and class content.	4.61	4.00	4.45	4.74	4.45
21.	Appreciating as a teacher.	4.67	4.50	4.83	4.51	4.63
22.	Being an appreciated leader of pedagogical activities.	4.46	4.00	4.62	4.49	4.39
23.	Supporting students in the learning process by recognizing questions and problems, addressing them, and responding to them.	4.65	4.50	4.90	4.57	4.66
	Overall	4.63	4.22	4.64	4.54	4.50

In Education, the respondents have the highest over-all evaluation on the level of importance in the pedagogical skills of lecturer in education (X-4.64) followed by the management (X-4.63). The College of Teacher has the priority of the pedagogical skills along the *supporting students in the learning process by recognizing questions and problems, addressing them, and responding to them* (X-4.90). It provides the students' centered learning process through the educational inquiry by recognizing questions and problems to ensure the pedagogical competence of the lecturer.

In support with this pedagogical skills needed by the lecturer in the field of teacher education with the mean rating of 4.83 which provides *good knowledge about teaching, appreciation of the teacher, developing course and teaching activities.* The educational consideration about the pedagogical skills recognizes the teacher's competence in the field of expertise as aligned with the *course and teaching activities* and in-depth understanding of the curriculum (X-4.79). There is also a need to *practice skillful listening reasonably* and patiently to the learners (X-4.76). Secondly, from all the educational analysis of the items relevant to the teacher's competence and expertise in pedagogy there is a need to be aware of the general goals, policies, and regulations of higher education (X- 4.72) In the Philippines, the Department of Education memorandum provides the implementation of the educational mandate and reforms to produce quality education in the basic education program. It is also needed to understand this educational goals, policies and regulations for the beginning teachers to adopt the actual situation in the Department of Education.

The less important pedagogical skills when ranked all the items in this section are the following: (1) the lecturer self-informing about the other parts of the course or programme (X- 4.34); and connection drawing between the content of the field and that of related fields (X- 4.38). These pedagogical skills are already integrated the teachers' competence in their field of specialization.

In information technology, it was found out that the highest level of importance in the pedagogical skill of the lecturer is providing an overview of course and class content. (X- 4.74). These are the level of importance in the pedagogical skills other than the course content of the subject matter from the mean rating of 4.60-4.69:

1. Explaining to his or her students how the course at hand relates to their educations as a whole. (4.69)
2. Continuously updating his or her (lecturer) knowledge (4.66)
3. Letting student participation on the discussion of learning goals and framework. (4.63)

The information technology students have common mean evaluation rating (X- 4.60) on the (1) skillful listening reasonably and patiently to his or her students. (X-60; (2) having students as the starting point when planning teaching.

Student Performance Assessment Skills

Basically, the student performance assessment skills are conformed with the management concepts along their field of expertise (management accounting, HRD accounting, HRD management, and etc.) as the course contents that defined more on strategic management and the financial viability of the enterprise.

Table 2
Level of Importance in the Student Performance Assessment Skills by the Senior Students of the University of Northern Philippine, Vigan City

No.	Description	M	SS	E	ST	W
1.	Providing clear information in good time.	4.67	5.00	4.79	4.63	4.77
2.	Giving prompt feedback.	4.46	4.00	4.52	4.51	4.37
3.	Using a variety of examination methods.	4.54	4.50	4.48	4.49	4.50
4.	Discussion sharing his or her student assessment with others.	4.48	4.00	4.45	4.54	4.37
5.	Abilities to promote related person for cooperation and participation of student assessment.	4.52	4.50	4.52	4.51	4.51
6.	Striving for clear information and effective communication after finished the assessment.	4.61	4.50	4.55	4.57	4.56
7.	Putting course evaluations to meaningful uses.	4.54	4.50	4.69	4.49	4.55
8.	Having development of evaluation tools.	4.63	4.00	4.48	4.49	4.40
9.	Having evaluation of the learning process with the students both in terms of results and process.	4.57	4.00	4.48	4.66	4.43
10.	Having analyses of learning problems (whether general or field specific), and responds to them or refer students as needed.	4.52	5.00	4.66	4.57	4.69
11.	Using current assessment approaches in the field.	4.51	4.00	4.55	4.51	4.39
12.	Applying rules consistently and living up to the agreements for assessment method.	4.48	5.00	4.66	4.57	4.68
13.	Making agreements about the students' tasks and making it clear what support they can expect.	4.72	4.50	4.72	4.51	4.61
14.	Responsibility acceptance for the task assigned.	4.72	4.50	4.83	4.66	4.68

15.	Opening mind to different ideas and perspectives.	4.70	4.50	4.69	4.71	4.65
16.	Being able to express what is important in his or her professional conduct, and to express the values, norms, and pedagogical approaches on which this is based.	4.76	4.00	4.72	4.71	4.55
17.	Being familiar with a variety of examination and assessment methods.	4.74	4.00	4.55	4.66	4.49
18.	Reflecting on personal behaviour systematically, applying feedback from others when doing so.	4.59	4.00	4.69	4.69	4.49
19.	Informing himself or herself bout student's previous knowledge and qualification.	4.52	4.50	4.76	4.51	4.57
20.	Recognizing behavioural problems in students, and when necessary refers them.	4.70	4.50	4.55	4.63	4.59
	Overall	4.60	4.38		4.58	4.54

In management, the senior students in management have high level of importance in the student performance assessment skills along *being able to express what is important in his or her professional conduct, and to express the values, norms, and pedagogical approaches on which this is based*(X- 4.76).Other consideration of management reflects the familiarity in a variety of examination and assessment methods (X- 4.74). The faculty of management provides further instruction as tto what is expected in the class such as *making agreements about the students' tasks and making it clear what support they can expect* (X-4.72). The instruction given to the students form part in the accepting the scope of the course content to be evaluated as part of the *assigned task* (X-4.72). These are usually accepted by the senior students which is relevant to the *opening mind to different ideas and perspectives* (X- 4.70). It must be noted that the senior students expect more understanding on the part of faculty as to their performance assessment skills. It should recognize the *behavioural problems in students, and when necessary refers them* (X 4.70).

When rank according to their evaluation, the less important items in the performance assessment skills are giving prompt feedback (X-4.46), discussion sharing his or her student assessment with others. (X- 4.48) and applying rules consistently and living up to the agreements for assessment method (X-4.48). Although, the items are still very important these are already presented mutual agreement with the senior students.

Education

In education, the senior students have high level of importance of student's performance assessment in *providing clear information in good time* (X-4.79) and *informing himself or herself about student's previous knowledge and qualification* (X-4.76). They seem to agree that learners' centered approach are always important in understanding performance assessment skills in the components of cognitive, affective and psycho-motor development relevant to the teachers' evaluation in the class. Furthermore, the importance of mutual agreement as to the instructional evaluation of the learning content. Likewise, the high level of professionalism is also important in expressing the values, norms, and pedagogical approaches relevant in their field of expertise. The less important for them showed that discussion sharing his or h4.45)

In Science and Technology, the information technology students have evaluated to have high level of importance in opening mind to different ideas and perspectives(X-4.71).This is important in the student performance assessment skills needed in the changing information technology perspectives in the areas of computer programming and website development. The IT professional needs in the adoption of the corporate strategy in the utilization of marketing promotion program of the highly competitive environment in the world market. This ensures the implementation of being able to express what is important in his or her professional conduct, and to express the values, norms, and pedagogical approaches on which this is based (X- 4.71).

Likewise, the IT students are less critical in their responses (X-4.49) in using a variety of examination methods; putting course evaluations to meaningful uses and having development of evaluation tools. Certainly, the students' performance assessment skills are more acceptable on the hands-on experience using the computer-based evaluation as what is needed in the corporate world.

On Classroom Management Skills

In management, the classroom management has high level of importance by *encouraging students to develop good study habits* (X- 4.87); *offering a safe environment where students and teachers treat each other with respect* (X- 4.85); and *stimulating students to be active learners* (4.83). The educational highlights in this response emphasize the students' view that the classroom management require the sense of respect given to the teachers and stimulate students to be active learners and giving encouragement to develop good study habits. The less important is regularly using student input in the teaching/learning process. (X-4.48)

Table 3
Level of Importance in the Classroom Management Skills as Evaluated by the Senior Students of the University of Northern Philippine

No.	Description	M	SS	E	ST	W
1.	Offering a safe environment where students and teachers treat each other with respect.	4.85	4.00	4.79	4.74	4.60
2.	Encouraging students to develop good study habits.	4.87	5.00	4.76	4.57	4.80
3.	Stimulating students to be actives learners.	4.83	5.00	4.79	4.71	4.83
4.	Being familiar with and show consideration for different learning styles.	4.57	4.00	4.69	4.57	4.46
5.	Informing about didactic knowledge about student learning in the subject area he or she teaches.	4.59	4.00	4.59	4.51	4.42
6.	Continually developing knowledge about the subject area in which he or she teaches.	4.67	4.00	4.59	4.69	4.49
7.	Being familiar with the requirements and connected with different teaching methods.	4.76	4.50	4.76	4.66	4.67
8.	Having good knowledge of different parts of the teaching process.	4.76	5.00	4.86	4.63	4.81
9.	Using different teaching methods.	4.63	4.50	4.62	4.51	4.57
10.	Varying teaching methods and content according to available resources and the situation at hand.	4.67	4.50	4.69	4.54	4.60
11.	Discussion of goals and framework with students.	4.70	4.50	4.69	4.49	4.59
12.	Mastering different teaching methods.	4.74	4.50	4.59	4.60	4.61
13.	Varying methods according to the student needs.	4.61	4.00	4.72	4.63	4.49
14.	Developing study guides or written teaching materials.	4.63	4.50	4.62	4.63	4.59
15.	Working well together with other teachers and personnel.	4.67	4.50	4.69	4.51	4.59
16.	Having good student results.	4.72	5.00	4.79	4.74	4.81
17.	Ensuring a learning environment where	4.65	4.50	4.66	4.63	4.61

	students can contribute their own input.					
18.	Regularly using student input in the teaching/learning process.	4.48	4.00	4.72	4.57	4.44
19.	Encouraging students to discuss norms and values.	4.72	4.00	4.79	4.71	4.56
20.	Challenges students to think about their own learning and development.	4.78	4.50	4.79	4.60	4.67
21.	Taking cultural, social, and emotional differences between students into consideration.	4.72	4.50	4.66	4.63	4.63
22.	Developing different learning path to respond to the student differences.	4.61	4.50	4.69	4.57	4.59
23.	Using written, audio-visual and digital teaching aids to achieve the teaching goals.	4.74	4.00	4.55	4.51	4.45
24.	Adapting existing materials and expand them personally (using questions suggestions, examples).	4.70	4.00	4.83	4.66	4.55
25.	Actively using the student's previous knowledge and connects to their experiences and interests.	4.72	4.50	4.72	4.60	4.64
26.	Employing different methods, recognizing the students differences (their different ways of learning, different levels, and different ways of working).	4.63	3.50	4.79	4.69	4.40
27.	Applies current insights and professional practice in their teaching.	4.74	3.50	4.79	4.60	4.41
28.	Making the content, form, structures, and relevance of the learning activity clear.	4.70	4.00	4.66	4.63	4.49
29.	Promoting everyone's cooperation and participation.	4.59	4.00	4.79	4.60	4.50
30.	Developing both individual and group activities.	4.76	4.00	4.69	4.69	4.53
	Overall	4.69	4.30	4.71	4.61	4.58

In Education, the senior students answered importance of classroom management by having good knowledge of different parts of the teaching process. (X-4.86) These are the common responses of the senior students in education reflecting their ideas about classroom management (X-4.79)

1. Applies current insights and professional practice in their teaching.
2. Promoting everyone's cooperation and participation.
3. Applies current insights and professional practice in their teaching.

4. Employing different methods, recognizing the students differences (their different ways of learning, different levels, and different ways of working).
5. Challenges students to think about their own learning and development.
6. Encouraging students to discuss norms and values.
7. Having good student results.
8. Offering a safe environment where students and teachers treat each other with respect.
9. Stimulating students to be actives learners.

The classroom management applies to the cooperation and participation in the teaching-learning process that needs to apply different methods and recognizing the student differences .The intention of this responses provides them to become active learners.

On Professional Development Skills

In management, the important professional skill (X-4.83) has been focused on continuously developing his or her knowledge by attending courses on teaching or pedagogical conferences; and striving for clear and effective communication with another teachers and students. The teaching and learning process requires the understanding of pedagogical concepts and effective communication as a means to enhance the professional skills in management.

Table 4

Level of Importance in the Professional Skills as Evaluated by the Senior Students of the University of Northern Philippine

No.	Description	M	SS	E	ST	W
1.	Continuously developing his or her knowledge by attending courses on teaching or pedagogical conferences.	4.83	4.00	4.76	4.74	4.58
2.	Pedagogical development and discussions about teaching are stimulated in various aspects.	4.63	4.00	4.66	4.63	4.48
3.	Perfect Presentation in Academic Areas, both of national and international conference.	4.63	4.50	4.45	4.49	4.52
4.	Having a clear concept of the role and responsibilities of the student and the teacher.	4.76	4.50	4.83	4.57	4.66
5.	Informing students about the reasons for his or her decisions on teaching.	4.57	3.50	4.59	4.57	4.31
6.	Planning teaching in accordance with what research has shown gives the best	4.61	3.50	4.72	4.57	4.35

	support to student learning.					
7.	Linking teaching to present research finding within the subject area in question.	4.57	3.50	4.66	4.60	4.33
8.	Continuously updating his or her knowledge.	4.74	4.00	4.86	4.46	4.51
9.	Seeking for information about subject related research, e.g. via journals or by attending conferences.	4.74	3.50	4.76	4.63	4.41
10.	Trying to attain coordination between different course sections and teachers.	4.67	4.00	4.72	4.69	4.52
11.	Working well together with other teachers and personnel.	4.72	5.00	4.79	4.71	4.81
12.	Engaging in educational development.	4.65	5.00	4.72	4.63	4.75
13.	Taking teacher training courses.	4.70	4.00	4.69	4.60	4.50
14.	Writing about teaching in educational journals.	4.59	4.00	4.45	4.66	4.42
15.	Informing about teaching experiences at for example conferences.	4.65	4.00	4.62	4.43	4.43
16.	Leadership acceptance and carrying out the adherent duties with good results	4.78	4.50	4.59	4.63	4.62
17.	Striving for clear and effective comm. with another teachers and students	4.83	4.00	4.69	4.69	4.55
18.	Can be the counsellor of students	4.74	4.50	4.69	4.69	4.65
	Average	4.69	4.11	4.68	4.61	4.52

The other important professional skills are leadership acceptance and carrying out the adherent duties with good results (X-4.78) ; having a clear concept of the role and responsibilities of the student and the teacher (X-4.76); working well together with other teachers and personnel (X-4.72); and can be the counsellor of students (X-4.74)

In education, the important professional skills provides continuously updating his or her knowledge. (X- 4.86). This followed by having a clear concept of the role and responsibilities of the student and the teacher. (X-4.83).The updating and enhancement of the subject contents required in the curriculum development have provided the important professional skills in the field of education. Likewise, the degree of professionalism in education is the specific role of the students and teachers in the delivery of the lessons that provided the effective means to achieve the educational objectives of the subject matter.

The other important professional skills reflect on working well together with other teachers and personnel (X-4.79); continuously developing his or her knowledge by attending courses on teaching or pedagogical conferences (X-4.76);and seeking for information about subject related research, e.g. via journals or by attending conferences. (X-4.76). The other matter of professionalism reflects in the pedagogy and research as a means to enhance further the quality of education .

In information technology, the important professional skill reflects continuously developing his or her knowledge by attending courses on teaching or pedagogical conferences (X-4.74).

Table 5

Executive Summary of the ASEAN Instructional Competency Standards

Items	Management		Social Science		Education		Science and Technology		As a Whole	
	☐	DR	☐	DR	☐	DR	☐	DR	☐	DR
Pedagogical Skills of Lecturers	4.63	VH	4.22	VH	4.64	VH	4.54	VH	4.50	VH
Student Performance Assessment Skills	4.60	VH	4.38	VH	4.62	VH	4.58	VH	4.54	VH
Classroom Management Skills	4.69	VH	4.30	VH	4.71	VH	4.61	VH	4.58	VH
Professional Development Skills	4.69	VH	4.11	H	4.68	VH	4.61	VH	4.52	VH
Grand Mean	4.65	VH	4.25	VH	4.66	VH	4.59	VH	4.54	VH

A. Pedagogical Skills of Lecturers in Management

In Management, the important pedagogical skills is focused on helping students develop a reflective attitude and critical thinking. (X-4.80) this is followed by continuously updating his or her (lecturer) knowledge (X-4.78) and being competent within his/her subject area. (X-4.76). Other relevant is having good curriculum knowledge with understanding. (X-4.74).

The intellectual skills is defined as the set of skills which includes the ability to carry out abstract logical thinking and learn the process of critical thinking. It also includes creative thinking or the generation of new ideas; visualization or "seeing things in the mind's eye"; and reasoning skills or the discovery of a rule or principle underlying the relationship between two or more objects and applying it when solving a problem. Hence, the accountancy graduate must demonstrate the following skills: analysis, problem solving and strategic/critical thinking. (Section 18a)

In the field of accountancy (Bachelor of Science in Accountancy), these are the important reflective attitude and critical thinking the accountancy graduate must demonstrate the following skills: (section 18)

1. *Analysis* – Ability to review, interpret, evaluate financial data and systems/ operational data/ controls in order to form conclusions and/or make recommendations on validity/usefulness/ correctness/ compliance within established policies, procedures, guidelines, agreements and/or legislation.

2. *Problem solving* – Discerning the true nature of a situation and evaluation of applicable principles and techniques. Innovative thinking, reliable evaluation of information, openness to constructive change and consideration of future contingencies and developments.

3. *Strategic/Critical Thinking* – Linking data, knowledge and insight together from different sources and disciplines to make informed decisions. Considering the "big picture" when making decisions, as well as potential threats to the vision, strategy, objectives and culture of the organization.

While in Hotel and Restaurant Administration (CMO No, 30, Series of 2006- Tourism Management, Hospitality Management, Hotel and Restaurant Management, and Travel) the critical thinking reflects in the **flexibility** (No.6) of curricula by mindful of the ever-changing landscape within which the tourism and the hospitality sectors operate, the curricula leave room for innovation and enhancement. Schools are encouraged to think global and act local, scan their milieu, understand their clientele and develop subjects to respond to the needs of their environment.

In the thinking skills of Hotel and restaurant Administration focuses on the following: thinks creatively, makes decisions, solves problems, visualizes, knows how to learn and reason. This is based on the orientation that the set of policies and standards consolidates all programs in tourism, hospitality management and related fields into a rational structure with two orientations: the macro and the micro.

1. The micro orientation pertains to the sectoral perspective. Programs with this orientation prepare the students for a career in management and/or entrepreneurship. They develop competency (knowledge, skills and attitude) necessary to manage and operate effectively, efficiently and profitably, the different enterprises in the various sectors comprising the tourism industry. (No. 5.1)

2. The macro orientation does not address the operation of any one particular sector nor enterprise, rather the program(s) teach the students to regard tourism on an aggregate perspective and prepare them for a career in policy-making and tourism development. (No. 5.2)

B. Student Performance Assessment Skills

The senior students in management have high level of importance in the student performance assessment skills along *being able to express what is important in his or her professional conduct, and to express the values, norms, and pedagogical approaches on which this is based*(X- 4.76). Basically, the student performance assessment skills are conformed with the management concepts along their field of expertise (management accounting, HRD accounting, HRD management, and etc.) as the course contents that defined more on strategic management and the financial viability of the enterprise.

1. Performs work activities effectively and efficiently to the standards expected in the operation required in the tourism Industry/hospitality sectors.
2. Undertakes task, functions, duties and activities in the operation of the hotels, restaurants, travel, government and non-government agencies in accordance with the competency standards
3. Analyzes situation, identifies problems, formulates solutions and implements corrective and/or mitigating measures and action.
4. Analyzes situation, identifies problems, formulates solutions and implements corrective and/or mitigating measures and action.

In the training of the HRA students (National Tourism Agency, Local Government Tourism Offices and Non-Government organizations), It is expected to have developed knowledge and competencies in at least five (5) of the following:
1. Organizing events such as festivals, conventions, meetings and travel shows
2. Tourism product conceptualization and development (familiarity with sustainable tourism principles and practices)
3. Building regulations and standards
4. Site planning regulation and standards
5. Designing and disseminating information materials (paper-based and

electronic media)

6. Formulating workable tourism market plan
7. Tourism policy and plan formulation relating to development strategies, investments, accreditation, business regulation, taxation, procurement and procedures
8. Structures and relationships among various political entities involved in tourism planning and development
9. Tourism related legislation
10. Monitoring and evaluating tourism projects through statistics gathering and research
11. Partnership building and fundraising: liaising and coordinating with private sector, civil society and government agencies
12. Community organizing and networking
13. Business communication skills and telephone courtesy
14. Business etiquette

B.   ASEAN Competency and Instructional Standards of Faculty for Accounting and Management, Tourism, Information Technology and Teacher Education

Educators are free to adopt the methods that work best in their particular cultures. However, they may need to be trained and encouraged to use a broad range of learner-centered teaching methods that include: (Section 44, Article IX)

a. Using case studies, projects and other means to simulate work
c. Adapting instructional methods and materials to the ever-changing environment
d. Pursuing a curriculum learn to learn on their own and carry out this skill with them after becoming professional accountants;
e. Using technology and e-learning; Encouraging students to be active participants in the learning process;
g. Using measurement and evaluation knowledge, skills, and professional values, ethics, and attitudes
h. Integrating knowledge, skills, professional values, ethics and attitudes across topics and disciplines to address many-sided and complex situations typical of profession
i. Emphasizing problem identification and problem-solving which encourages identifying relevant information, making logical assessments and communicating clear conclusions;
j. Exploring research findings; and Stimulating students to develop professional skepticism and professional judgment.

Delivering all of these teaching methods in a purely academic environment is not the only solution. Integration of education and knowledge. A well-designed program of on-the-job training can deliver many of the required experiences. Supervisors, mentors and others involved in practical experience may need to be trained in the most effective way of planning practical experience.

Other learning methods include:
a) Working in groups and in-office environments;
b. Integration of professional knowledge, skills, values, ethics and values across topics practice in solving problem ; and
c. Reflection and post-implementation work reviews as a means of learning.

I. Accountancy

The BSA graduate must demonstrate the following skills: (section 18)

A. Intellectual Aspect

This set of skills includes the ability to carry out abstract logical thinking and learn the process of critical thinking. It also includes creative thinking or the generation of new ideas; visualization or "seeing things in the mind's eye"; and reasoning skills or the discovery of a rule or principle underlying the relationship between two or more objects and applying it when solving a problem. Hence, the BSA graduate must demonstrate the following skills.

1. *Analysis* – Ability to review, interpret, evaluate financial data and systems/ operational data/ controls in order to form conclusions and/or make recommendations on validity/usefulness/ correctness/ compliance within established policies, procedures, guidelines, agreements and/or legislation.
2. *Problem solving* – Discerning the true nature of a situation and evaluation of applicable principles and techniques. Innovative thinking, reliable evaluation of information, openness to constructive change and consideration of future contingencies and developments
3. *Strategic/Critical Thinking* – Linking data, knowledge and insight together from different sources and disciplines to make informed decisions. Considering the "big picture"

when making decisions, as well as potential threats to the vision, strategy, objectives and culture of the organization.

B. Interpersonal Aspect

This involves developing the ability of the BSA graduate to work in groups and being a team player. It includes the skills to participate as member of a team and contributing to group effort; teaching others new skills; working to satisfy clients' expectations; negotiation skills and working with diversity or working well with men and women from diverse backgrounds.

Hence, the BSA graduate must demonstrate attributes such as being:
- A team player
- Persuasive, confident and diplomatic
- Discreet, open minded and patient
- Capable for hard work and able to respond well to pressure

C. Communication

This refers to active listening skills and the ability to communicate ffectively one's points of view, both orally and in writing, at all organizational levels; being able to justify one's position, deliver impressive presentations and to persuade and convince others. The BSA graduate should demonstrate skills such as the ability to:

- Explain verbally and/or in writing financial/ statistical/administrative matters/ policies/ procedures/ regulatory matters/audit results at a level appropriate to the audience.
- Ask clear, concise and relevant questions to obtain desired information to perform a task.
- Negotiate effectively.

Values that the BSA graduate should possess include:

A. Professional Ethics

Since the objectives of the accountancy profession are to work in accordance with the highest standards of professionalism, to attain the higher level of performance and generally to meet the public interest, the need for CPAs to conform to the ethical standards of the profession becomes vital.

These include: Integrity - Avoiding actual or apparent conflicts of interest and; Objectivity and independence - Communicating information; and due care –

Maintaining and training from disclosing confidential advise all appropriate parties of any potential conflict; refraining from engaging in any activity that would prejudice their ability to carry out their duties ethically; refusing any gift, favor or hospitality that would influence or appear to influence their actions; refraining from either actively or passively subverting the attainment of the organization's legitimate and ethical objectives; recognizing and communicating professional limitations or other constraints that would preclude responsible judgment or successful performance of an activity; communicating unfavorable as well as favorable information and professional judgments or opinions; and refraining from engaging in or supporting any activity that would discredit the profession. fairly and objectively; and disclosing fully all relevant information that could reasonably be expected to influence an intended users understanding of the reports, comments and recommendations presented.

Professional competence and appropriate level of professional competence by ongoing development of knowledge and skills; performing one's professional duties in accordance with relevant laws, regulations and technical standards; preparing objective and complete reports and recommendations after appropriate analysis of relevant and reliable information.

Confidentiality - information acquired in the course of their work, except when authorized, unless legally obligated to do so; informing staff as appropriate regarding the confidentiality of information acquired in the course of their work and monitor their activities to assure the maintenance of that confidentiality; and refraining from using or appearing to use confidential information acquired in the course of their work for unethical or illegal advantage either personally or through third parties.

Professional behavior - Discharging one's professional responsibilities with competence and diligence and performing one's services to the best of a member's ability with concern for the best interest of those for whom the services are performed and consistent with the profession's responsibility to the public; obligation of self-discipline above and beyond the requirements of laws and regulations; and unswerving commitment to honorable behavior, even at the sacrifice of personal advantage

II. Hotel and Restaurant Administration
(CHED Memorandum Order No. 30, Series of 2006)
Bachelor of Science in Tourism Management (BSTM)
Bachelor of Science in Hospitality Management (BSHM)
Bachelor of Science in Hotel and Restaurant Management (BSHRM)
Bachelor of Science in Travel Management

Tourism is the world's largest industry, generating in 2003 over USD 514 Billion in receipts from 697 million tourists and employing hundreds of million people worldwide. Almost 760 million traveled across borders in 2004; several times more traveled domestically. The probability of one being able to visit foreign lands in his lifetime has never been higher. (Section 1- Background of the Tourism Industry)

The aforementioned factors have ramifications on the Philippine tourism education system. A good starting point for reform was to make a thorough review of the management-oriented curriculum that has, since the 70's, pervaded among tourism and hospitality schools. To produce graduates that will not only survive but also thrive in a borderless economy, a paradigm shift from supply-driven to market-driven curriculum in terms of content and structure was adopted. To be more responsive to the needs of the industry, the new program emphasizes skills and competencies instead of just managerial theory and is scheduled in such a way as to provide more but focused options for the students in terms of career paths. The course line-up incorporates subjects on sustainable development and international standards and practices to address issues that arise from market imperfections and the challenges of globalization. Finally, the curriculum is designed to allow flexibility and creativity on the part of higher educational institutions. (Section 2- Rationale)

Against this overview, and considering sustainable development as the key to optimal tourism growth, this set of programs on tourism, hospitality management and related fields was developed to support the tourism industry and to address its manpower needs more particularly, in preparation for the full implementation of the General Agreement of Trade and Services (GATS) under the aegis of the World Trade Organization.

Competency Standards

The Graduates of BSTM, BSHM, BSHRM, BSTrM and/or bachelor degree in other related fields shall possess the following competencies: (Section 8. Skill, Competencies and Qualities-)

A. Five Competencies

1. **Resources**: identifies goal-relevant activities, ranks them, allocates resources
2. **Interpersonal**: works with others
3. **Information**: acquires and evaluates information
4. **Systems**: understands complex interrelationships
5. **Technology**: works with a variety of technologies

B. Skills and Personal Qualities

1. **Basic skills**: reads, writes, performs arithmetic and mathematical operations, listens and speaks;
2. **Thinking skills**: thinks creatively, makes decisions, solves problems, visualizes, knows how to learn and reason; and
3. **Personal qualities**: possesses a sense of responsibility, self-esteem, sociability, self-management, integrity, and honesty

CURRICULA

This set of curricula has the following features: (Article V-Curricula; Section 9-Curricula Description)

1. **Common core**. All the programs share a set of common core. Under the general umbrella of Tourism, graduates of these programs possess a common set of core and specific competencies developed from the general education, business and tourism/hospitality subjects.
2. **Competency-based**. Job readiness of the graduates is the focus of the curricula. Competencies are matched with the competency standards required by of the industry based on the job positions that the graduates will eventually occupy upon graduation.
3. **Industry-driven**. Industry participated in the identification of job entry positions and development of competencies standards.
4. **Curriculum design**. Professional subjects in the first two years are procedural, and the last two years are supervisory. Implicitly, the

curriculum design enables the students to leave school after completing the first two years and take on entry- level positions in accommodation, food and beverages, travel agencies, government or non-government agencies. The last two years will hone the students' supervisory competency to prepare them for supervisory positions as they progress with their careers.

5. **Orientation**. This set of policies and standards consolidates all programs in tourism, hospitality management and related fields into a rational structure with two orientations: the macro and the micro.

   5.1 The micro orientation pertains to the sectoral perspective. Programs with this orientation prepare the students for a career in management and/or entrepreneurship. They develop competency (knowledge, skills and attitude) necessary to manage and operate effectively, efficiently and profitably, the different enterprises in the various sectors comprising the tourism industry.

   5.2. The macro orientation does not address the operation of any one particular sector nor enterprise, rather the program(s) teach the students to regard tourism on an aggregate perspective and prepare them for a career in policy-making and tourism development.

6. **Flexibility**. Mindful of the ever-changing landscape within which the tourism and the hospitality sectors operate, the curricula leave room for innovation and enhancement. Schools are encouraged to think global and act local, scan their milieu, understand their clientele and develop subjects to respond to the needs of their environment.

III. **Teacher Education Teacher Education Curriculum (CHED Memorandum Order No. 30, Series 2004)Revised Policies and Standards for Undergraduate Teacher Education Curriculum**

1. Bachelor of Elementary Education (BEED)
2. Bachelor of Secondary Education

Quality pre-service teacher education is a key factor in quality Philippine education. In the Philippines, the pre-service preparation of the teachers for the primary and secondary educational sectors is very important function and responsibility that has been assigned to higher education institutions. (Section 1)

Program Description and General Objectives

The BEED is structured to meet the needs of professional teachers for elementary schools and special education programs in the Philippines, and as the BSEd for the needs of professional teachers for secondary schools in the Philippines.

The BEED aims to develop elementary school teachers who are either; (Section 4)

a. Generalists who can teach across the different learning areas in grade school.
b. Special Education teachers or;
c. Pre- school teachers

Teacher Education is an applied discipline which draws from many of the basic discipline in the social sciences, the Science and technology fields And also the Humanities and related fields. (Allied Programs- Section 5)

Competency Standards

Graduate of BEEd and BSEd programs are teachers who. (Article IV, Section 6)

1. Have the basic and higher level literacy, Communication, numeracy critical thinking, learning skills needed for higher learning.
2. Have a deep and principled understanding of the learning processes and the role of the teacher in facilitating these processes in their students;
3. Have a deep and principled understanding of how educational processes relate to larger historical, social cultural and political processes.
4. Have a meaningful and comprehensive knowledge of the subject matter they will teach;
5. Can apply a wide range of teaching process skills (including curriculum development, lesson planning, material development, educational assessment and teaching approaches);
6. Have a direct experience in the field and classroom
7. Can demonstrate and practice the professional and ethical requirements of the teaching professions;
8. Can facilitate learning diverse types of learners, in diverse type of learning environments, using a wide range of teaching knowledge and skills;
9. Can reflect on the relationships among teaching process skills, the learning processing in the students, the nature of the content/subject matter, and the broader social forces encumbering the school and educational processes in order to constantly improve their teaching knowledge, skills and practices.

10. Can be creative and innovative in thinking of the alternative teaching approaches, take informed risks in trying out these innovative approaches and evaluate the effectiveness of such approaches in improving student learning; and
11. Are willing and capable to continue learning in order to better fulfill their mission as teachers.

The curriculum herein is designed to prepare professional teachers for practice in primary and secondary schools in the Philippines. The design features include various components that correspond to the basic and specialized knowledge and skills that will be needed by a practicing professional teacher: foundational general education knowledge and skills, theoretical knowledge about teaching and learning methodological skills that allow them more options and greater flexibility in designing and implementing learning environment that will maximize their students' learning, once they are in the teaching service. (Article V ,Section 7, Curriculum Description)

a)   **General Education Courses** . General education and legislated courses shall follow existing requirements. The CHED Memorandum No. 59 series 1996 (63 units) is the recommended track for the teacher education programs. In addition, the course requirements for the selected general education courses are specified in this curriculum (refer to section 17) (Section 9)

b)   **Professional Education Courses.** These courses represent component of the curriculum that aims to develop the range of knowledge and skills needed in the practice of the teaching profession. These courses are divided into three broad categories: (Section 10)
- Theory and concepts courses,
- Methods and strategies courses ,and
- Field study courses.

c)   **Theory and Concepts Courses** . The following are theory and concepts courses that provide the broad frame works within which students can understand, rationalize and reflect on the various methods, strategies, processes, issue and other matters related to the teaching profession. (Section 11)
- Child and adolescent development
- Facilitating human learning
- Social dimensions of education
- The Teaching professions

d) **Methods and Strategies Courses.** The Following are the Methods and strategies courses in the program that aim to develop in students a wide range of skills to facilitate and evaluate learning in diverse types of the students in a variety of learning environment. (Section 12)

- **Field study courses** . The following series of courses are the field study courses that are intended to provide students with practical learning experiences in which they can observe verify, reflect on, and actually experience different components of the teaching learning processes in actual school settings. The experience will begin with field observation and gradually intensify until students undertake practice teaching. (Section 13)

- **Special Topics Courses** .Students will have the opportunity to explore special topics and issues related to their field by taking three one-unit elective seminars on a range of topics chosen by the teacher education institution, based on their perceived needs of the students and the expertise of their faculty. (Section 14)

Information Technology Education (CHED Memorandum Order No. 53, Series of 2006 Policies and Standards for Information Technology Education (ITE) Programs)

The field of Information Technology (IT) is ever dynamic; its advancement and development had been rapid and its evolvement is a continuous process. To face the challenges of advancement, the Commission recognizes the need to be responsive according to the current needs of the country. Hence, it is essential and important that the country's **IT** capability should be continually developed and strengthened to be at par globally. (Article 1, Introduction – Section 1. Rational and Background)

It is the objective of the Commission to develop and promote the Policies and Standards [PS] for Information Technology Education to provide a minimum standard for Higher Education Institutions (HEIs) offering or intending to offer quality ITE programs. The PS is developed with consultations from all stakeholders.

From the academe to industry. The PS contains provisions that cultivate the culture of excellence in offering the ITE programs. This is in line with the vision of the Commission to have HEIs produce competent graduates that shall cater to the needs of the **IT** industry. The P8 is also designed for all HEIs to exercise their innovativeness and creativity in the development of its curriculum for the offering of ITE programs.

Program Specifications

The degree programs corresponding respectively to these specific areas are the following: (Degree Programs ,Article III, Section 3)

a) **Bachelor of Science in Computer Science (BSCS)** ~ the study of concepts and theories. algorithmic foundations, implementation and application of information and computing solutions. (Section 3.1)

b) **Bachelor of Science in Information Technology (BSIT)** - the study of utilization of computers and computer software to plan, install, customize. operate. manage, administer and maintain information technology infrastructure. (Section 3.2)

c) **Bachelor of Science in Information Systems (BSIS) n** the study of design and implementation of solutions that integrate information technology with business processes. The BSIS shall replace the Bachelor of Science in Information Management [BSIM) program. (Section 3.3)

Program Description.

The objectives of the three {3] programs in ITE are as follows: (Section 4. Program, Description)

a) The Bachelor of Science in Computer Science IBSCS) program prepares students to be IT professionals and researchers. and to be proficient in designing and developing computing solutions. (4.1.1)

b) The Bachelor of Science in Information Technology (BSIT) program prepares students to be IT professionals, be well versed on application installation, operation. Development, maintenance and administration, and familiar with hardware installation. Operation, and maintenance. (4.1.2)

c) The Bachelor of Science in Information Systems (BSIS) program prepares students to be IT professionals and be expert on design and implementation of IS for business processes. (4.1.3)

Specific professions/careers/occupations or trades that the graduates of these programs may pursue. — After satisfactorily completing all the requirements leading to a BSCS. BSIT, or BSIS degree. students may qualify for but not limited to the following entry level positions: (4.2)

1.Bachelor of Science in Computer Science (BSCS)
- Applications Developer
- Computer Science Instructor
- Database Programmer / Designer
- Information Security Engineer
- Quality Assurance Engineer
- Researcher
- Systems Developer
- Systems Analyst

Bachelor of Science in Information Technology (BSIT)
- Applications developer
- Database Administrator
- Entrepreneur in IT Industry
- Information Security Administrator
- Information Technology Instructor
- Network Administrator
- Network Engineer
- Systems Analyst
- Technical Support Specialist
- Test Engineer
- Web Administrator / Web Master
- Web Developer

Bachelor of Science in Information Systems (BSIS)

- Business Process Analyst
- Data Quality Specialist
- Entrepreneur in IT industry
- IS Instructor
- Systems Auditor
- Quality Assurance Analyst
- Systems Implementation Officer
- Technical Support Specialist

Competency Standards

Competency refers to specific skills, knowledge and attitude that may be demonstrated through performance, while standards are common set of expectations. Graduates of either BSCS, BSIT, or BSIS programs. are expected to have acquired but not limited to the following competencies: (Section 6, Article IV)

é.1 Personal Skills

Personal-discipline skills

Critical-thinking skills

Inter and intra person motivation skills

a Problem solving skills

- Planning and organizing skiils
- Ethical thinking

0 Entrepreneurial thinking

- Innovative
- Perseverance in pursuing goals and continuous improvement

6.2 Interpersonal Skills

1- Team work and collaborative skills

0 Oral and written communication skills

0 Conflict resolution skills

6.3 Technical Understanding

6.3.i Bachelor of Science in Computer Science (BSCS)

- Application of fundamental computer concepts as problem solving skills
- Design and implementation of computer-based solutions
- Recognition and application of technical standards and interoperability

- Research in Computer Science related areas
- Integration of knowledge learned in different areas of Computer Science

6.3.2 Bachelor of Science in Information Technology (BSIT)

- Systems analysis and design
- Operation of database, networks and multimedia systems
- Software integration, testing and documentation
- Systems management and administration

Principles of accounting

6.3.3 Bachelor of Science in Information Systems (BSIS)

- Information abstraction, representation and organization
- Computing architectures and delivery systems
- Concepts of information and system distribution
- Information management and system development
- Computing tools in knowledge application

Expansion of the International Linkages on Academic and Research Collaboration with Suan Dusit Rajabhat University (SDRU)

The expansion of academic exchange and collaboration of UNP-CTE with Suan Dusit Rajabhat University (SDRU) at Suphanburi Campus was the cultural diversity program on Chinese Language and role of the UNP in the publication of academic materials for the Confucius Institute of Maritime Silk Road.

A. Suan Dusit Rajabhat University at Suphanburi through Confucius Institute (CI) in Collaboration with Romchatra Foundation and Confucius Institute of the Maritime Silk Road(CIMSR)

The expansion of academic exchange and collaboration of Suan Dusit Rajabhat University (SDRU) at Suphanburi Campus was the cultural diversity program on Chinese Language and role of the UNP to publish academic materials for the Confucius Institute of Maritime Silk Road. The SDRU research team led by Dr. Prakit Bhulapatna (left photo), Dean of Graduate School was able to gather data by sending the questionnaires to each respondent university which were brought back to Thailand by the university representatives from the 5 countries who also attended the Focus Group Discussion conducted in January 12-17, 2015.

This was the reason that the research team expanded the academic collaboration on ASEAN cultural diversity through Suan Dusit Rajabhat University at Suphanburi through Confucius Institute (CI)started the expanded collaboration with the assistance of Romchatra Foundation and Confucius Institute of the Maritime Silk Road (CIMSR)

The sustained academic exchange and collaboration with the Romchatra Foundation at the Confucius Classroom Traimitwittayalai at Timit Wittayalai at Charoenkung Road, Samphantawaong District Bangkok, Thailand.   The Romchatra Foundation and UNP conducted series of academic collaboration such as Global Initiative in Basketball at Trimit Wittayalai High School, Academic lecture series on the Traimit model and career path program for the foreign students.

B. **Benchmarking the Confucius Classroom /Institute with the strategic opportunity for the establishment of this center in the University of Northern Philippines with the current MOA agreement with Romchatra Foundation :**

1) The foundation provides the diplomatic ties with China through the Confucius Classroom/ Institutes in order to strengthen educational cooperation between China and Philippines, support and promote the development of Chinese language education of primary and middle schools, and increase mutual understanding and friendship between the young people of China and the Philippines.

2) The Confucius Classroom/ Institutes can serve the following Chinese teaching courses and programs according to the local instance:
   a) Teach Chinese and Sponsor cultural activities and Chinese competitions;
   b) Train teachers to teach Chinese in primary and middle schools;
   c) Organize summer and winter camp to China for primary and middle school students;
   d) Compile teaching materials.

C. **Student Exchange Program-Tan Trao University, Tuyen Quang Province, Vietnam**

The College of Teacher Education has established a Student Exchange Program through the Memorandum of Agreement (MOA) between Tan Trao University and University of Northern Philippines issued last March 6,

2015 . The MOA manifested the Higher Education collaboration in research and extension programs, cultural and scientific , interests, faculty, staff and student exchanges and other activities for the advancement of global excellence in education, governance, business, technology and health.

A number of CTE faculty attended the International Conference held at Tan Trao University, Vietnam on May 22, 2015. The title of the International Conference was " Assessing Primary Students by Approaching and Evaluating their Competence A Possible Approach to Pedagogic Institutions in Vietnam and same Southeast Asian Countries." (May 22, 2015) This was the offshoot of the research collaboration n with the Suan Dusit which the University of Northern Philippines and Tan Trao University participated as the institutional members in the completion of ASEAN research on educational training competence.

In the international conference at Tan Trao University, the faculty members of the College of Teacher Education participated the academic exchange program in the areas of pedagogy, MTB-MLE and Science Education. The five (5) researches were presented during the conference.

1. Implementation of the K to 12 program in the Laboratory Schools of the College of Teacher Education, University of Northern Philippines.

2. The Culture-Based Multidisciplinary Model of the Mother Tongue Based- Multilingual Education (MTB-MLE) of the Primary Schools in the Philippines.

3. Correlation Analysis of Licensure Examination for Teacher and Academic Performance of BEEd Students.

4. Interpersonal   Conflict Management Style of Future Basic Education Teachers Misconceptions in Astronomy.

In the concluding study about the international partnership with the ASEAN University through the academic collaboration with Tan Trao University has the educational impact in the areas of educational administration, cultural diversity, language proficiency, pedagogical assessment and teaching-learning process. The CTE-Graduate Studies has shared the faculty expertise in the field of educational administration with the actual exposures of the visiting professors of Tan Trao University to bring Vietnamese students to learn and experience the culture, history and tradition of the Ilocanos. Furthermore, the educational impact of the twinning program was the implementation of the practice teaching abroad that compensated the expertise of the faculty and students to teach the Vietnamese students and faculty about the English language. Likewise, the faculty exchange program provided the teaching opportunity to share the best practices in the field of pedagogy.

D. Continuation of the Research Collaboration of Suan Dusit Rajabhat University

The second research collaboration conducted by Suan Dusit University (2018) with University of Northern Philippines, Tan Trao University, (Vietnam) Dong Kham Chang Teacher College (Laos), Universitas Negeri Jakarta (Indonesia) entitled " The Context and Trend to Develop the Pre-working Training Course for Promoting the Competency, Capacity and Ability in the Business Service Field in ASEAN countries."

The investigation of this research had 3 main objectives:
1. to study, survey and analyze the context, trend, competency, capacity and ability in the business service field in ASEAN countries;
2. to develop the competency standard and in the business service field to promote the worker in ASEAN countries; and
3. to discuss the competency standard that are relevant to the need of the ASEAN workers.

The instrument of this research was a questionnaire, and divided into three-parts of topic: (a) personal and service skills; (b) the communicative skills; and (c) organizational and perspective in the business field.

Based on the result of the study, the overall opinion on the competency that it should have or should be the organizational and perspective on the highest need followed by personal and service skills of the business officer and the communicative skills came last as highly need. From the workshop and the focus group of the expert, it can be concluded that thinking skills are also the best way to develop the human in all careers because of many jobs need the human who also has awareness in their duties, responsibilities and concern in their job.

The core competency is the major competency that every officer in ASEAN's country must have and should have. Because, the core competency is also mixed the valuable concept of the working career in the business service field such:

1) Customers and colleges are also including the establishing goals, providing the motivation provision and the developing each others.

2) Thinking skills are also including the analytical and critical thinking skills, forward thinking skills, and strategic thinking skills.

3) Communicative skills are also including the diagnostic information gathering persuasive communicative, interpersonal awareness, influencing others in the business service, an oral communication, written communication skills, attention to communication.

Moreover, in this research developing the functional competency that can be seen from the following details :

1. The Cooperative Relationships and Team Working are also including the building collaborative relationships in the business service field customer orientation in the business service products and services and fostering teamwork and empowering others in the business service.

2. The Management and Organizational Empowering are also including the managing change in the business service jobs and managing performance in the business service jobs.

Moreover, both of four sub-categories of the thinking skills such: (1) the analytical and critical thinking skills; (2) the forward thinking skills; (3) conceptual thinking skills; and (4) the strategic thinking skills are suitable for this field of work. From the group discussion can be concluded that the "Establish the goals" should be the first priority of management in any field of work as well as the business service, because the organization can set the goals and develops a plan to help fulfill the service mission.

The comparison and discussion made clear that " the core competency standard" are adopted in a several area of the business service jobs from the survey research and focus group discussion . In spite of the core competency is looking like the main organ of the human body, but it cannot avoid the functional competency is also the supporting organ of the body too. Additionally, the group discussion is also analyzed that the "Cooperative Relationships and Team Working" can be done by the good relationship of the colleagues and partner, so the business service jobs of the ASEAN should be established the organization in cooperation.

Chapter 8
Academic Exchange and Research Collaboration in the Teacher Education Program of the University of Northern Philippines and Tan Trao University

Abstract

The academic collaboration of the College Teacher Education with Tan Trao University has the educational impact in the areas of educational administration, cultural diversity, language proficiency, pedagogical assessment and teaching-learning process. It has shared the faculty expertise in the field of educational administration with the actual exposures of the visiting professors of Tan Trao University to bring Vietnamese students to learn and experience the culture, history and tradition of the Ilocanos. Furthermore, the academic exchange has achieved greater access to student and faculty exchange program through language proficiency training, cultural diversity and pedagogical assessment participation of the stakeholders.

I. Introduction

The Tan Trao University, Vietnam renewed the Memorandum of Agreement signed last March 10, 2016 for the academic collaboration and student exchange program that deployed qualified student teachers for the College of Teacher Education. It also provided student teachers of Tan Trao University to apply real world teaching experience on cultural diversity. There was a substantial financial logistic support utilized in bringing sustained student and faculty exchange program for Vietnam.

1. The academic collaboration of the International Conference with the theme "Assessing Primary Students by Approaching and Evaluating their Competence-A Possible Approach to Pedagogic Institutions in Vietnam."

2. The participation of student exchange program of two (2) BSEd students in the fourth-month internship to teach English Language for the faculty and students of Tan Trao University in 2016.

3. Student Exchange Program - The Vietnamese students were exposed to the CTE Best Practices in classroom instruction,

Ilokano language and culture (MTB-MLE), teacher education extra-curricular activities last May 5-30, 2017. The accepted Vietnamese students were specialized in primary schools, literature education, physical and environment science, land and environment science.

4. Pre-Service Teacher Exchange Program of Tan Trao University with the participation of the Senior High School Teachers in providing academic support of the K to 12 curricula, Ilocano culture, Vigan Cultural Heritage activities and English Language Proficiency class for the Vietnamese students.

In partnership with the UNP Center for International Studies, the College of Teacher Education accepted ten students from the Tan Trao University for exposure on May 5-30, 2017. The students were accompanied by their professors. They were exposed to the CTE Best Practices in classroom instruction, co-curriculum activities, extra-curricular activities, extension and lectures on orthography and culture heritage. The said Vietnamese students underwent a rigid selection process so that the best 10 excellent students were sent to the UNP-CTE to undergo the May 5-30, 2017 exposure

The ten Vietnamese students who were accepted for exposure to the CTE are: 1. Tran Thi Nghia - Primary School 2. Linh Huru Khurong - Land and Environment Science 3. Tran Hien Quang - Land and Environment Science 4. Phung Tien Thong - Literature Education 5. Hoang Thi Trang - Language Education 6. Nguyen Thi Lan Anh - Land and Environment Science 7. Nguyen Ngoc Quynh - Primary School 8. Nguyen Thi Phrong Thao- Primary School 9. Nguyen Thu Uyen - Primary School 10. Tran Van Bac - Physical and Environment Science.

II. Objectives of the Study

The general objective of the study is to determine the educational outcome and impact through qualitative and documentary analysis of the twinning agreement between the University of Northern Philippines and Tan Trao University.

Specifically, the objectives of the study are the following:

1. Identify the program outcome and impact of the research presentation and collaboration on teaching and learning process which adopted the pedagogical practice as institutional mentoring process for the international partnership with Tan Trao University.

2. Describe the potent catalyst of the emerging research and international collaboration in Vietnam by the College of Teacher Education.

3. Describe the College of Teacher Education Exchange Program on cultural diversity and language development program.

4. Evaluate the sustained international linkage and partnership with Tan Trao University.

III. Methodology

The qualitative analysis of the academic collaboration on student exchange, in-country facilitation and other thematic results of the twinning agreement provided the discussion as to the academic activities for the sustained implementation of the program. The study utilized the thematic discussion about the actual sustained international linkages along education supervision, pedagogical assessment, cultural diversity, in-country experience on cultural diversity, language proficiency and student exchange program. The educational outcome and impact was determined by the actual experience of the stakeholders in the student exchange program including the direct academic benefits as a result of the collaborative performance in the twinning programs.

IV. RESULTS AND DISCUSSION

The research study presents the program outcomes and impact of the twinning agreement between the University of Northern Philippines and Tan Trao University along the thematic international linkages on educational supervision, students exchange program, cultural diversity, language education and other areas of academic collaboration.

A. Program Outcome and Impact of the Research Presentation and Collaboration on Teaching and Learning Process Adopted in the Educational Supervision for the International partnership with Tan Trao University.

The academic collaboration of Tan Trao University in the teacher education program provides the continuing support of the international research presentations in the area of educational administration and the supervision of the teaching- learning process. The Tan Trao University presented the 1st International Conference in Vietnam as an offshoot of the faculty exchange program of Suan Dusit University that supported this activity.

The rationale of the 1st conference adhered to the idea of holistic education. The university administration of Tan Trao supported this holistic education which has become a popular teaching and learning approach particularly for primary education in Western countries, but it may appear new to Vietnamese education and perhaps to some South East Asian countries. The key characteristics of *Holistic education* are instead of educating students with academic aspects only, educator should see the student's development as a *'whole'*: hard skills (academic ability); soft skills (presentation, independence, critical thinking…).

The program outcome revolves from the benchmarking of the educational management adopted from the best practices of the Southeast Asian countries particularly the teacher education program that anchored on the policy research of the Blended Education program. The university officials of Tan Trao made mention of the program outcome of the academic collaboration in Vietnam that "Taking account from *Holistic education*, the 1st International Conference at Tan Trao University will raise the issue of whether we should assess students at primary level through exams and marks, or instead, students will be assessed by teachers' comments and evaluations about different skills and abilities at a particular period of time. The theme of the conference also focuses on current assessment system of all students in general and primary students in particular in Vietnam and some South East Asian countries.

This was held in Tuyen Quang, the former temporary capital of Vietnam in the resistance war against French colony. Tuyen Quang has complex history in both pre-modern and modern Vietnam which makes it "a place of history". Tan Trao University is also named towards a historical milestone. Tan Trao is a newly founded university, but it has attracted large numbers of young scholars, these staffs are expected to be the key people in implementing and renovating of what we learn from the conference.

It has shown in the academic collaboration of the Tan Trao University had given opportunity to provide sustained support in the educational management practices and teaching-learning process. The educational impact of the strong support of the Graduate School on the ideas and concepts of Educational Administration the best practice of the teacher education program emerged the adoption of the twinning program in the student exchange program as deeply rooted by the research collaboration.

B. The Potent Catalyst of the Emerging Research and International Collaboration in Vietnam by the Graduate Studies for Education

The 1st International Conference at Tan Trao University became the potent Catalyst in the implementation of the academic collaboration and exchange which was started in May 2015 that continued the support of the College of Teacher Education in the University of Northern Philippines. The international collaboration of Tan Trao University started the signing of Memorandum of Agreement (MOA) Between the University of Northern Philippines and Tan Trao University, Vietnam for Research Collaboration, Academic and Student Exchange Program on May 22, 2015. This was attended by Mr. Albert R. Tejero, Vice President for Finance and Administration to represent the University President with CTE faculty and students.

The research studies presented in the 1st International Conference with the theme "Assessing Primary Students by Approaching and Evaluating their Competence A Possible Approach to Pedagogic Institutions in Vietnam and same Southeast Asian Countries:" were the following:

1. Implementation of the K to 12 program in the Laboratory Schools of the College of Teacher Education, University of Northern Philippines.

2. The Culture-Based Multidisciplinary Model of the Mother Tongue Based- Multilingual Education (MTB-MLE) of the Primary Schools in the Philippines

3. Correlation Analysis of Licensure Examination for Teacher and Academic Performance of BEEd Students

4. Interpersonal Conflict Management Style of Future Basic Education Teachers

5. Misconceptions in Astronomy of the Third Year Elementary Education Students, University of Northern Philippines

The program outcome of the 1st conference provided the opportunity to expand the twinning agreement on the teaching-learning process by the faculty and student exchange program that resulted to the crediting of the international linkage points for the application of Center of Development in the field of teacher education. This was the reason that the evaluators of the CHED panel for Center of Development to consider the sustained international linkages of the College of Teacher Education.

C. Academic Exchange Program on Cultural Diversity and Language Development Program

The continuing academic collaboration with Tan Trao University improved the technical assistance on the Student Exchange Program with the exposure of the Vietnamese students on the Cultural Diversity and Language Development program last May 2017. The partnership title of the student exchange program was "A Taste of UNP Culture: The Vietnamese Faculty and Students in UNP- The CTE Exchange Program in Partnership with the Center for International Studies."

In partnership with the UNP Center for International Studies through the Blended program of the College of Teacher Education accepted ten students from the Tan Trao University for exposure on May 5-30, 2017. The students were accompanied by their professors. They were exposed to the CTE Best Practices in classroom instruction, co-curriculum activities, extra-curricular activities, extension and lectures on orthography and culture heritage. The said Vietnamese students underwent a rigid selection process so that the best 10 excellent students were sent to the UNP-CTE to undergo the May 5-30, 2017 exposure.

The ten Vietnamese students who were accepted for exposure to the College of Teacher Education, University of Northern Philippines:
1. Tran Thi Nghia - Primary School
2. Linh Huru Khurong - Land and Environment Science
3. Tran Hien Quang - Land and Environment Science
4. Phung Tien Thong - Literature   Education
5. Hoang Thi Trang - Language Education
6. Nguyen Thi Lan Anh - Land and Environment Science
7. Nguyen Ngoc Quynh - Primary School
 8. Nguyen Thi Phrong Thao- Primary School
 9. Nguyen Thu Uyen - Primary School
10. Tran Van Bac - Physical and Environment Science

The College of Teacher Education on the Vietnamese Students' Exchange Program showcases the many faces of Filipino hospitality and UNP's brand of globally competitive instruction, research and extension.

The Vietnamese Student Exchange Program was implemented with various academic activities in the teacher training which included classroom observations at the Laboratory Schools and at the undergraduate courses; field exposures in agricultural and fishing communities; upland communities; program and various activities they were exposed to the Ilokano culture and language.

One of the Vietnamese Students wrote in his testimony on the Internship Report of the Student Exchange Program in the College of Teacher Education:

…Then I found out a bit information about everything I see in the Philippines. Not only being exchange student but also exchange knowledge and ideas. I think it was good for me when I get to know all things I like and want. Now I know a little bit about the culture of the country and people in the Philippines. I see that Philippines is actually a beautiful country with all helpful people and beautiful sight. UNP is a very perfect place to study research and expand my knowledge. And your place City of Vigan is also a worthy place to stay. So many feelings and emotions involved cannot explain through words. The place where I want to spend some more time…

Nguyen Ngoc Quynh

The College of Teacher Education (CTE) implemented the Vietnamese Students' Exchange Program with the support of the Center for International Studies with the program outcome of the insights in the international linkages to support the supervisory program for the teaching-learning process to enhance the experiential knowledge on cultural diversity and language development. The educational impact of the Vietnamese Students' Exchange program ensures the continuing support of the university officials of Tan Trao University to give more Vietnamese students and request that the CTE students and faculty would teach English proficiency program.

It is also expected to continue giving priority of the student exchange program to be emerged in the CTE as to the best practices on educational administration by sending Vietnamese students' in the Tan Trao University, College of Education those are major in Primary School, Literature Education, and Environment Science to implement the twinning program.

D. Student Exchange Program on Practice Teaching Abroad

The College of Teacher Education has established a Student Exchange Program through the Memorandum of Agreement (MOA) between Tan Trao University and University of Northern Philippines issued last March 6, 2015 . The MOA manifested the Higher Education collaboration in research and extension programs, cultural and scientific , interests, faculty, staff and student exchanges and other activities for the advancement of global excellence in education, governance, business, technology and health.

This was properly endorsed by the Commission on Higher Education in compliance with the provisions of CMO No. 22, S. 2013 entitled " Revised Policies, Standards and Guidelines on Student Internship Abroad Program (SIAP). The Chairperson of CHED approved the International Internship/Training for two months. The international internship was justified by its outcome-based initiative for the practice teaching at Tan Trao University with this expected program outcome:

To fully realize the vision and mission of the University, the College of Teacher Education, a newly designated Center of Development along teacher education in the region, collaborated with other higher education institutions in the ASEAN region to become partners in transforming and molding the faculty and the future educators with the values, ideals and aspirations of the ASEAN community. Thus, the exposure of these future teachers through their Practice Teaching Internship in ASEAN countries like Vietnam will definitely equip them with the necessary capabilities to responded to the needs and demands of the ASEAN and global community.

The language competence of the Filipino students was given opportunity to be deployed in the Practice Teaching Abroad in Tan Trao University, Tuyen Quang Province, Vietnam on July 15-November 2016. During the four-month internship, they taught in English classes, proof read English documents and final teaching demonstration. " First I have learned to adjust where people speak alien language and to the students with their level of competency. I have learned to realize that English is not just learned out of necessity but it is a lifelong skill which they can never take away from you." quipped Racachot when asked about the things she learned during the said intern.

In the publication of The Rabii (August-December 2016) through the article "CTE goes Global," the International Internship was implemented by the four month journey of the two student-teachers included tasks namely ; conducting English classes inside and outside the university; assisting in the development of teading materials and activities related to English language and proof read-reading English documents for the University. They also conducted the final demonstration in the said university.

In the practice teaching abroad, the host university provided one way airfare, transport, accommodation and subsistence daily allowance (no less than 2,500,000 Dong per month) to the student teachers.

E. Partnering Cultural Diversity of Tan Trao University of the Vietnamese Internship for the Student Exchange Program

The sustained international linkages with Tan Trao University was implemented last March 2018 with the Student Exchange theme " On Heart , One Soul, One Family: Partnering Cultural Diversity." There were 8 delegates who participated in the 2018 Student Exchange Program as part of the twinning agreement on cultural immersion between Tan Trao University and University of Northern Philippines.

1. Lam Lai Dang
2. Ma Thi Huong
3. Dang Bich Ngoc
4. Do Thi Ha Thrang
5. Tran Thi Thuy Tien
6. Hoang Phuong Thao
7. Kita Bounkhampha
8. Dam Xuan Quynh

The enriching cultural immersion in the student exchange program implemented the experiential learning on the Ilocano culture and tradition, the festivals in the UNESCO Heritage City of Vigan as the Seven Wonder Cities of the World, the pedagogical exposures in the basic education through their academic exposures in the CTE Laboratory Schools and the cultural engagement with the Filipino Society. The experiential learning had given opportunity to enhance their insights in the pre-service education with cultural exposures in the UNESCO Heritage city of Vigan.

These were the significant cultural and academic reflections shared by the 2018 Student Exchange program of Tan Trao University in Vietnam :

The insight of Lam Lai Dang reflected from the relevance of the learning environment in the promotion of universal peace and security. This important insight ensured the contribution of ASEAN peace and security which was done through cultural exchange and adoption of quality and excellence in the Higher Education Program .

I learned a lot of things in UNP. It is like a new home to me. The education is so good and the environment is at peace. I want to come back and pursue father my studies...

Lam Lai Dang

The experiential learning of the Vietnamese Student Exchange Program provided the support of cultural diversity as to their experiences and exposure in the festivities of the UNESCO Heritage City of Vigan such as the local cuisine, local dances, and songs. Furthermore, the most important cultural experience was the learning of the native tongue and the English language. The UNESCO Heritage City of Vigan as the Seven Wonder Cities of the World was the window of ensuring the richness of learning for the ASEAN Culture, History and Tradition.

... We felt that the educational environment in this place is very friendly, the UNP students helped us very much especially the caring attention of teachers. I learned a lot at UNP. From local foods, dances and songs academic activities. How I wish I could come back again in UNP to pursue further studies.

Ma Thi Huong

We learned a lot in our internship at UNP where we observed classes. We learned to dance, and the most important is we learned much the English language. My Stay in the Philippines is worth coming...

Dang Bich Ngoc

... I love the university, the students and the people of Vigan. It was a nice place to stay and a good place to study...

Tran Thi Thuy Tien

The CTE teachers were given the opportunity to interact and help the Vietnamese students the Filipino hospitality of generosity, compassion, love and peace-loving people. This was appreciated and recognized to the efforts made by the teachers who had shown their genuine compassion and professionalism to deal the students of the pre-service education.

UNP is really a good place to study. The teachers are good, caring and generous. They make us feel at home and like second parents to us. The students whom we met at the people whom we met in the community. Surely, I will miss a lot, the beaches, the beautiful plaza…

Hoang Phuong Thao

This is one of the best opportunities have ever experienced. The first time I came to UNP, I was so excited and happy, all the teachers were there available to help, whether it was a school activity or not. That gave me a lot of learning experiences in language, culture and other academic activities.

Filipinos speak English very well making their second language. UNP has a good environment to study and improve life skills and I got a lot of friends here. After my return to my own country (Laos) I will take these lessons learned and share it to all my friends. I hope I will come back again in the future.

Kita

The other students appreciated so much the hospitality even when Dam Xuan Quynh got sick in her stay at UNP, she was so thankful about the personal touched of Filipino caring other people :

It was a short stay but a wonderful experience. From the classroom to the community, and to the beaches. I felt hoe the teachers were so caring especially when I got sick. I am so thankful that I came here because in short while I learned a lot. I was able to improve my English which I really need in the future. How I wish I can come back again.

Dam Xuan Quynh

To all the officials, teachers and students of the University makes me proud of having stayed in this institution. They are so friendly and caring. I learned a lot from the classroom, the community and the people.

Do Thi Ha Thrang

Table 1

Sustained International Linkage and Partnership
with Tan Trao University

Nature of Assistance	Number of Activities	Program Outcomes and Impact
International Conference	3	Presentation of best practices in educational management, teaching-learning process, language proficiency, MTB-MLE
English Language Proficiency and Sharing of history, tradition and culture	5	Student Exchange
Twinning Agreement on Research for Teaching competence	4	Sharing of best-practices in educational assessment
Academic Visit and Benchmarking	3	Faculty and Students exchange activities
Blended Education Program	1	Doctor of Education program under the Blended Education on International Studies
Facilitation of Teacher Education Experiences	7	Faculty lecture and academic exchange for language proficiency
Faculty Exchange Exposure	1	Language performance
Academic Partnership	4	International conference and research collaboration

The program outcome and impact ensures the common sharing of academic resources in the implementation of international conferences and academic collaboration in the student exchange program. The international conferences emerged the first sustainable academic collaboration that provided the opportunity of Tan Trao University to adopt the best practices in the field of educational administration, teaching process, evaluation and assessment of learning, language proficiency and implementation of the MTB-MLE. The sustained impact of the twinning agreement defined more on the expertise of the University of Northern Philippines to act as host in the Student Exchange Program for the Vietnamese students with qualitative impact of the experiential learning about cultural diversity, language proficiency, teaching-learning process and understanding the culture of the Filipinos.

Conclusion

The academic collaboration of the College of Teacher Education with Tan Trao University has the educational impact in the areas of educational administration, cultural diversity, language proficiency, pedagogical assessment and teaching-learning process. The CTE-Graduate Studies has shared the faculty expertise in the field of educational administration with the actual exposures of the visiting professors of Tan Trao University to bring Vietnamese students to learn and experience the culture, history and tradition of the Ilocanos. Furthermore, the educational impact of the twinning program was the implementation of the practice teaching abroad that compensated the expertise of the faculty and students to teach the Vietnamese students and faculty about the English language. Likewise, the faculty exchange program provided the teaching opportunity to share the best practices in the field of pedagogy.

Potent Catalyst for Best Practices in Academic Collaboration and Exchange with Foreign Universities for Teacher Education Program of the ASEAN Community

This chapter presents the participation of Tan Trao University to collaborate with the College of Teacher Education, University of Northern Philippines in the Student and Faculty Exchange program to support the Socio-Cultural Blueprint of the ASEAN Integration for 2025. The Best Practices of the College of Teacher Education on the areas of cultural diversity, MTB-MLE, language proficiency, educational supervision and administration and pedagogy became the centerpiece of academic collaboration and exchange relevant to the ASEAN Integration. It expected that continuity of the students' exchange program provided the educational impact particularly to the Vietnamese Students to learn English language in contextualized setting that can better understand culture and tradition of the ASEAN people.

The Signing of Memorandum of Agreement (MOA) Between the University of Northern Philippines and Tan Trao University, Vietnam for Research Collaboration, Academic and Student Exchange Program on May 22, 2015.

A. International Collaboration and Research Presentation in Educational Assessment and Evaluation

A number of CTE faculty attended the International Conference held at Tan Trao University, Vietnam on May 22, 2015. The title of the International Conference was " Assessing Primary Students by Approaching and Evaluating their Competence A Possible Approach to Pedagogic Institutions in Vietnam and same Southeast Asian Countries." (May 22, 2015) This was the offshoot of the research collaboration n with the Suan Dusit which the University of Northern Philippines and Tan Trao University participated as the institutional members in the completion of ASEAN research on educational training competence.

In the international conference at Tan Trao University, the faculty members of the College of Teacher Education participated the academic exchange program in the areas of pedagogy, MTB-MLE and Science Education. The five (5) researches were presented during the conference.

1. Implementation of the K to 12 program in the Laboratory Schools of the College of Teacher Education, University of Northern Philippines.
2. The Culture-Based Multidisciplinary Model of the Mother Tongue Based- Multilingual Education (MTB-MLE) of the Primary Schools in the Philippines.
3. Correlation Analysis of Licensure Examination for Teacher and Academic Performance of BEEd Students.
4. Interpersonal Conflict Management Style of Future Basic Education Teachers Misconceptions in Astronomy.

B. Student Exchange Program of Tan Trao University and University of Northern Philippines

The College of Teacher Education has established a Student Exchange Program with ASEAN Universities. One of these is the Student Exchange Program between UNP and Tan Trao University.

• Marielle Ann A. Verzosa and Rosan R. Racachot, 4th year BSEd students pioneered the first Practice Teaching Abroad in Tan Trao University, Tuyen Quang Province, Vietnam on July 15- November 2016 .

"I have learned that teaching is a lifelong skill which nobody can take away from you." quipped Racachot when asked about the things she learned during the said intern.

Dr. Luz Relon, Practice Teaching Coordinator pause for a souvenir photo with Vietnamese Exchange Students

During the four-month English classes, proof-read final teaching~~ments and demonstration~~

Student Exchange Program from Tan Trao University, May 5-30, 2017

A Taste of UNP Culture: The Vietnamese Faculty and Students in UNP- The CTE Exchange Program in Partnership with the Center for International Studies

- In partnership with the UNP Center for International Studies, the College of Teacher Education accepted ten students from the Tan Trao University for exposure on May 5-30, 2017. The students were accompanied by their professor. They were exposed to the CTE Best Practices in classroom instruction, cocurriculum activities, extra-curricular activities, extension and lectures on orthography and culture heritage. The said Vietnamese students underwent a rigid selection process so that the best 10 excellent students were sent to the UNP-CTE to undergo the May 5-30, 2017 exposure.

The ten Vietnamese students who were accepted for exposure to the CTE are:

1. Tran Thi Nghia — Primary School
2. Linh Huru Khurong -Land and Environment Science
3. Tran Hien Quang -Land and Environment Science
4. Phung Tien Thong -Literature   Education
5. Hoang Thi Trang -Language Education
6. Nguyen Thi Lan Anh -Land and Environment Science
7. Nguyen Ngoc Quynh -Primary School
8. Nguyen Thi Phrong Thao- Primary School
9. Nguyen Thu Uyen -Primary School
10. Tran Van Bac -Physical and Environment Science

Tan Trao University's students are choosen to practice internships at the University of the Northern Philippines

According to the Memorandum of Understanding signed between Tan Trao University and the University of the Northern Philippines, so Tan Trao University's students have to pass many rounds of interviews and to win a selection process. Finally, Tan Trao University has chosen 10 excellent students in studying as well as they can communicate fluent in English to make a practice at the University of the Northern Philippines.

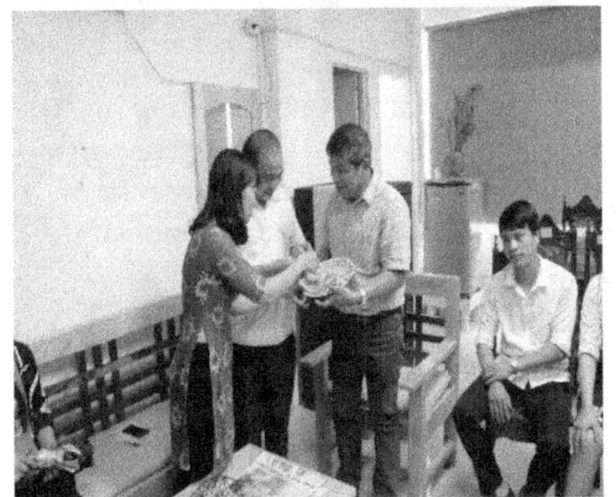

UNP showcases the many faces of Filipino hospitality and UNP's brand of globally competitive instruction, research and extension.

A Vietnamese student belts out a song while the other delegates prepare for their respective parts during the send-off program tendered by the   College of Teacher Education

The Vietnamese Student Exchange Program was implemented with various academic activities in the teacher training   which   included   classroom observations at the Laboratory Schools and at the undergraduate courses; field exposures in agricultural and fishing communities; upland   communities; program and various activities they were exposed to the Ilokano culture and language. The academic exposures were also included the student collaboration of the BEEd, BSIE and BSEd programs and educational engagement with CTE student organizations like the Young Mind Educators Club (YMEC) of the BEED, Social Science Club of the BSED major in Social Sciences, FITE for BSIE program.

One of the Vietnamese Students wrote in his testimony on the Internship

Report of the Student Exchange Program in the College of Teacher Education:

…Then I found out a bit information about everything I see in the Philippines. Not only being exchange student but also exchange knowledge and ideas. I think it was good for me when I get to know all things I like and want. Now I know a little bit about the culture of the country and people in the Philippines. I see that Philippines is actually a beautiful country with all helpful people and beautiful sight. UNP is a very perfect place to study research and expand my knowledge. And your place City of Vigan is also a worthy place to stay. So many feelings and emotions involved cannot explain through words. The place where I want to spend some more time…

Nguyen Ngoc Quynh
Education Student major in Primary School

After the monthly exposure the Vietnamese students pause with the faculty and selected students of the College of Teacher Education during the send-off program

Chapter 9
The Academic Development Initiatives of the ASEAN Universities for the Socio-Cultural Community (ASCC) – Blueprint 2025

The ASEAN Universities are committed to implement the blueprint ASCC 2025 by committing to lift the quality of life of its peoples through cooperative activities that are people-oriented, people-centered, environmentally friendly, and geared towards the promotion of sustainable development. The nature of the Socio-Cultural Community for the ASEAN universities provides the educational support for the inclusive education, access to higher education, pro- students development programs and the participation of the academic exchange such as the support on cultural diversity, language proficiency, pedagogical innovation, research collaboration to ensure the improvement of quality education that can further translated in the commitment to lift the quality of life of the ASEAN people.

The academic community may further enhance the support of the ASEAN Socio-Cultural Community that conforms the ASCC 2025 vision that engages and benefits the peoples and is inclusive, sustainable, resilient, and dynamic. It aims to realize:

1. A committed, participative and socially-responsible community through an accountable and inclusive mechanism for the benefit of all ASEAN peoples, upheld by the principles of good governance;

2. An inclusive community that promotes high quality of life, equitable access to opportunities for all and promotes and protects human rights of women, children, youths, the elderly/older persons, persons with disabilities, migrant workers, and vulnerable and marginalized groups;

3. A sustainable community that promotes social development and environmental protection through effective mechanisms to meet the current and future needs of the peoples;

1. A resilient community with enhanced capacity and capability to adapt and respond to social and economic vulnerabilities, disasters, climate change as well as emerging threats, and challenges; and

2. A dynamic and harmonious community that is aware and proud of its identity, culture, and heritage with the strengthened ability to

innovate and proactively contribute to the global community.

The Higher Education Institutions (HEIs) in the ASEAN Countries are given the wide range of educational thrusts that can be taken from the aims of the ASCC 2025 by providing the support of good governance through a socially-responsible community with inclusiveness and accountability. The HEIs may provide the academic support through access to education, scholarship programs, and other relevant educational programs such as Alternative Education and Special Education. The inclusivity of education may also be promoted by the development theme of good governance that can apply flagship educational programs that can be done in academic exchange and collaboration with the ASEAN universities. These are part of the inclusive community that promotes high quality of life, equitable access to opportunities for all and promotes and protects human rights of women, children, youths, the elderly/older persons, persons with disabilities, migrant workers, and vulnerable and marginalized groups. Basically, these are in considerations with the social development and the inclusion of environmental protection to respond the emerging threats of climate change.

Primarily, the implementation of academic collaboration, students and faculty exchange, inter-country facilitation, research partnerships and other activities for the sustained international linkages in the ASEAN universities. This is in line with the ASCC aim on a dynamic and harmonious community that is aware and proud of its identity, culture, and heritage with the strengthened ability to innovate and proactively contribute to the global community.

The Aligned Characteristics and Elements of ASEAN Socio-Cultural Community Blueprint 2025 for the Higher Education Institutions

A. Engages and Benefits of the ASCC 2025

The ASEAN Universities can work out the multi-sectoral and multi-stakeholder engagements as development partners in academia through the inter-cultural dialogue by deepening the sense of ASEAN identity. This can be done by the following academic collaboration and exchange through twinning agreement on the following themes:

1. The cultural immersion with the partner universities to understand the ASEAN culture, tradition and history.

2. The research collaboration that gives the opportunity to share the educational experiences on culture and the arts, science and technology, pedagogical practices, and other field of interest.

3. The student and faculty exchange program to enhance the teaching-learning exposures in the academe.

4. The inter-country facilitation to support the adopt the best practices in managing the HEI and academic activities on instruction, research, extension and production.

The key result areas and corresponding strategic measures are as follows:

A.1. Engaged Stakeholders in ASEAN processes

The ASEAN Universities can conduct training and conferences by promoting public awareness the role of ASCC relevant to the educational initiatives for the participation on research and policy development to achieve quality education to the stakeholders. The varied field of expertise may pursue the advocacy of good governance, sustainable development, environmental program and inclusive education to provide substantial knowledge to contribute economic, socio-cultural, educational development in the ASEAN region.

A.2. Empowered People and Strengthened Institutions

The ASEAN Universities have the academic capability and competence to conduct research and produce instructional materials, published books and journals relevant to the topics on climate change, science and technology, gender and development, politics and governance, ICT and cultural identity of the ASEAN countries. These publications provide the substantial academic contributions to empower institutions in giving the needed information on institutional capacity to enhance the quality of life of the stakeholders.

B. INCLUSIVE

The participation of the ASEAN Universities in inclusive growth has to do with the ASCC thrust to move towards a more inclusive community. This would entail the promotion of equitable access to opportunities for ASEAN peoples, and the promotion and protection of human rights of women, children, youths, the elderly/ older persons, persons with disabilities, migrant workers, ethnic minority groups, and vulnerable and marginalized groups, throughout their life cycle, guided by a life-cycle approach and adhering to rights-based principles in the promotion of ASEAN policies and programmes in the ASCC Pillar.

This can be done by providing the conduct of training-workshop, capacity building, conference presentations and publications of research findings to address the concerns and challenges related to welfare, social protection, women empowerment, gender equality, promotion and protection of human rights, equitable access to opportunities, poverty eradication, health, decent work, education and information. As the program outcome of the support in the ASEAN Universities the promotion of an improved quality of life, addresses barriers to the enjoyment of equitable access to opportunities by ASEAN peoples, and that promotes and protects human rights.

The key result areas and corresponding strategic measures are as follows:

B.1. Reducing Barriers

The ASEAN universities have the capacity and competence to deal with the pressing issues and concerns in providing insights on social protection, quality care, access to ICT, and support of vulnerable groups. The regional cooperation of the ASEAN Universities gives the opportunity to work together in finding solutions to the common concerns and issues in reducing barriers particularly in promoting equitable access to social protection, support of the marginalized and vulnerable groups, access on ICT, and support of special needs and senior citizens including the persons with disabilities.

B.2. Equitable Access for All

The ASEAN Universities have the academic expertise and competence to give technical assistance to the government agencies and other partner agencies to promote the regional platforms for the equitable opportunities, participation and effective engagement of women, children, youths, the elderly/older persons, persons with disabilities, people living in remote and border areas, and vulnerable groups. The other areas of concern in the purview of "Equitable Access for All" includes gender mainstreaming, social protection, universal health coverage, food safety, poverty eradication, employment and decent work, and trafficking in persons; health services and education including early childhood education and vocational education, skills training, and promotion of skills recognition.

In the case of teacher education program for the ASEAN Universities, it reflects to the promotion of early childhood education that may include the universal access to education, support of special needs, capacity building program for basic education (K-12 contextualized Curricula) in the improvement of teaching-learning process, pedagogical training, instructional materials development and other education support. Furthermore, the educational support of the Senior High School on the technical-vocational education through skills training and promotion of skills recognition.

The other considerations ASEAN Universities to further provide the academic support on the principles of good governance and the inclusivity of development programs to promote, enhance and strengthen the following:

1. Support of the gender and development to strengthen women's welfare

2. Promote human capital development, economic self-reliance and sustainable livelihood, especially among the poor, through access to education, employment opportunities, entrepreneurship and micro-finance;

3. Promote continuous efforts toward multi-dimensional poverty eradication through multi-sectoral, multi-stakeholder and community-based approaches;

4. Build an enabling environment to provide the unemployed, poor and other marginalized groups equitable access to resources, opportunities, and safeguard measures to prevent them from falling under the negative influence of violent extremism and threats;

5. Ensure inclusive, participatory and representative decision making at all levels with special attention to the needs of those in disadvantaged situations, including ethnic minority groups, children, youths, women, persons with disabilities, and the elderly/older persons;

6. Promote inclusive growth through appropriate measures at the national level to ensure that the poor and vulnerable have equitable access to economic and other opportunities;

7. Promote equitable opportunities to quality education and access to information with priority given to the advancement of universal access to education;

8. Promote a community that is healthy, caring, sustainable and productive, and one that practices healthy lifestyle resilient to health threats and has universal access to healthcare; and

9. Promote increased accessibility for persons with disabilities and other vulnerable groups in keeping with the universal design facilities.

The ASEAN Universities may initiate research agenda in higher education to support the "Equitable Access to All" that can be considered the educational development themes on GAD, support of vulnerable groups, pro-poor programs, inclusive communities, ICT, universal access to education, vulnerable groups and other relevant themes for inclusivity of higher education. These are important development programs wherein the ASEAN Universities can present empirically tested policies along the identified variables of " Equitable Access to All."

B.3. Promotion and Protection of Human Rights

The ASEAN Universities may work well the promotion and protection of human rights particularly in engaging the communities to educate them about the ideas of social justice, human rights, fundamental freedoms and other social development programs to ensure the improvement of quality life. These have been studied by the general education subjects (Social Science particularly Political Science) in providing the fundamental human rights and freedom as part of the professional training of students in the ASEAN Universities. The social engagements of the academe would contribute to the better understanding about the fundamental rights and privileges particularly those depressed and underserved communities.

These are the identified strategic measures to ensure the promotion and protection of human rights in the ASCC 2025:

i. Promote regional inter-sectoral mechanisms towards a holistic and multi-disciplinary approach in enhancing quality care, well-being, gender equality, social justice, human rights and fundamental freedoms, especially the vulnerable groups, in response to all hazards and emerging social and economic risks/threats;

ii. Promote sustainable financing mechanism for social protection, particularly universal health coverage, early childhood care and development, financial risk protection for disaster risk reduction and climate change adaptation, and social pension, through strategic partnerships with private sector and other relevant stakeholders;

iii. Provide regional platforms for dialogue and support initiatives to address issues of traditional practices that impinge upon the fulfilment of rights;

iv. Support accelerated implementation among ASEAN Member States to extend coverage, accessibility, availability, comprehensiveness, quality, equality, affordability and sustainability of social services and social protection;

v. Enhance the effective implementation of relevant ASEAN declarations and instruments related to human rights;

vi. Enhance regional initiatives to promote and protect the rights of women and children as well as persons with disabilities especially through the work of the ASEAN Commission on the Promotion and Protection of the Rights of Women and Children (ACWC);

vii. Enhance regional initiatives and stakeholder participation to promote the elimination of all forms of discrimination–institutionalized or otherwise–exploitation, trafficking, harmful practices, and violence and abuse against children, women, persons with disabilities, youths, migrant workers, the elderly/older persons, and victims/survivors of trafficking in persons, ethnic minority groups, and vulnerable and marginalized groups;

viii. Encourage intergenerational relationships, families and communities in promoting and protecting the rights of the elderly/older persons, and providing quality care and protection of the elderly/older persons, in accordance with the Brunei Darussalam Declaration on Strengthening Family Institution: Caring for the Elderly; and

ix. Enhance regional initiatives in accordance with the ASEAN Declaration on the Protection and Promotion of the Rights of Migrant Workers to improve the protection and promotion of the rights of workers and migrant workers.

The development themes for research, instruction and community engagement in the multi-disciplinary research presentation and instructional development for the academic support of the following: (1) Social Justice and Protection; (2) Early Childhood Care and Development; (3) Protection on the rights of workers and migrant workers; (4) Care of the Elderly; (5) Constitutional Rights and Privileges; and (6) Protection of the Vulnerable and Marginalized Groups.

C. SUSTAINABLE

The ASEAN Universities provide the support in this area to achieve sustainable environment in the face of social changes and economic development. It has to promote and ensure balanced social development and sustainable environment that meet the needs of the peoples at all times. The aim is to strive for an ASEAN Community with equitable access to sustainable environment that can support its social development and its capacity to work towards sustainable development.

The key result areas and corresponding strategic measures are as follows:

C.1. Conservation and Sustainable Management of Biodiversity and Natural Resources

The strategic measures on sustainable development of the ASCC 2025 may work well with the relevant course offering of the ASEAN Universities in the areas of ecosystem development, forest management; biodiversity; and coast management. The academic community has the expertise and competence to conduct policy research, program advocacy, and capacity building to ensure the promotion and conservation of biodiversity and natural resources.

These are the following strategic framework of the ASCC 2025 to ensure the implementation of Biodiversity and Natural Resources:

i. Strengthen regional cooperation to protect, restore and promote sustainable use of terrestrial ecosystems resources, combat desertification, halt biodiversity loss, and halt and reverse land degradation;

ii. Strengthen regional cooperation on sustainable forest management in the context of forest fire prevention and control, including through the implementation of the ASEAN Agreement on Transboundary Haze Pollution, to effectively address transboundary haze pollution;

iii. Promote cooperation for the protection, restoration and sustainable use of coastal and marine environment, respond and deal with the risk of pollution and threats to marine ecosystem and coastal environment, in particular in respect of ecologically sensitive areas;

iv. Adopt good management practices and strengthen policies to address the impact of development projects on coastal and international waters and transboundary environmental issues, including pollution, illegal movement and disposal of hazardous substances and waste, and in doing so, utilize existing regional and international institutions and agreements;

v. Enhance policy and capacity development and best practices to conserve, develop and sustainably manage marine, wetlands, peatlands, biodiversity, and land and water resources;

vi. Promote capacity building in a continuous effort to have sustainable management of ecosystems and natural resources;

vii. Promote cooperation on environmental management towards sustainable use of ecosystems and natural resources through environmental education, community engagement and public outreach;

viii. Strengthen global and regional partnerships and support the implementation of relevant international agreements and frameworks;

ix. Promote the role of the ASEAN Centre for Biodiversity as the centre of excellence in conservation and sustainable use of biodiversity; and

x. Support the full implementation of the Strategic Plan for Biodiversity 2011-2020 and the Aichi Targets.

C.2. Environmentally Sustainable Cities

The support of the ASEAN Universities on environmentally sustainable cities through the engineering and architecture courses has its relevance in the urban planning for green city, infrastructure support on environment friendly buildings including access to clean water and air, clean health sanitation and provisions of facilities for the PWDs, elderly persons and persons with special needs.

Strategic Measures on policy research and program intervention for environmentally sustainable cities:

i. Enhance participatory and integrated approaches in urban planning and management for sustainable urbanization towards a clean and green ASEAN;

ii. Strengthen the capacity of national and local institutions to implement strategies and programmes towards liveable cities;

iii. Promote coordination among relevant sectors to provide access to clean land, green public space, clean air, clean and safe water, and sanitation;

iv. Promote cities that are child-, youths-, the elderly/older persons and persons with disabilities-friendly through enhanced coordination with relevant sectors to provide sustainable and accessible infrastructure systems;

v. Strengthen positive economic, social and environmental linkages among urban, peri-urban and rural areas; and

vi. Strengthen policies and strategies for the effective impact management of population growth and migration on cities.

C.3. Sustainable Climate

The ASEAN Universities can support the sustainable climate in the development of technology-based research to respond and mitigate effects of climate change and propose research studies to ensure the assessment of natural calamities and monitoring of Greenhouse Gas. (GHG) The development of instructional material support to disseminate studies for climate change and ensure the safety of vulnerable and marginalized communities.

These are the strategic measures identified in the ASCC 2025 to ensure the implementation of development policies and programs for sustainable climate.

i. Strengthen human and institutional capacity in implementing climate change adaptation and mitigation, especially on vulnerable and marginalized communities;

ii. Facilitate the development of comprehensive and coherent responses to climate change challenges, such as but not limited to multi-stakeholder and multi-sectoral approaches;

iii. Leverage on private sector and community to have access to new and innovative financing mechanisms to address climate change;

iv. Strengthen the capacity of sectoral institutions and local governments in conducting Greenhouse Gas (GHG) inventory, and vulnerability assessments and adaptation needs;

v. Strengthen the effort of government, private sector and community in reducing GHG emission from main activities of development;

vi. Mainstream climate change risk management and GHG emission reduction on sectoral planning; and

vii. Strengthen global partnerships and support the implementation of relevant international agreements and frameworks, e.g. the United Nations Framework Convention on Climate Change (UNFCCC).

The universal curriculum content for sustainable climate can be achieved by the concepts of Greenhouse Gas (GHG), financing programs for climate change by identifying potential areas of natural calamities such as floods, erosion and other forms of natural hazards that can be addressed to ensure human safety.

C.4. Sustainable Consumption and Production

The ASEAN Universities have the academic expertise and competence to promote environmental education in its curricula, community engagements, and capacity building to ensure the proper implementation of waste management and environment friendly technologies in order to achieve sustainable consumption and production.

These are the strategic measures adopted in this area to ensure the implementation of policies and research along environmentally-sound technologies, environmental education and waste management:

i.   Strengthen public-private partnerships to promote the adoption of environmentally-sound technologies for maximizing resource efficiency;

ii. Promote environmental education (including eco-school practice), awareness, and capacity to adopt sustainable consumption and green lifestyle at all levels;

iii. Enhance capacity of relevant stakeholders to implement sound waste management and energy efficiency; and

iv. Promote the integration of Sustainable Consumption and Production strategy and best practices into national and regional policies or as part of CSR activities.

It is expected that the ASEAN Universities to initiative development researches and programs on the adoption of best practices on CSR along green lifestyle, eco-system development, technology-based facilities and equipment for waste management and energy for sustainable development.

D. RESILIENT

Based on the implementation of ASEAN Resilience, it expounded the ASCC 2025 for the resilient communities that it must be integrated, comprehensive, and inclusive approaches are necessary to build resilient communities in the ASEAN region post-2015. Resilience is an essential aspect of human security and sustainable environment which is addressed by integrating policies, capacity and institution-building, stakeholder partnerships in disaster risk reduction, humanitarian assistance, and community empowerment, among others. Resilience has to be inclusive, non-discriminatory and incorporates market and technology-based policies, including contributions from the private sector as well as the scientific and academic communities.

Through the Declaration on Institutionalizing the Resilience of ASEAN and its Communities and Peoples to Disasters and Climate Change adopted during the 26th ASEAN Summit in Kuala Lumpur, Malaysia on 27 April 2015, the Leaders committed "to forge a more resilient future by reducing existing disaster and climate-related risks, preventing the generation of new risks and adapting to a changing climate through the implementation of economic, social, cultural, physical, and environmental measures which address exposure and vulnerability, and thus strengthen resilience."

The objective of this Characteristic is to achieve an enhanced capacity to collectively respond and adapt to current challenges and emerging threats. This recognizes that socio-cultural resilience has cross-pillar linkages within the ASEAN Community as an effective force for moderation for the common good, and one that is prepared for natural and human-induced disasters, and socio-economic crises, while fully embracing the principles of comprehensive security. (ASCC Blueprint 2025)

The ASEAN Universities have the development competence to ensure an integrated, comprehensive, and inclusive approaches to build resilient communities in the ASEAN region. The University research agenda and program advocacy on socio-cultural resilience may be adopted along human security and sustainable environment which is addressed by integrating policies, capacity and institution-building, stakeholder partnerships in disaster risk reduction, humanitarian assistance, and community empowerment, among other.

The key result areas and corresponding strategic measures are as follows: (ASCC, Blueprint 2025)

D.1. A Disaster Resilient ASEAN that is able to Anticipate, Respond, Cope, Adapt, and Build Back Better, Smarter, and Faster

The program implementation on disaster resilient ASEAN may be proposed for the academe through international linkages for academic collaboration, inter-country facilitation and capacity building to identify potential resilient communities to work out on the adoption of synergize initiative in disaster risk reduction, climate change adaptation and mitigation, humanitarian actions and sustainable development. These are the broad academic framework to support Disaster Resilient ASEAN that may produce dynamic initiative with the partner universities in the implementation of this program.

The ASCC Blueprint 2025 identified the following strategic measures for the Disaster Resilient ASEAN :

i. Enhance regional mechanisms and capacities to enable ASEAN to respond together to disasters within and outside the region;

ii. Promote regional standards, including methodologies and tools to assess, record, calculate the disaster losses and damages, and share non-sensitive data and create common information system, to enhance interoperability, ensure unity of action, and strengthen resilience;

iii. Promote local communities' resilience by integrating principles of resilience in risk reduction, preparedness, response, recovery, and rehabilitation measures;

iv. Promote policy coherence and interlinkages, and synergize initiatives on disaster risk reduction, climate change adaptation and mitigation, humanitarian actions and sustainable development;

v. Institutionalize resilience by strengthening institutional and adaptive capacities to reduce existing risks and prevent future risks;

vi. Harness local wisdom and traditional knowledge to foster a culture of resilience; and

vii. Enhance capacity, technology and community resilience to the impact of unexploded ordnance on the livelihood of people, especially the vulnerable groups in rural areas.

In these strategic measures, the ASEAN Universities can initiate multi-stakeholder collaboration with partner agencies to implement the ASCC 2025 Blueprint on broad policy research adoption and program advocacy for resilient communities to respond disaster risk reduction, climate change adaptation and mitigation, humanitarian actions and sustainable development.

D.2. A Safer ASEAN that is able to Respond to all Health-related Hazards including Biological, Chemical, and Radiological-nuclear, and Emerging Threats

The ASEAN Universities can initiate the participation of the medical and health related courses and technological sciences programs to respond the intervention measures for the health-related hazards, including biological, chemical, radiological-nuclear hazards and emerging threats.

These are the strategic measures to respond to all health-related hazards: (ASCC Blueprint 2025)

i. Strengthen health systems to be resilient in preparedness for effective response to health-related hazards, including biological, chemical, radiological-nuclear hazards and emerging threats;

ii. Promote regional standards to enhance interoperability, ensure unity of action and strengthen collective resilience; and

iii. Enhance institutional and human capacities and approaches to support the effective implementation of policies, strategies and programmes in preparing and responding to all health-related hazards and emerging threats.

D.3. A Climate Adaptive ASEAN with Enhanced Institutional and Human Capacities to Adapt to the Impacts of Climate Change

The significance of the Climate Adaptive ASEAN considers the indigenous and traditional knowledge and practices in responding and adapting to the impacts of climate change. The ASEAN Universities can initiate relevant research studies that can be utilized as evidence-based policies to the best practices of implementing Climate Adaptive ASEAN.

These are the critical platforms for the strategic measures of Climate Adaptive ASEAN presented in the ASCC Blueprint 2025:

i. Expand regional cross-sectoral platforms and establish shared strategies to respond to the impacts of climate change;

ii. Promote sound scientific and evidence-based policies on climate change adaptation; and

iii. Promote and consider indigenous and traditional knowledge and practices in responding and adapting to the impacts of climate change.

D.4. Strengthened Social Protection for Women, Children, Youths, the Elderly/Older Persons, Persons with Disabilities, Ethnic Minority Groups, Migrant Workers, Vulnerable and Marginalized Groups, and People Living in At-risk Areas, including People Living in Remote and Border Areas and Climate Sensitive Areas, to Reduce Vulnerabilities in Times of Climate Change-related Crises, Disasters and other Environmental Changes

The ASEAN Universities can initiative research studies on reducing exposure and vulnerability to climate-related extreme events and other economic, social and environmental shocks and disasters. This can be done through vulnerability assessment to resilient communities including target response measures to reduce incidence of disasters and crises in the area.

Strategic Measures

i. Encourage risk and vulnerability assessments and other scientific and evidence-based measures for policies and plans to ensure targeted response measures; and

ii. Establish platforms to empower people living in at-risk areas to become resilient by reducing their exposure and vulnerability to climate-related extreme events and other economic, social and environmental shocks and disasters.

D.5. Enhanced and Optimized Financing Systems, Food, Water, Energy Availability, and other Social Safety Nets in Times of Crises by making Resources more Available, Accessible, Affordable and Sustainable

The ASEAN Universities are given opportunity to conduct policy research and program advocacy on social safety nets about the availability, accessibility, affordability and sustainability in the implementation of disaster risk reduction and climate change adaptation. The social engagement is important providing pro-poor services (targeting the vulnerable and marginalized groups) such as policy research on supporting insurance mechanisms; research studies about the food adequacy, and accessibility of affordable energy services.

Strategic Measures

i. Enhance cross-sectoral and cross-pillar coordination to ensure food adequacy and accessibility at the household level, especially vulnerable households, and ability to cope with disaster, food price shocks and scarcity by developing adaptive mechanisms and strategies;

ii. Enhance cross-sectoral and cross-pillar coordination to ensure availability and accessibility of affordable energy services at the household level and promote utilization of renewable energy and green technologies;

iii. Enhance cross-sectoral and cross-pillar coordination to ensure availability of clean water, sanitation facilities and electricity to households in times of crises;

iv. Enhance the targeting of poor, vulnerable and marginalized groups in times of crises; and

v. Explore the possibility of establishing financial and insurance mechanisms and strategies for disaster risk reduction and climate change adaptation.

D.6. Endeavour towards a "Drug-Free" ASEAN

The ASEAN Universities may initiate social engagements with resilient communities for the conduct of information dissemination, capacity building and conduct of research studies on ill-effects of dangerous drugs including treatment and rehabilitation program for drug abuse problems.

These are the critical strategic measures to ensure the implementation of " Drug-Free" ASEAN:

i. Support the coordination with relevant stakeholders in policy formulation, develop and implement preventive programmes for different target groups, adopt and utilize effective treatment and rehabilitation and after-care programmes, and research on drug abuse problems; and

ii. Enhance community awareness and social responsibility on the ill-effects of dangerous drugs through community engagement, advocacy and other relevant activities.

E. DYNAMIC

The ASEAN Universities are able to strengthen the ability to continuously innovate and be a proactive member of the global community. Furthermore, the ASCC 2025 aims to provide an enabling environment with policies and institutions that engender people and firms to be more open and adaptive, creative, innovative, and entrepreneurial.

The key result areas and corresponding strategic measures are as follows: (NSCC 2015)

E.1. Towards an Open and Adaptive ASEAN

The ASEAN Universities promote greater people-to-people interaction can be done through the faculty and students exchange program to support varied academic endeavor in the region. The open and adaptive ASEAN may conduct cultural exchange program, pedagogical training of ICT Support (21st century learning skills), good governance on the best practices of Civil Service and other various forms of academic collaborative festivals.

These are the strategic measures to support the Open Adaptive ASEAN by 2025:

i. Encourage freedom of universal access to information and communication technology in accordance with national legislations;

ii. Promote a culture of tolerance, understanding and mutual respect for religions and interfaith dialogue;

iii. Showcase ASEAN to the outside world using various approaches e.g. ASEAN arts, film festivals and heritage programmes;

iv. Project a common ASEAN voice in global socio-cultural fora and negotiations, where appropriate;

v. Promote greater people-to-people interaction and mobility within and outside ASEAN;

vi. Promote cooperation in sports and develop comprehensive and inclusive sports programmes to encourage healthy and active lifestyles;

vii. Strengthen capacity and capability of both the ASEAN civil service and public sectors to respond to emerging challenges and the needs of the peoples through efficient, effective, transparent and accountable public services, participatory and innovative approaches, and collaboration;

viii. Provide opportunities for relevant stakeholders for knowledge sharing, which include exchange of best practices and studies;

ix. Encourage volunteerism among ASEAN Member States to strengthen the ASEAN Community;

x. Project ASEAN's visibility through comprehensive, multi-stakeholder branding efforts, which are represented by common ASEAN identifiers, such as ASEAN Day, ASEAN Flag, ASEAN Anthem and ASEAN Emblem; and

xi. Promote measures to ensure a caring society, social harmony and values of humanity, and spirit of community.

E.2. Towards a Creative, Innovative and Responsive ASEAN

The ASEAN Universities are given opportunity to design academic cooperation particularly in the promotion of innovative ASEAN approach to higher education with areas of interest along Global Research Network, Life Long learning, Community Service and other forms of academic endeavors. The academe has the expertise and competence to generate new ideas to respond this strategic measure on creative, innovative and responsive ASEAN.

These are the specific strategic measures to ensure creative , innovative and responsive ASEAN by 2025:

i.   Enhance the competitiveness of ASEAN human resources through the promotion of life-long learning, pathways, equivalencies and skills development as well as the use of information and communication technologies across age groups;

ii. Promote an innovative ASEAN approach to higher education, incorporating academics, community service, regional placement, and entrepreneurship incubation and support;

iii. Encourage regional cooperation in the areas of education, training and research, and strengthen ASEAN's role in regional and global research network by promoting initiatives and providing incentives and support for research and development, including research publications;

iv. Promote the free flow of ideas, knowledge, expertise, and skills to inject dynamism within the region;

Furthermore, the creative, innovative and responsive advocacy for the Higher Education Institutions are the strengthen curricula and system of education in science, technology and other disciplines through the following; (ASCC 2025)

i.   Encourage and support creative industry and pursuits, such as film, music, and animation;

ii. Promote ASEAN as a centre for human resource development and training;

iii.   Strengthen regional and global cooperation in enhancing the quality and competitiveness of higher education institutions;

iv.   Encourage the government, private sector and community to develop a system of continuous training and re-training to support lifelong learning and workforce development; and

v.   Promote registration of intellectual property rights (IPR), and strengthen its cooperation and implementation in ASEAN in areas such as food safety, medicines, traditional cultural assets and biodiversity-based products.

E.3. Engender a Culture of Entrepreneurship in ASEAN

The ASEAN Universities have the development responsibility to cascade corporate practices in business environment through the development of creative and inclusive social entrepreneurship that would support the youth, persons with disabilities, women and vulnerable groups. These are other important functions of ASEAN Universities to strengthen the support of vulnerable, depressed and underprivilege communities to empower them in creating sustained social entrepreneurship.

These are the identified strategic measures to engender a culture of entrepreneurship in ASEAN 2025:

i. Strengthen the supportive environment for socially and environmentally responsible entrepreneurship, such as mentoring, providing seed money, venture and crowd funding, and marketing support;

ii. Promote and nurture creative and inclusive social entrepreneurship for youths, persons with disabilities, women and vulnerable and marginalized groups; and

iii. Encourage institutional and technical innovations in the provision of social services and health care.

III. Implementation and Review of the ASCC 2025

The institutional mechanism represents the ASCC Blueprint 2025 which is guided by the ASEAN Charter as well as other key ASEAN instruments and documents, which provide the principles and frameworks for ASEAN socio-cultural cooperation and their implementation. Such implementation is also guided by relevant domestic laws, regulations and policies. In addition to this implementation and review of ASCC 2025 , the ASEAN Universities may direct the implementation of the strategic measures along Institutional Mechanisms, Strategies, ASEAN Institutional Capacity, Resource Communication and Review .

Operational Implementation of the Aligned Characteristics and Elements of ASEAN Socio-Cultural Community Blueprint 2025 for the Higher Education Institutions

The aligned characteristics and Elements of ASEAN Socio-Cultural Community Blueprint 2025 (ASCC 2025) specifies the common ground of implementing the ASEAN Universities as to the development roles in promoting quality and excellence in higher education program. It expected that this initiative of the aligned characteristics and benefits of the ASCC 2025 with the program outcomes and impact relevant to ASEAN culture, tradition and history; research collaboration and conference; student and faculty exchange programs, inter-country facilitation, and other academic collaborations. The ASCC 2025 will ensure the greater role of the ASEAN Universities to initiate, innovate, and participate the common benefits in the higher education program for the advancement of learnings and academic excellence including the improvement of quality life for all ASEAN people.

A. **Engages and Benefits of the ASEAN Universities in the ASCC 2025**

1. The cultural immersion with the partner universities to understand the ASEAN culture, tradition and history.

2. The research collaboration that gives the opportunity to share the educational experiences on culture and the arts, science and technology, pedagogical practices, and other field of interest.

3. The student and faculty exchange program to enhance the teaching-learning exposures in the academe.

5. The inter-country facilitation to support the adopt the best practices in managing the HEI and academic activities on instruction, research, extension and production.

The ASEAN Universities can work out the multi-sectoral and multi-stakeholder engagements as development partners in academia through the inter-cultural dialogue by deepening the sense of ASEAN identity. This can be done by the following academic collaboration and exchange through twinning agreement on the following themes:

The key result areas and corresponding strategic measures are as follows:

A.1. Engaged Stakeholders in ASEAN processes

The ASEAN Universities can conduct training and conferences by promoting public awareness the role of ASCC relevant to the educational initiatives for the participation on research and policy development to achieve quality education to the stakeholders. The varied field of expertise may pursue the advocacy of good governance, sustainable development, environmental program and inclusive education to provide substantial knowledge to contribute economic, socio-cultural, educational development in the ASEAN region.

A.2. Empowered People and Strengthened Institutions

The ASEAN Universities have the academic capability and competence to conduct research and produce instructional materials, published books and journals relevant to the topics on climate change, science and technology, gender and development, politics and governance, ICT and cultural identity of the ASEAN countries. These publications provide the substantial academic contributions to empower institutions in giving the needed information on institutional capacity to enhance the quality of life of the stakeholders.

B. INCLUSIVE

The participation of the ASEAN Universities in inclusive growth has to do with the ASCC thrust to move towards a more inclusive community. This would entail the promotion of equitable access to opportunities for ASEAN peoples, and the promotion and protection of human rights of women, children, youths, the elderly/ older persons, persons with disabilities, migrant workers, ethnic minority groups, and vulnerable and marginalized groups, throughout their life cycle, guided by a life-cycle approach and adhering to rights-based principles in the promotion of ASEAN policies and programmes in the ASCC Pillar.

This can be done by providing the conduct of conferences, capacity training, presentation and publications of research findings to address the concerns and challenges related to welfare, social protection, women empowerment, gender equality, promotion and protection of human rights, equitable access to opportunities, poverty eradication, health, decent work, education and information. As the program outcome of the support in the ASEAN Universities the promotion of an improved quality of life, addresses barriers to the enjoyment of equitable access to opportunities by ASEAN peoples, and that promotes and protects human rights.

The key result areas and corresponding strategic measures are as follows: (ASCC 2025)

B.1. Reducing Barriers

The ASEAN universities have the capacity and competence to deal with the pressing issues and concerns in providing insights on social protection, quality care, access to ICT, and support of vulnerable groups. The regional cooperation of the ASEAN Universities gives the opportunity to work together in finding solutions to the common concerns and issues in reducing barriers particularly in promoting equitable access to social protection, support of the marginalized and vulnerable groups, access on ICT, and support of special needs and senior citizens including the persons with disabilities.

B.2. Equitable Access for All

The ASEAN Universities have the academic expertise and competence to give technical assistance to the government agencies and other partner agencies to promote the regional platforms for the equitable opportunities, participation and effective engagement of women, children, youths, the elderly/older persons, persons with disabilities, people living in remote and border areas, and vulnerable groups. The other areas of concern in the purview of "Equitable Access for All" includes gender mainstreaming, social protection, universal health coverage, food safety, poverty eradication, employment and decent work, and trafficking in persons; health services and education including early childhood education and vocational education, skills training, and promotion of skills recognition.

In the case of teacher education program for the ASEAN Universities, it reflects to the promotion of early childhood education that may include the universal access to education, support of special needs, capacity building program for basic education in the improvement of teaching-learning process, pedagogical training, instructional materials development and other education support. Furthermore, the educational support of the Senior High School on the technical-vocational education through skills training and promotion of skills recognition.

The ASEAN Universities may initiate research agenda in higher education to support the "Equitable Access to All" that can be considered the educational development themes on GAD, support of vulnerable groups, pro-poor programs, inclusive communities, ICT, universal access to education, vulnerable groups and other relevant themes for inclusivity of higher education. These are important development programs wherein the ASEAN Universities can present empirically tested policies along the identified variables of "Equitable Access to All."

B.3. Promotion and Protection of Human Rights

The ASEAN Universities may work well the promotion and protection of human rights particularly in engaging the communities to educate them about the ideas of social justice, human rights, fundamental freedoms and other social development program to ensure the improvement of quality life. These have been studied by the general education subjects (Social Science particularly Political Science) in providing the fundamental human rights and freedom as part of the professional training of students in the ASEAN Universities. The social engagements of the academe would contribute to the better understanding about the fundamental rights and privileges particularly those depressed and underserved communities.

The development themes for research, instruction and community engagement in the multi-disciplinary research presentation and instructional development for the academic support of the following: (1) Social Justice and Protection; (2) Early Childhood Care and Development; (3) Protection on the rights of workers and migrant workers; (4) Care of the Elderly; (5) Constitutional Rights and Privileges; and (6) Protection of the Vulnerable and Marginalized Groups.

C. SUSTAINABLE

The ASEAN Universities provide the support in this area to achieve sustainable environment in the face of social changes and economic development. It has to promote and ensure balanced social development and sustainable environment that meet the needs of the peoples at all times. The aim is to strive for an ASEAN Community with equitable access to sustainable environment that can support its social development and its capacity to work towards sustainable development.

C.1. Conservation and Sustainable Management of Biodiversity and Natural Resources

The strategic measures on sustainable development of the ASCC 2025 may work well with the relevant course offering of the ASEAN Universities in the areas of ecosystem development, forest management; biodiversity; and coast management. The academic community has the expertise and competence to conduct policy research, program advocacy, and capacity building to ensure the promotion and conservation of biodiversity and natural resources.

C.2. Environmentally Sustainable Cities

The support of the ASEAN Universities on environmentally sustainable cities through the engineering and architecture courses has its relevance in the urban planning for green city, infrastructure support on environment friendly buildings including access to clean water and air, clean health sanitation and provisions of facilities for the PWDs, elderly persons and persons with special needs.

C.3. Sustainable Climate

The ASEAN Universities can support the sustainable climate in the development of technology-based research to respond and mitigate effects of climate change and propose research studies to ensure the assessment of natural calamities and monitoring of Greenhouse Gas. (GHG) The development of instructional material support to disseminate studies for climate change and ensure the safety of vulnerable and marginalized communities.

The universal curriculum content for sustainable climate can be achieved by the concepts of Greenhouse Gas (GHG), financing programs for climate change by identifying potential areas of natural calamities such as floods, erosion and other forms of natural hazards that can be addressed to ensure human safety.

C.4. Sustainable Consumption and Production

The ASEAN Universities have the academic expertise and competence to promote environmental education in its curricula, community engagements, and capacity building to ensure the proper implementation of waste management and environment friendly technologies in order to achieve sustainable consumption and production.

It is expected that the ASEAN Universities to initiative development researches and programs on the adoption of best practices on CSR along green lifestyle, eco-system development, technology-based facilities and equipment for waste management and energy for sustainable development.

D. RESILIENT

Based on the implementation of ASEAN Resilience, it expounded the ASCC 2025 for the resilient communities that it must be integrated, comprehensive, and inclusive approaches are necessary to build resilient communities in the ASEAN region post-2015. Resilience is an essential aspect of human security and sustainable environment which is addressed by integrating policies, capacity and institution-building, stakeholder partnerships in disaster risk reduction, humanitarian assistance, and community empowerment, among others. Resilience has to be inclusive, non-discriminatory and incorporates market and technology-based policies, including contributions from the private sector as well as the scientific and academic communities. Through the Declaration on Institutionalizing the

Resilience of ASEAN and its Communities and Peoples to Disasters and Climate Change adopted during the 26th ASEAN Summit in Kuala Lumpur, Malaysia on 27 April 2015, the Leaders committed "to forge a more resilient future by reducing existing disaster and climate-related risks, preventing the generation of new risks and adapting to a changing climate through the implementation of economic, social, cultural, physical, and environmental measures which address exposure and vulnerability, and thus strengthen resilience."

The objective of this Characteristic is to achieve an enhanced capacity to collectively respond and adapt to current challenges and emerging threats. This recognizes that socio-cultural resilience has cross-pillar linkages within the ASEAN Community as an effective force for moderation for the common good, and one that is prepared for natural and human-induced disasters, and socio-economic crises, while fully embracing the principles of comprehensive security. (ASCC Blueprint 2025)

The ASEAN Universities have the development competence to ensure an integrated, comprehensive, and inclusive approaches to build resilient communities in the ASEAN region. The University research agenda and program advocacy on socio-cultural resilience may be adopted along human security and sustainable environment which is addressed by integrating policies, capacity and institution-building, stakeholder partnerships in disaster risk reduction, humanitarian assistance, and community empowerment, among other.

The key result areas and corresponding strategic measures are as follows: (ASCC, Blueprint 2025)

D.1. A Disaster Resilient ASEAN that is able to Anticipate, Respond, Cope, Adapt, and Build Back Better, Smarter, and Faster .

The program implementation on disaster resilient ASEAN may be proposed for the academe through international linkages for academic collaboration, inter-country facilitation and capacity building to identify potential resilient communities to work out on the adoption of synergize initiative in disaster risk reduction, climate change adaptation and mitigation, humanitarian actions and sustainable development. These are the broad academic framework to support Disaster Resilient ASEAN that may produce dynamic initiative with the partner universities in the implementation of this program.

In these strategic measures, the ASEAN Universities can initiate multi-stakeholder collaboration with partner agencies to implement the ASCC 2025 Blueprint on broad policy research adoption and program advocacy for resilient communities to respond disaster risk reduction, climate change adaptation and mitigation, humanitarian actions and sustainable development.

D.2. A Safer ASEAN that is able to Respond to all Health-related Hazards including Biological, Chemical, and Radiological-nuclear, and Emerging Threats

The ASEAN Universities can initiate the participation of the medical and health related courses and technological sciences programs to respond the intervention measures for the health-related hazards, including biological, chemical, radiological-nuclear hazards and emerging threats.

D.3. A Climate Adaptive ASEAN with Enhanced Institutional and Human Capacities to Adapt to the Impacts of Climate Change

The significance of the Climate Adaptive ASEAN considers the indigenous and traditional knowledge and practices in responding and adapting to the impacts of climate change. The ASEAN Universities can initiate relevant research studies that can be utilized as evidence-based policies to the best practices of implementing Climate Adaptive ASEAN.

D.4. Strengthened Social Protection for Women, Children, Youths, the Elderly/Older Persons, Persons with Disabilities, Ethnic Minority Groups, Migrant Workers, Vulnerable and Marginalized Groups, and People Living in At-risk Areas, including People Living in Remote and Border Areas and Climate Sensitive Areas, to Reduce Vulnerabilities in Times of Climate Change-related Crises, Disasters and other Environmental Changes

The ASEAN Universities can initiative research studies on reducing exposure and vulnerability to climate-related extreme events and other economic, social and environmental shocks and disasters. This can be done through vulnerability assessment to resilient communities including target response measures to reduce incidence of disasters and crises in the area.

D.5. Enhanced and Optimized Financing Systems, Food,

Water, Energy Availability, and other Social Safety Nets in Times of Crises by making Resources more Available, Accessible, Affordable and Sustainable

The ASEAN Universities are given opportunity to conduct policy research and program advocacy on social safety nets about the availability, accessibility, affordability and sustainability in the implementation of disaster risk reduction and climate change adaptation. The social engagement is important providing pro-poor services (targeting the vulnerable and marginalized groups) such as policy research on supporting insurance mechanisms; research studies about the food adequacy, and accessibility of affordable energy services.

D.6. Endeavour towards a "Drug-Free" ASEAN

The ASEAN Universities may initiate social engagements with resilient communities for the conduct of information dissemination, capacity building and conduct of research studies on ill-effects of dangerous drugs including treatment and rehabilitation program for drug abuse problems.

E. DYNAMIC

The ASEAN Universities are able to strengthen the ability to continuously innovate and be a proactive member of the global community. Furthermore, the ASCC 2025 aims to provide an enabling environment with policies and institutions that engender people and firms to be more open and adaptive, creative, innovative, and entrepreneurial.

E.1. Towards an Open and Adaptive ASEAN

The ASEAN Universities promote greater people-to-people interaction can be done through the faculty and students exchange program to support varied academic endeavor in the region. The open and adaptive ASEAN may conduct cultural exchange program, pedagogical training of ICT Support (21st century learning skills), good governance on the best practices of Civil Service and other various forms of academic collaborative festivals.

E.2. Towards a Creative, Innovative and Responsive ASEAN

The ASEAN Universities are given opportunity to design academic cooperation particularly in the promotion of innovative ASEAN approach to higher education with areas of interest along Global Research Network, Life Long learning, Community Service and other forms of academic endeavors. The academe has the expertise and competence to generate new ideas to respond this strategic measure on creative, innovative and responsive ASEAN.

E.3. Engender a Culture of Entrepreneurship in ASEAN

The ASEAN Universities have the development responsibility to cascade corporate practices in business environment through the development of creative and inclusive social entrepreneurship that would support the youth, persons with disabilities, women and vulnerable groups. These are other important functions of ASEAN Universities to strengthen the support of vulnerable, depressed and underprivilege communities to empower them in creating sustained social entrepreneurship.

Chapter 10

ASEAN Socio-cultural Community Blueprint 2025

I. INTRODUCTION

The ASEAN's socio-economic progress in these two and a half decades is heralded by remarkable human and sustainable development. At the heart of the ASEAN Socio-Cultural Community (ASCC) is the commitment to lift the quality of life of its peoples through cooperative activities that are people-oriented, people-centred, environmentally friendly, and geared towards the promotion of sustainable development. The ASCC 2025 opens a world of opportunities to collectively deliver and fully realize human development, resiliency and sustainable development as we face new and emerging challenges together.

The ASCC's strategy and planning mechanism, the ASCC Blueprint, was substantially implemented from 2009 to 2015 and was shown to be effective in developing and strengthening the coherence of policy frameworks and institutions to advance Human Development, Social Justice and Rights, Social Protection and Welfare, Environmental Sustainability, ASEAN Awareness, and Narrowing the Development Gap. More concretely, the ASCC has helped to heighten commitment in the form of policy and legal frameworks, such as the Declaration on Non-Communicable Diseases in ASEAN and the Declaration on Elimination of Violence Against Women and Elimination of Violence Against Children in ASEAN.

The region has also shown collective will, for example, in offering quick, tangible action in humanitarian assistance through the ASEAN Coordinating Centre for Humanitarian Assistance (AHA Centre). Underlying these initiatives are important development outcomes spurring social changes in the region: the proportion of people living on less than USD1.25 per day fell from one in two persons to one in eight persons in the last two decades; the net enrolment rate for children of primary school age rose from 92 percent in 1999 to 94 percent in 2012; proportion of seats held by women in parliaments increased from 12 percent in 2000 to 18.5 percent in 2012; maternal mortality per 100,000 live births fell from 371.2 in 1990 to 103.7 in 2012; and the proportion of urban population living in slums decreased from 40 percent in 2000 to 31 percent in 20121.

Against this backdrop of intensified regional cooperation, the region has witnessed extreme poverty dramatically declining in a number of ASEAN Member States.

The region also experienced an expanding middle class, improving health and ASEAN Statistical Report: The Millennium Development Goals (2011): UN MDG Report (2012); HIV/AIDS Regional Report (2012) and Report of the ASEAN Regional Assessment of MDG Achievement and Post-2015 Development Priorities (2015) education, a growing workforce serving regional and global labour needs, a rapidly rising urban population that generates new services, city infrastructure development, and evolving lifestyles. Nevertheless, more needs to be done to secure the benefits and results of progress. Tens of millions remain in extreme poverty. Intra-ASEAN migration is on the rise, from 1.5 million in 1990 to 6.5 million in 20132. Almost 50 percent of international migrants are women, who are increasingly migrating to seek employment opportunities. An estimated one in eight migrant workers is a young person between the ages of 15 and 243.

Public health scourges of communicable and emerging infectious diseases like drug-resistant malaria and tuberculosis are still a significant presence and threat in a few ASEAN Member States. Millions are still deprived of full primary education due to the lack of access to schools and high drop-out rates.

Hunger, as reflected in malnutrition, remains a problem in a significant share of the populace in a few ASEAN Member States. Similarly, a large percentage of the population in a number of ASEAN Member States are very vulnerable to poverty or sliding deeper into poverty from significant food price hikes, as the 2007- 2008 global food price surge shows. Progress in social protection, justice, rights, inclusion and identity must also address extremism. A number of ASEAN Member States remain vulnerable to natural and human-induced disasters, which tend to disproportionately and adversely affect the poor and low income populace.

Pollution and resource degradation are also increasingly serious problems in a number of ASEAN Member States. ASEAN is also among the most highly vulnerable regions to climate change and will need to find solutions to adapt to climate change in building a resilient ASEAN.

Going beyond the current progress in the ASCC and the region in general, ASEAN's experiences, aspirations and destiny will be closely intertwined and influenced by global developments and challenges. As the year 2015 draws to a close, the global community of nations through the United Nations is forging commitment with all its 193 member states to realize in the next fifteen years a comprehensive and far-reaching set of universal and transformative goals and targets for the 2030 Agenda for Sustainable Development. This will continue and build upon the gains of the Millennium Development Goals and rally broad-based support on addressing challenges to sustainable development such as poverty, rising inequalities within and among countries, violent extremism and natural resource depletion and climate change among many others.

Thus, at this critical juncture for the ASEAN Community, cognizant of the challenges and opportunities regionally and globally, the ASCC 2025 vision is for an ASEAN Community that engages and benefits the peoples and is inclusive, sustainable, resilient, and dynamic. It aims to realize:

3. A committed, participative and socially-responsible community through an accountable and inclusive mechanism for the benefit of all ASEAN peoples, upheld by the principles of good governance;

4. An inclusive community that promotes high quality of life, equitable access to opportunities for all and promotes and protects human rights of women, children, youths, the elderly/older persons, persons with disabilities, migrant workers, and vulnerable and marginalized groups;

5. A sustainable community that promotes social development and environmental protection through effective mechanisms to meet the current and future needs of the peoples;

6. A resilient community with enhanced capacity and capability to adapt and respond to social and economic vulnerabilities, disasters, climate change as well as emerging threats, and challenges; and

7. A dynamic and harmonious community that is aware and proud of its identity, culture, and heritage with the strengthened ability to innovate and proactively contribute to the global community.

II. Characteristics and Elements of ASEAN Socio-Cultural Community Blueprint 2025

A. Engages and Benefits to the people

The ASEAN Community shall be characterized as one that engages and benefits its peoples, upheld by the principles of good governance.It focuses on multi-sectoral and multi-stakeholder engagements, including Dialogue and Development Partners, sub-regional organizations, academia, local governments in provinces, townships, municipalities and cities, private-public partnerships, community engagement, tripartite engagement with the labor sector, social enterprises, government organization, non-governmental organization, civil society organization (GO-NGO/CSO) engagement, corporate social responsibility (CSR), inter-faith and inter-cultural dialogue, with emphasis on raising and sustaining awareness and caring societies of ASEAN, as well as deepening the sense of ASEAN identity.

The objective is to enhance commitment, participation and social responsibility of ASEAN peoples through an accountable and engaging mechanism for the benefit of all, towards a community of engaged and empowered ASEAN peoples who are provided the platforms to participate in ASEAN processes as well as to enjoy the benefits from the various initiatives.

The key result areas and corresponding strategic measures are as follows:

A.1. Engaged Stakeholders in ASEAN processes

Strategic Measures :

i. Institutionalize ASEAN policies on relevant stakeholders' consultations and engagement in the work of ASEAN Organs and Bodies including policy making initiatives, integration of impact assessment into policy development, programme development, implementation and monitoring, among others; and

ii. Promote partnership frameworks and guidelines in engaging the stakeholders for the effective implementation of ASEAN initiatives and promotion of public awareness of ASCC programs and accomplishments.

A.2. Empowered People and Strengthened Institutions

Strategic Measures :

i. Increase competencies and resilience of relevant stakeholders with advanced technological and managerial skills so as to improve institutional capacity to address current challenges and emerging trends, such as disasters, pandemics and climate change;

ii. Harness the use of information and communication technologies across different age groups as a means to connect with the regional and global community;

iii. Promote participation of local governments/authorities, provinces, townships, municipalities and cities through the central government in the development of ASEAN capacity building programs that benefit their respective communities;

iv. Promote non-discriminatory laws, policies and practices by developing effective, responsive, accountable and transparent institutions at all levels;

v. Strengthen civil service through effective capacity building, human resource development and collaboration programs among ASEAN Member States;

vi. Promote ASEAN awareness among government officials, students, children, youths and all stakeholders as part of building ASEAN identity; and

vii. Work towards achieving gender equality and the empowerment of all women and girls.

B. Inclusive

In realising the overarching goals of an ASEAN Community 2025, the ASCC is envisioned to move towards a more inclusive community. This would entail the promotion of equitable access to opportunities for ASEAN peoples, and the promotion and protection of human rights of women, children, youths, the elderly/ older persons, persons with disabilities, migrant workers, ethnic minority groups, and vulnerable and marginalised groups, throughout their life cycle, guided by a life-cycle approach and adhering to rights-based principles in the promotion of ASEAN policies and programmes in the ASCC Pillar.

Complementing the inclusive growth agenda of the ASEAN Economic Community (AEC), this Characteristic focuses on addressing the concerns of all peoples of ASEAN on matters related to welfare, social protection, women empowerment, gender equality, promotion and protection of human rights, equitable access to opportunities, poverty eradication, health, decent work, education and information.

12. The objective of this Characteristic is an inclusive ASEAN Community that promotes an improved quality of life, addresses barriers to the enjoyment of equitable access to opportunities by ASEAN peoples, and that promotes and protects human rights.

13. The key result areas and corresponding strategic measures are as follows:

B.1. Reducing Barriers

Strategic Measures:

i. Reduce inequality and promote equitable access to social protection and enjoyment of human rights by all and participation in societies, such as developing and implementing frameworks, guidelines and mechanisms for elimination of all forms of discrimination, violence, exploitation, abuse and neglect;

ii. Provide guidelines for quality care and support for women, children, youths, the elderly/older persons, persons with disabilities, migrant workers, ethnic minority groups, and vulnerable and marginalized groups;

iii. Provide regional mechanisms to promote access to information and communication technologies for all;

iv. Promote regional cooperation initiatives to support ASEAN Member States in implementing the Bali Declaration on the Enhancement of the Role and Participation of the Persons with Disabilities in ASEAN Community and the ASEAN Decade of Persons with Disabilities (2011-2020); and

v. Promote regional cooperation initiatives to support ASEAN Member States to be well prepared for ageing society.

B.2. Equitable Access for All

Strategic Measures :

i. Enhance regional platforms to promote equitable opportunities, participation and effective engagement of women, children, youths, the elderly/older persons, persons with disabilities, people living in remote and border areas, and vulnerable groups in the development and implementation of ASEAN policies and programmes;

ii. Develop regional strategies and enhance institutional capacity for gender mainstreaming in ASEAN policies, programmes and budgets across pillars and sectors;

iii. Enhance effectiveness of the implementation of strategies and programmes under ASCC and promote their harmonization with those of ASEAN Political-Security Community (APSC) and AEC, particularly in the areas of social protection, universal health coverage, food safety, poverty eradication, employment and decent work, and trafficking in persons;

iv. Provide mechanisms and enhance institutional capacity to promote greater access to basic social services for all, such as health services and education including early childhood education and vocational education, skills training, and promotion of skills recognition;

v. Support ASEAN Member States' initiatives in strengthening national gender and age-disaggregated databases and analyses, including on poverty and equity, and establish a reliable regional database for key sectors to support ASEAN policies and programmes;

vi. Promote human capital development, economic self-reliance and sustainable livelihood, especially among the poor, through access to education, employment opportunities, entrepreneurship and micro-finance;

vii. Promote continuous efforts toward multi-dimensional poverty eradication through multi-sectoral, multi-stakeholder and community-based approaches;

viii.   Build an enabling environment to provide the unemployed, poor and other marginalized groups equitable access to resources, opportunities, and safeguard measures to prevent them from falling under the negative influence of violent extremism and threats;

ix.   Ensure inclusive, participatory and representative decision making at all levels with special attention to the needs of those in disadvantaged situations, including ethnic minority groups, children, youths, women, persons with disabilities, and the elderly/older persons;

x.   Promote inclusive growth through appropriate measures at the national level to ensure that the poor and vulnerable have equitable access to economic and other opportunities;

xi.   Promote equitable opportunities to quality education and access to information with priority given to the advancement of universal access to education;

xii.   Promote a community that is healthy, caring, sustainable and productive, and one that practices healthy lifestyle resilient to health threats and has universal access to healthcare; and

xiii.   Promote increased accessibility for persons with disabilities and other vulnerable groups in keeping with the universal design facilities.

B.3. Promotion and Protection of Human Rights

Strategic Measures :

x. Promote regional inter-sectoral mechanisms towards a holistic and multi-disciplinary approach in enhancing quality care, well-being, gender equality, social justice, human rights and fundamental freedoms, especially the vulnerable groups, in response to all hazards and emerging social and economic risks/threats;

xi. Promote sustainable financing mechanism for social protection, particularly universal health coverage, early childhood care and development, financial risk protection for disaster risk reduction and climate change adaptation, and social pension, through strategic partnerships with private sector and other relevant stakeholders;

xii. Provide regional platforms for dialogue and support initiatives to address issues of traditional practices that impinge upon the fulfilment of rights;

xiii. Support accelerated implementation among ASEAN Member States to extend coverage, accessibility, availability, comprehensiveness, quality, equality, affordability and sustainability of social services and social protection;

xiv. Enhance the effective implementation of relevant ASEAN declarations and instruments related to human rights;

xv. Enhance regional initiatives to promote and protect the rights of women and children as well as persons with disabilities especially through the work of the ASEAN Commission on the Promotion and Protection of the Rights of Women and Children (ACWC);

xvi. Enhance regional initiatives and stakeholder participation to promote the elimination of all forms of discrimination–institutionalized or otherwise–exploitation, trafficking, harmful practices, and violence and abuse against children, women, persons with disabilities, youths, migrant workers, the elderly/older persons, and victims/survivors of trafficking in persons, ethnic minority groups, and vulnerable and marginalized groups;

xvii. Encourage intergenerational relationships, families and communities in promoting and protecting the rights of the elderly/older persons, and providing quality care and protection of the elderly/older persons, in accordance with the Brunei Darussalam Declaration on Strengthening Family Institution: Caring for the Elderly; and

xviii. Enhance regional initiatives in accordance with the ASEAN Declaration on the Protection and Promotion of the Rights of Migrant Workers to improve the protection and promotion of the rights of workers and migrant workers.

C. Sustainable

In moving towards the realization of the overarching goals of an ASEAN Community 2025, the ASCC envisions the achievement of a sustainable environment in the face of social changes and economic development.

The objective of this Characteristic is to promote and ensure balanced social development and sustainable environment that meet the needs of the peoples at all times. The aim is to strive for an ASEAN Community with equitable access to sustainable environment that can support its social development and its capacity to work towards sustainable development.

The key result areas and corresponding strategic measures are as follows:

C.1. Conservation and Sustainable Management of Biodiversity and Natural Resources

Strategic Measures :

xi. Strengthen regional cooperation to protect, restore and promote sustainable use of terrestrial ecosystems resources, combat desertification, halt biodiversity loss, and halt and reverse land degradation;

xii. Strengthen regional cooperation on sustainable forest management in the context of forest fire prevention and control, including through the implementation of the ASEAN Agreement on Transboundary Haze Pollution, to effectively address transboundary haze pollution;

xiii. Promote cooperation for the protection, restoration and sustainable use of coastal and marine environment, respond and deal with the risk of pollution and threats to marine ecosystem and coastal environment, in particular in respect of ecologically sensitive areas;

xiv. Adopt good management practices and strengthen policies to address the impact of development projects on coastal and international waters and transboundary environmental issues, including pollution, illegal movement and disposal of hazardous substances and waste, and in doing so, utilize existing regional and international institutions and agreements;

xv. Enhance policy and capacity development and best practices to conserve, develop and sustainably manage marine, wetlands, peatlands, biodiversity, and land and water resources;

xvi. Promote capacity building in a continuous effort to have sustainable management of ecosystems and natural resources;

xvii. Promote cooperation on environmental management towards sustainable use of ecosystems and natural resources through environmental education, community engagement and public outreach;

xviii. Strengthen global and regional partnerships and support the implementation of relevant international agreements and frameworks;

xix. Promote the role of the ASEAN Centre for Biodiversity as the centre of excellence in conservation and sustainable use of biodiversity; and

xx. Support the full implementation of the Strategic Plan for Biodiversity 2011-2020 and the Aichi Targets.

C.2. Environmentally Sustainable Cities

Strategic Measures

vii. Enhance participatory and integrated approaches in urban planning and management for sustainable urbanization towards a clean and green ASEAN;

viii. Strengthen the capacity of national and local institutions to implement strategies and programmes towards liveable cities;

ix. Promote coordination among relevant sectors to provide access to clean land, green public space, clean air, clean and safe water, and sanitation;

x. Promote cities that are child-, youths-, the elderly/older persons and persons with disabilities-friendly through enhanced coordination with relevant sectors to provide sustainable and accessible infrastructure systems;

xi. Strengthen positive economic, social and environmental linkages among urban, peri-urban and rural areas; and

xii. Strengthen policies and strategies for the effective impact management of population growth and migration on cities.

C.3. Sustainable Climate

Strategic Measures

viii. Strengthen human and institutional capacity in implementing climate change adaptation and mitigation, especially on vulnerable and marginalized communities;

ix. Facilitate the development of comprehensive and coherent responses to climate change challenges, such as but not limited to multi-stakeholder and multi-sectoral approaches;

x. Leverage on private sector and community to have access to new and innovative financing mechanisms to address climate change;

xi. Strengthen the capacity of sectoral institutions and local governments in conducting Greenhouse Gas (GHG) inventory, and vulnerability assessments and adaptation needs;

xii. Strengthen the effort of government, private sector and community in reducing GHG emission from main activities of development;

xiii. Mainstream climate change risk management and GHG emission reduction on sectoral planning; and

xiv. Strengthen global partnerships and support the implementation of relevant international agreements and frameworks, e.g. the United Nations Framework Convention on Climate Change (UNFCCC).

C.4. Sustainable Consumption and Production

Strategic Measures

v.   Strengthen public-private partnerships to promote the adoption of environmentally-sound technologies for maximizing resource efficiency;

vi. Promote environmental education (including eco-school practice), awareness, and capacity to adopt sustainable consumption and green lifestyle at all levels;

vii. Enhance capacity of relevant stakeholders to implement sound waste management and energy efficiency; and

viii. Promote the integration of Sustainable Consumption and Production strategy and best practices into national and regional policies or as part of CSR activities.

D. RESILIENT

Integrated, comprehensive, and inclusive approaches are necessary to build resilient communities in the ASEAN region post-2015. Resilience is an essential aspect of human security and sustainable environment which is addressed by integrating policies, capacity and institution-building, stakeholder partnerships in disaster risk reduction, humanitarian assistance, and community empowerment, among others. Resilience has to be inclusive, non-discriminatory and incorporates market and technology-based policies, including contributions from the private sector as well as the scientific and academic communities. Through the Declaration on Institutionalizing the Resilience of ASEAN and its Communities and Peoples to Disasters and Climate Change adopted during the 26th ASEAN Summit in Kuala Lumpur, Malaysia on 27 April 2015, the Leaders committed "to forge a more resilient future by reducing existing disaster and climate-related risks, preventing the generation of new risks and adapting to a changing climate through the implementation of economic, social, cultural, physical, and environmental measures which address exposure and vulnerability, and thus strengthen resilience."

The objective of this Characteristic is to achieve an enhanced capacity to collectively respond and adapt to current challenges and emerging threats. This recognizes that socio-cultural resilience has cross-pillar linkages within the ASEAN Community as an effective force for moderation for the common good, and one that is prepared for natural and human-induced disasters, and socio-economic crises, while fully embracing the principles of comprehensive security.

The key result areas and corresponding strategic measures are as follows:

D.1. A Disaster Resilient ASEAN that is able to Anticipate, Respond, Cope, Adapt, and Build Back Better, Smarter, and Faster

Strategic Measures

viii. Enhance regional mechanisms and capacities to enable ASEAN to respond together to disasters within and outside the region;

ix. Promote regional standards, including methodologies and tools to assess, record, calculate the disaster losses and damages, and share non-sensitive data and create common information system, to enhance interoperability, ensure unity of action, and strengthen resilience;

x. Promote local communities' resilience by integrating principles of resilience in risk reduction, preparedness, response, recovery, and rehabilitation measures;

xi. Promote policy coherence and interlinkages, and synergize initiatives on disaster risk reduction, climate change adaptation and mitigation, humanitarian actions and sustainable development;

xii. Institutionalize resilience by strengthening institutional and adaptive capacities to reduce existing risks and prevent future risks;

xiii. Harness local wisdom and traditional knowledge to foster a culture of resilience; and

xiv. Enhance capacity, technology and community resilience to the impact of unexploded ordnance on the livelihood of people, especially the vulnerable groups in rural areas.

D.2. A Safer ASEAN that is able to Respond to all Health-related Hazards including Biological, Chemical, and Radiological-nuclear, and Emerging Threats

Strategic Measures

> iv. Strengthen health systems to be resilient in preparedness for effective response to health-related hazards, including biological, chemical, radiological-nuclear hazards and emerging threats;

> v. Promote regional standards to enhance interoperability, ensure unity of action and strengthen collective resilience; and

> vi. Enhance institutional and human capacities and approaches to support the effective implementation of policies, strategies and programmes in preparing and responding to all health-related hazards and emerging threats.

D.3. A Climate Adaptive ASEAN with Enhanced Institutional and Human Capacities to Adapt to the Impacts of Climate Change

Strategic Measures

> iv. Expand regional cross-sectoral platforms and establish shared strategies to respond to the impacts of climate change;

> v. Promote sound scientific and evidence-based policies on climate change adaptation; and

> vi. Promote and consider indigenous and traditional knowledge and practices in responding and adapting to the impacts of climate change.

D.4. Strengthened Social Protection for Women, Children, Youths, the Elderly/Older Persons, Persons with Disabilities, Ethnic Minority Groups, Migrant Workers, Vulnerable and Marginalized Groups, and People Living in At-risk Areas, including People Living in Remote and Border Areas and Climate Sensitive Areas, to Reduce Vulnerabilities in Times of Climate Change-related Crises, Disasters and other Environmental Changes

Strategic Measures

    iii. Encourage risk and vulnerability assessments and other scientific and evidence-based measures for policies and plans to ensure targeted response measures; and

    iv. Establish platforms to empower people living in at-risk areas to become resilient by reducing their exposure and vulnerability to climate-related extreme events and other economic, social and environmental shocks and disasters.

D.5. Enhanced and Optimized Financing Systems, Food, Water, Energy Availability, and other Social Safety Nets in Times of Crises by making Resources more Available, Accessible, Affordable and Sustainable

Strategic Measures

    vi. Enhance cross-sectoral and cross-pillar coordination to ensure food adequacy and accessibility at the household level, especially vulnerable households, and ability to cope with disaster, food price shocks and scarcity by developing adaptive mechanisms and strategies;

    vii. Enhance cross-sectoral and cross-pillar coordination to ensure availability and accessibility of affordable energy services at the household level and promote utilization of renewable energy and green technologies;

    viii. Enhance cross-sectoral and cross-pillar coordination to ensure availability of clean water, sanitation facilities and electricity to households in times of crises;

ix. Enhance the targeting of poor, vulnerable and marginalized groups in times of crises; and

x. Explore the possibility of establishing financial and insurance mechanisms and strategies for disaster risk reduction and climate change adaptation.

D.6. Endeavour towards a "Drug-Free" ASEAN

Strategic Measures

iii. Support the coordination with relevant stakeholders in policy formulation, develop and implement preventive programmes for different target groups, adopt and utilize effective treatment and rehabilitation and after-care programmes, and research on drug abuse problems; and

iv. Enhance community awareness and social responsibility on the ill-effects of dangerous drugs through community engagement, advocacy and other relevant activities.

E. Dynamic

The objective of this Characteristic is to strengthen the ability to continuously innovate and be a proactive member of the global community. It aims to provide an enabling environment with policies and institutions that engender people and firms to be more open and adaptive, creative, innovative, and entrepreneurial.

The key result areas and corresponding strategic measures are as follows:

E.1. Towards an Open and Adaptive ASEAN

Strategic Measures

xii. Encourage freedom of universal access to information and communication technology in accordance with national legislations;

xiii. Promote a culture of tolerance, understanding and mutual respect for religions and interfaith dialogue;

xiv. Showcase ASEAN to the outside world using various approaches e.g. ASEAN arts, film festivals and heritage programmes;

xv. Project a common ASEAN voice in global socio-cultural fora and negotiations, where appropriate;

xvi. Promote greater people-to-people interaction and mobility within and outside ASEAN;

xvii. Promote cooperation in sports and develop comprehensive and inclusive sports programmes to encourage healthy and active lifestyles;

xviii. Strengthen capacity and capability of both the ASEAN civil service and public sectors to respond to emerging challenges and the needs of the peoples through efficient, effective, transparent and accountable public services, participatory and innovative approaches, and collaboration;

xix. Provide opportunities for relevant stakeholders for knowledge sharing, which include exchange of best practices and studies;

xx. Encourage volunteerism among ASEAN Member States to strengthen the ASEAN Community;

xxi. Project ASEAN's visibility through comprehensive, multi-stakeholder branding efforts, which are represented by common ASEAN identifiers, such as ASEAN Day, ASEAN Flag, ASEAN Anthem and ASEAN Emblem; and

xxii. Promote measures to ensure a caring society, social harmony and values of humanity, and spirit of community.

E.2. Towards a Creative, Innovative and Responsive ASEAN

Strategic Measures

v. Enhance the competitiveness of ASEAN human resources through the promotion of life-long learning, pathways, equivalencies and skills development as well as the use of information and communication technologies across age groups;

vi. Promote an innovative ASEAN approach to higher education, incorporating academics, community service, regional placement, and entrepreneurship incubation and support;

vii. Encourage regional cooperation in the areas of education, training and research, and strengthen ASEAN's role in regional and global research network by promoting initiatives and providing incentives and support for research and development, including research publications;

viii. Promote the free flow of ideas, knowledge, expertise, and skills to inject dynamism within the region;

Strengthen curricula and system of education in science, technology and creative disciplines;

vi. Encourage and support creative industry and pursuits, such as film, music, and animation;

vii. Promote ASEAN as a centre for human resource development and training;

viii. Strengthen regional and global cooperation in enhancing the quality and competitiveness of higher education institutions;

ix. Encourage the government, private sector and community to develop a system of continuous training and re-training to support lifelong learning and workforce development; and

x. Promote registration of intellectual property rights (IPR), and strengthen its cooperation and implementation in ASEAN in areas such as food safety, medicines, traditional cultural assets and biodiversity-based products.

E.3. Engender a Culture of Entrepreneurship in ASEAN

Strategic Measures

iv. Strengthen the supportive environment for socially and environmentally responsible entrepreneurship, such as mentoring, providing seed money, venture and crowd funding, and marketing support;

v. Promote and nurture creative and inclusive social entrepreneurship for youths, persons with disabilities, women and vulnerable and marginalized groups; and

vi. Encourage institutional and technical innovations in the provision of social services and health care.

III. IMPLEMENTATION AND REVIEW

A. Implementation Mechanism

The ASCC Blueprint 2025 is guided by the ASEAN Charter as well as other key ASEAN instruments and documents, which provide the principles and frameworks for ASEAN socio-cultural cooperation and their implementation. Such implementation is also guided by relevant domestic laws, regulations and policies.

A.1. Institutional Mechanism

The sectoral bodies under the ASCC shall be responsible for operationalizing the strategic measures relevant to their mandate by translating them into specific action lines or programmes, projects and activities as part of their respective sectoral work plans. For strategic measures that are cross-cutting and require collaboration with sectoral bodies from the APSC and AEC Pillars, an institutionalized cross-pillar and cross-sectoral coordination strategy shall be employed where the lead sectoral bodies in collaboration with cooperating bodies will develop their respective sectoral work plans, anchored on the corresponding strategic measures relevant to their sectors and based on the SMART (Specific, Measurable, Achievable, Realistic, and Time-bound) approach to ensure realization.

The ASCC Council is responsible for overseeing the implementation of the ASCC Blueprint 2025 and with the support of the Senior Officials Committee for the ASCC (SOCA) and the sectoral bodies, shall be the principal body responsible for coordinating matters that require cross-sectoral and cross- pillar collaboration. The ASEAN Secretariat shall continue to convene and enhance the Senior Officials Coordinating Conference on the ASEAN Socio- Cultural Community (SOC-COM) mechanism to provide a platform for broad participation and engagement of sectoral bodies within ASCC and from other pillars (through their chairpersons/ vice-chairs), the Committee of Permanent Representatives to ASEAN (CPR), entities associated with ASEAN, and other relevant stakeholders, including sub- regional organizations.

The ASCC Council and the sectoral bodies under its purview shall promote multi- stakeholder engagement to share expertise and resources, transfer of knowledge and technology, monitor implementation, and act as partners in carrying out regional cooperation initiatives of mutual interest. Participative monitoring review mechanisms shall be encouraged.

Dialogue partners and regional entities associated with the ASEAN shall be encouraged to support the implementation of the ASCC Blueprint 2025 through mutually-beneficial cooperation frameworks where the programmes, projects and activities are in line with the vision, objectives and strategic measures in the ASCC Blueprint 2025.

A.2. Implementation Strategies

27. The implementation of the ASCC Blueprint 2025 shall employ strategies and approaches that will maximize the role of ASEAN Organs and Bodies, encourage stakeholder engagement and enhance capacity building mechanisms in disseminating relevant knowledge to the peoples of ASEAN. It shall promote the provision of platforms for relevant stakeholders and groups to fully participate in programmes, meetings and other initiatives of ASEAN Organs and Bodies, as well as the opportunities for partnerships and collaborations. It shall also promote public private partnerships (PPP), social entrepreneurship and CSR for inclusive and sustainable socio-cultural development. It will likewise develop capacity building mechanisms for relevant stakeholders in the ASCC who are able to cascade the relevant knowledge to the peoples of ASEAN. Furthermore, the ASCC will intensify strategies, work programmes and initiatives of sectoral bodies under the ASCC Pillar to narrow the development gap.

A.3. Strengthened ASEAN Institutional Capacity and Presence

28. The ASEAN Secretariat shall also enhance its capacities and responsiveness to support the work of the ASCC and in collaboration with other sectors, pillars, and other stakeholders. Cognizant of the recommendations by the High Level Task Force on Strengthening the ASEAN Secretariat and Reviewing the ASEAN Organs, the ASCC Council and sectoral bodies under its purview, with the support of the ASEAN Secretariat shall take concrete steps to carry out the recommendations towards an enhanced ASEAN institutional capacity and presence.

National Focal Points of Sectoral Bodies shall be encouraged to strengthen their coordination with their National Secretariats and ASCC National Focal Points in ensuring timely sharing of information, effective and efficient consultation with capitals and in promoting public awareness on the work and achievements of the ASCC.

B. RESOURCES

In keeping with the principles of ownership and enhancing ASEAN Centrality and in order to support the implementation of strategic measures in the ASCC Blueprint 2025, ASEAN Member States are encouraged to provide resources to support, when appropriate, the projects and work of the sectoral bodies.

Indicative multi-year and annual budget is necessary to support the implementation of the ASCC Blueprint 2025 to foster the predictability of availability of funds.

Sectoral bodies have to ensure financial sustainability if they plan to establish centres to support the implementation of the ASCC Blueprint 2025 or their sectoral work plans.

To ensure sustainability of projects and established mechanisms, resources in the form of funds, technical expertise and knowledge assets from Dialogue Partners, International Organizations and other partners, will be mobilized by the ASEAN Member States and respective ASEAN Organs and Bodies. Resource mobilization strategies would also garner the support of philanthropists from among the business sector and individuals for the implementation of the ASCC Blueprint 2025.

C. COMMUNICATION

In line with the ASEAN Communications Master Plan (ACMP), the ASCC in close collaboration with relevant ASEAN Organs and Bodies and stakeholders will develop necessary platforms, mechanisms, strategies and initiatives to promote awareness and appreciation of the ASCC Blueprint 2025 in order to achieve greater communication impact.

D. REVIEW

The review and assessment of ASCC Blueprint 2025 implementation shall utilize the existing Monitoring and Evaluation (M&E) system that consists of implementation-focused monitoring system and the ASCC

Scorecard. Building on the current ASCC Scorecard, the sectoral bodies will revisit their sectoral indicators to ensure that other dimensions of the ASCC Blueprint 2025 will be considered in enhancing the current scorecard and its indicators, based on accepted regional results-based management standards. An M&E Work Plan will be drawn up that consists of internal monitoring by the respective sectoral bodies and evaluation that may engage other stakeholders.

The M&E system shall build upon the ASCC Scorecard used in assessing the progress of implementation of the ASCC Blueprint 2009-2015 and consider the lessons learned and recommendations from the ASCC Scorecard Assessment Results. This shall be reflected in a results framework that will be developed to monitor and assess progress of the ASCC Blueprint 2025. Building on the ASCC Scorecard, the sectoral bodies will revisit their sectoral indicators to ensure that other dimensions of the new ASCC Blueprint 2025 will be considered in enhancing the current scorecard and its indicators.

A Results Framework shall form part of this M&E system where higher-order or outcome-based objectives, key result areas (KRA) and indicators are compiled, synthesized and aligned with the Characteristics and Elements in this Blueprint. The Results Framework maps and clusters such objectives, KRAs, and indicators in terms of their relation to the Blueprint components. In addition, the Results Framework provides the basis for monitoring Blueprint implementation by establishing the provisional targets and timelines. The matrix also provides information for resource mobilization purposes by breaking down resource requirements into Annual/Multi-Year funding targets. Such targets may be expressed in funds, expertise, training or other inputs.

The Results Framework of the ASCC Blueprint 2025 shall be guided by the following key concepts:

Objectives: A specific end result desired or expected to occur as a consequence, at least in part, of an intervention or activity. The blueprint clearly spells out the objectives under each characteristic of
(1) Engages and Benefits the Peoples;
(2) Inclusive;
(3) Sustainable;
(4) Resilient and
(5) Dynamic;

Key Result Areas: Areas corresponding to the objective where results or changes are expected to occur. Results are changes in a state or condition that derive from a cause-and-effect relationship.
The blueprint has specified the key result areas under each objective of the characteristic;

Key Performance Indicators: Quantitative or qualitative factor or variable that provides a simple and reliable means to measure achievement, to reflect the changes connected to an intervention, or to help assess the performance of a development actor or intervention; and

Strategic Measures: Outcome-oriented action statements to deliver desired changes in the KRAs. Outcomes represent changes in the institutional and behavioural capacities for development conditions that occur between the completion of outputs and the achievement of the objectives.

A Mid-Term Evaluation, covering the period of 2016-2020, and an End-of-Term Evaluation, covering the period of 2021-2025, will be conducted to monitor progress and evaluate outcomes/impacts of the achievement of the objectives of the ASCC Blueprint 2025.

Other appropriate approaches and methodologies, such as systematic collection of data, qualitative and quantitative evaluations, policy analyses, development of indicators, polls and impact studies, are encouraged to assess the impact of policies/programmes/projects arising from this blueprint that may be done at regional and sectoral levels.

In support of the SMART approach, indicative result/outcome-based indicators should be developed to measure impacts of the implementation of strategic measures.

As part of the M&E system, the ASCC shall also establish a compliance monitoring system for the implementation of all ASEAN Declarations relevant to the ASCC Pillar

Chapter 11

Conference Paper : International Conference on Assessing Primary Students by Approaching and Evaluating their Competency: A Possible to Pedagogic Institutions in Vietnam and Some South Asian Countries At: Tan Trao University, Trug Mon commune, Yen Son District, Tuyen Quang Province, Vietnam (May 2015)

I. The Culture-based Multidisciplinary Model of the Mother Tongue based-Multilingual Education (MTB-MLE) of the Primary Schools in the Philippines

Abstract

The culture-based multidisciplinary analysis provides the relevant instructional materials needed for the primary education in the curriculum guide for primary education subjects in relation to the implementation of the Mother Tongue-Based – Multilingual Education (MTB-MLE) as guided by the implementation of DepEd Order No.74.,s. 2009 and DepEd No. 31, s.2012.The Mother Tongue Based -Multilingual Education (MTB-MLE) is the government's banner program for education as a salient part of the implementation of the K to 12 Basic Education Program. Its significance is underscored by the passing of Republic Act 10523, otherwise known as the "Enhanced Basic Education Act of 2013." This is define as the education, formal or non - formal, in which the learner's mother tongue and additional languages are used in the classroom. Learners begin their education in the language they understand best - their mother tongue - and develop a strong foundation in their mother language before adding additional languages.

Research stresses the fact that children with a solid foundation in their mother tongue develop stronger literacy abilities in the school language. This educational model of the mother tongue provides a social research to validate and interpret the varied terms in the first language that is acceptable on its usage to particular ethnographic and cultural experiences by the learners and teachers. In this study, the critical variables in the social researches in the basic education provide the right mother tongue usage based acceptable Ilokano terms in Northern Philippines. The educational model presents the research design applicable in the mother tongue through the key informant groups responding the social and academic research as to the acceptability of the Ilocano term (Mother Tongue) as to its instructional utilization in the K to 12 curriculum.

II. Introduction

The concept of the MTB-MLE adopted by the Department of Education defines it as education, formal or non - formal, in which the learner's mother tongue and additional languages are used in the classroom. Learners begin their education in the language they understand best - their mother tongue - and develop a strong foundation in their mother language before additional languages. The end goal of the MTB-MLE reflects from the development of the Filipino children in the lifelong learning to become competent in the different learning areas in the L1 (Mother Tongue), L2 (Filipino, the national language) and L3 (English, the global language). As pointed out by Cummins (2000), children who come to school with a solid foundation in their mother tongue develop stronger literacy abilities in the school language. When parents and other caregivers (e.g. grandparents) are able to spend time with their children and tell stories or discuss issues with them in a way that develops their mother tongue vocabulary and concepts, children come to school well-prepared to learn the school language and succeed educationally. Children's knowledge and skills transfer across languages from the mother tongue they have learned in the home to the school language.

UNESCO (2003) supported the Mother Tongue as medium of instruction in primary education since the early 1950's. Years of research have shown that children who begin their education in their mother tongue make a better start, and continue to perform better, than those for whom school starts with a new language. The same applies to adults seeking to become literate. This conclusion is now widely implemented, although we still hear of governments that insist on imposing a foreign language of instruction on young children, either in a mistaken attempt at modernity or to express the pre-eminence of a social dominant group (UNESCO 2003).

In the Philippines, the Department of Education in support of the UNESCO study it included the building proficiency in the Mother Tongue-Based Multilingual Education in the K to 12 curriculum through the following : (1) In Kindergarten to Grade 3, the child's dominant language is used as the language of learning; (2) Filipino and English language proficiency is developed from Kindergarten to Grade 3 but very gradually; (3) Mother Tongue is used in instruction and learning materials of other learning areas ; and (4) The learners retain their ethnic identity, culture, heritage and values. This will serve as their passport to enter and achieve well in the mainstream educational system and in the end, contribute productively to their community and to the larger society as well as Multilingual, Multiliterate, and Multi-Cultural Citizens of the country.

III. Research Objectives

The study aims to discuss the Culture-Based Multidisciplinary Model of the Mother Tongue Based-Multilingual Education (MTB-MLE) of the Primary Schools in the Philippines. The following are specific objectives of the study:

1. To expound the concept and principles of the K to 12 Mother Tongue Curriculum in the primary education

1. To identify the research studies of the Mother Tongue Instruction in Early Childhood Education.
2. To present the educational significance of the K to 12 Curriculum to the Primary Education Program as implemented in Laboratory School, University of Northern Philippines.
3. To describe the implementation of the Lingua Franca as Learning Area of the MTB-MLE in the Philippines.
4. To present the Culture-Based Multidisciplinary Analysis of the MTB-MLE of the K to 12 Program in Northern Philippines.

IV. Research Methodology

The research design of the study provides the discussion on a qualitative analysis in the implementation of the MTB-MLE of the K to 12 Basic Education Program for Kindergarten, Grade 1 and Grade 2. The MTB-MLE provides the educational components on the basis of the K to 12 Curriculum Guide of the Department of Education in the Philippines. It also presented the research studies conducted by the UNESCO in the program advocacy to utilize the mother tongue as the medium of instruction in the primary education. The Department of Education implement the mother tongue through specific educational situs such as DepEd Order No. 16, s.2012 and DepEd Order No. 28, s.2013. The researchers also utilized the previous studies in MTB-MLE as the educational model to present Culture-Based Multidisciplinary Analysis of the MTB-MLE of the K to 12 Program in Northern Philippines.

V. Concept and Principles of the K to 12 Mother Tongue Curriculum in the   Primary Education

The Department of Education implemented the Mother Tongue–Based Multilingual Education (MTB-MLE) is the government's banner program for education as a salient part of the implementation of the K to 12 Basic Education Program. Its significance is underscored by the passing of Republic Act 10523, otherwise known as the "Enhanced Basic Education Act of 2013."

In this Act, the basic education is delivered in languages understood by the learners as the language plays a strategic role in shaping the formative years of learners. For kindergarten and the first three (3) years of elementary education, instruction, teaching materials and assessment is the regional or native language of the learners. The mother language or first Language (LI) refers to language or languages first learned by a child, which he/she identifies with, is identified as a native language user of by others, which he/she knows best, or uses most. This includes Filipino sign language used by individuals with pertinent disabilities. The regional or native language refers to the traditional speech variety or variety of Filipino sign language existing in a region, area or place.

The educational standards and principles of the Mother Tongue Based-Multilingual Education (MTB-MLE) reflects to the adherence which starts from where the learners are and from what they already knew proceeding from the known to the unknown. The curriculum standards and principles of the basic education are the following that also reflected of the MTB-MLE program in the Philippines: (a) learner-centered, inclusive and developmentally appropriate; (b) relevant, responsive and research-based; (c) culture sensitive; and (d) contextualized and global. Furthermore, the pedagogical approaches are constructivist; inquiry-based; reflective; collaborative and integrative. It uses the spiral progression approach to ensure mastery of knowledge and skills after each level. The curriculum is also flexible enough to enable and allow schools to localize, indigenize and enhance the same based on their respective educational and social contexts. What is important provision in the MTB-MLE is the production and development of locally produced teaching materials that is now devolve to the regional and division education units.

In the Philippines, the Department of Education designed the two-track method to be used for the effective implementation of the MTB-MLE, that is the primer track to focus on accuracy and the story track to focus on meaning. Learning via the two-track method to gain proficiency in literacy as well as comprehend academic content and gain curriculum mastery, creative and critical thinking skills for decisive decision-making.

The MTB-MLE provides the following educational components relevant to the implementation of the K to 12 Curriculum: (K to 12 Curriculum Guide, Department of Education)

1. **Literacy.** We only learn to read once. Learning to read in the L1 develops skills that transfer to reading any other languages. Comprehension in reading other languages only occurs after oral proficiency has developed such that vocabulary of the written L2 text is already part of the learners' spoken vocabulary.

2. **Prior knowledge.** Engaging learners in a discussion of what is already familiar to them using the home language and culture enables better learning of the curriculum through integration and application of that knowledge into current knowledge schemes.

3. **Cognitive development and higher order thinking skills (HOTS).** Using the learners' mother tongue provides a strong foundation by developing cognitive skills and comprehension of the academic content from day one. The knowledge, skills, attitudes, and values gained through the mother tongue better support learning of other languages and learning through other languages later. As learners articulate their thoughts and expand ideas, both language and critical thinking are strengthened. MTB-MLE cultivates critical thinking through talking about ideas in the familiar language. When teaching only in the L2, critical thinking is postponed until L2 is sufficiently developed to support such analysis.

4. **Strong Bridge.** MTB-MLE provides a good bridge to listening, speaking, reading, and writing the L2s (L2, L3) of the classroom using sound educational principles for building fluency and confidence in using the other languages for lifelong learning. Reading in the L2 is only introduced after basic L1 reading fluency and L2 oral proficiency are developed. Comprehension in reading the L2 occurs after the development of that spoken L2. Once sufficient oral and written proficiency in the L2 are developed, a gradual transition

to using the L2 as medium of instruction can progress without the L1 support.

5. **Scaffolding.** In L2 teaching, the L1 is used to support learning when the L2 is not sufficiently developed to be used alone. The L1 is used for expression and the teacher facilitates the development of the L2 to enable learners to adequately express ideas in the L2. In this way, the L1 strengthens the learning of the L2 by supporting the L2 development for communication.

6. **Teaching for meaning and accuracy.** Decoding text requires accuracy, while comprehending texts requires decoding skills within a meaningful context. Both meaning and accuracy are important, but in classrooms that teach only L2, there is often primary focus on accuracy until the L2 is sufficiently learned. This delays actual meaningful learning until the L2 can support that learning.

V. The Research Studies of the Mother Tongue Instruction in Early Childhood Education

Research stresses the fact that children with a solid foundation in their mother tongue develop stronger literacy abilities in the school language. Their knowledge and skills transfer across languages. This bridge enables the learners to use both or all their languages for success in school and for lifelong learning. In terms of cognitive development, the school activities will engage learners to move well beyond the basic what-questions to cover all higher order thinking skills in L1 which they can transfer to the other languages once enough Filipino or English has been acquired to use these skills in thinking and articulating thoughts.

A growing body of empirical research and theory on language acquisition and bi/multilingual learning complement a rights based rationale for basing early education in children's mother tongue before introducing a second language as a medium of instruction. In its report, "Strong Foundations: Early Childhood Care and Education", UNESCO (2007) points out the overlooked advantages of mother tongue based multilingual education in the early years. (Ball, 2010)

(1)   When children are offered opportunities to learn in their mother tongue, they are more likely to enrol and succeed in school (Kosonen, 2005).

(2)   Their parents are more likely to communicate with teachers and participate in their children's learning (Benson, 2002).

(3)   Mother tongue based education especially benefits disadvantaged groups, including children from rural and Indigenous communities (Hovens, 2002).

(4)   In the majority world, mother tongue based education can especially benefit girls, who tend to have less exposure to an official language and have been found to stay in school longer, achieve better, and repeat grades less often when they are taught in their mother tongue (UNESCO Bangkok, 2005).

Research confirms that children learn best in their mother tongue as a foundation for and bilingual and multilingual education. Studies show that six to eight years of education in a language are necessary to develop the level of literacy and verbal proficiency required for academic achievement in secondary school. (Thomas & Collier, 2002)
.

Research shows that children's ability to learn a second or additional languages (e.g., a lingua franca and an international language) does not suffer when their mother tongue is the primary language of instruction throughout primary school. Fluency and literacy in the mother tongue lay a cognitive and linguistic foundation for learning additional languages. When children receive formal instruction in their first language throughout primary school and then gradually transition to academic learning in the second language, they learn the second language quickly. If they continue to have opportunities to develop their first language skills in secondary school, they emerge as fully bilingual (or multilingual) learners. If, however, children are forced to switch abruptly or transition too soon from learning in their mother tongue to schooling in a second language, their first language acquisition may be attenuated or even lost. Even more importantly, their self-confidence as learners and their interest in what they are learning may decline, leading to lack of motivation, school failure, and early school leaving.

VI. Implementation of the Lingua Franca as Learning Area of the MTB-MLE in the Philippines

In School Year (SY) 2012-2013, the Mother Tongue Based-Multilingual Education was implemented in all public schools specifically in

Kindergarten, Grades 1, 2 and 3 as part of the K to 12 Basic Education Program with the support the goal of "Every Child-A-Reader and A-Writer by Grade 1." (DepEd Order No. 16, s.2012). There were eight major languages or Lingua Franca and others offered as learning area and utilized as language of instruction : (DepEd Order No. 16, s.2012)

1. Tagalog;		5. Hiligaynon;
2. Kapampangan;		6. Waray;
3. Pangasinense;		7. Tausug;
4. Iloko;		8. Maguindanaoan

The languages of instruction expanded to the other mother tongue languages of specific regions and divisions (Geographical Location) for the School Year (SY) 2013-2014 . The MTB-MLE aims to improve the pupil's language and cognitive development, as well as his/her socio-cultural awareness as provided in the enclosure of DepEd Order No. 16, s. 2012. The child's language will serve as the fundamental language for literacy and learning. This was implemented as the languages of instruction for Grade 1 pupils who speak the same languages. (DepEd Order No. 28, s.2013)

1.   Ybanaq   (Region II – Tuguegarao City, Cagayan , Isabela)
2.   Ivatan   (Region II- Batanes Group of Islands)
3.   Sambal   (Region III- Zambales)
4.   Akianon   (Region VI Aklan, Capiz)
5.   Kinaray-a (Region Vi Capiz, Aklan)
6.   Yakan   (ARMM- Basilan Province)
7.   Suriqaonon (Caraga- Surigao City and Provinces)

There are available learning materials identified in the Department of Education based on the previous educational projects in the indigenous materials used in the MTB-MLE. Based on DepEd Order No. 16, s.2012, the Lingua Franca Project (1999-2001) and the Lubuagan Project (1999 to present) have provided valuable inputs in the implementation of the MTB-MLE. Nine hundred twenty-one (921) schools including those for children of indigenous people have been modeling MTB-MLE with support from the   following:

1. Basic Education Assistance for Mindanao (BEAM)
2. Third Elementary Education Program (TEEP)
3. Translators Association of the Philippines (TAP)
4. Save the Children, and the Summer Institute of Linguistics (SIL).

These were some of the previous Lingua Franca projects supported by the Department of Education as invaluable inputs in the implementation of the MTB-MLE. However, there are teachers are complaining about the lack of instructional materials in the mother tongue language.

V. Culture-Based Multidisciplinary Analysis of the MTB-MLE of the K to 12 Program in Northern Philippines

As part of the Culture-Based Multidisciplinary Model in the MTB-MLE, the enhancement for the instructional materials in Northern Philippines can be done through key informants' derivatives for those who are experts in the mother tongue language translations. Previous studies cultured-based research in mother tongue utilizing the key informants' were presented in the International Nakem Conferences as part of the enhancement of the mother tongue language translations.

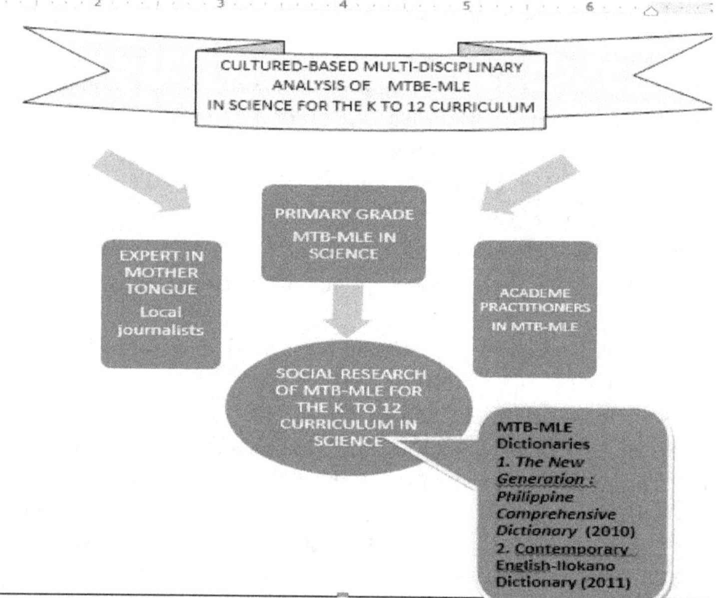

In the illustration of the culture-based multidisciplinary analysis of MTB-MLE in Science for the K to 12 Curriculum, it provides the reproduction of Ilokano instructional materials as to the usage in the mother tongue in Northern Philippines.

Basically, the researchers of the mother tongue can be presented in the following :

1. Expert in mother tongue language translations. There are three group of key informants identified in this study .These are the group 1 and 2 key informants to translate the meaning of the science terms. The native language translations of the key informants are derive from its experience and expertise in providing information about the local news in the community.

2. The key informant group 1 has experience and expertise in literary works such as writers in Bannawag, Liwayway and other local magazines available in the locality.

3. The key informant group 2 has experience and expertise as local journalists and broadcasters in radio and television in the locality.

4. The key informant group 3 has experience and expertise as teaching and translating literary works in Ilocano , they are instructors and retired teachers in SUCs

5. The key informant group 4 has been MTB-MLE practitioners teaching grade 1-3 in the basic education program.

6. The Grade 1-3 practitioners in MTB-MLE as they are assigned to teach in primary grade whose medium of instruction is the mother tongue. They have training in the various MTB-MLE programs particularly the old instructional materials collected such as songs, poems and literary works .

7. The English–Ilocano Dictionaries provide information and data based from *The New Generation : Philippine Comprehensive Dictionary* (2010) for D1 and Contemporary English-Ilokano Dictionary (2011) for D2 which were utilized to verify and validate the Ilocano and Filipino translations in science for the MTB-MLE in Grade 3.

These are the qualitative observations and findings in the focused group discussions and actual experiences on social research of the Mother Tongue Based-Multilingual Education (MTB-MLE) in Sciences for the K to 12 curriculum:

1. The Local journalists, Broadcasters and Literary Experts are inclined to translate Ilocano terms adoptable in media broadcasting. The science terms identified to translate in Ilocano have more inclined to translate at a deeper literary meaning of the Ilocano society. However, general Ilocano terms are commonly translated similar with the other group respondents and Ilocano-speaking residents of Metro Vigan. The cultural experiences and expertise are given in consideration to the knowledge in Ilokano society as given emphasis on the translations of science terms.

2. The retired teachers and faculty with expertise in Ilocano translation are more inclined to follow similar translations, however, commonly used terms have the same translation with other Ilocanos –speaking residents of Metro Vigan.

3. The general terms in the Mother Tongue and other easily accessible terms used in the class.

4. The 1-3 grade teachers are consistent in the translations of the Ilocano terms which are acceptable in both social research and instruction. The main instrument of the Ilocano translation materials are taken in songs, poem and short story on general translation   in sciences.

In a focused group discussion , as to the demonstration teaching conducted in the Nakem International Conference of the MTB-MLE showed interesting findings that the regionalistic and ethnographic consideration are varied in the presentation of the demonstration lessons with cultural lineage translation. This regional clustering of languages is distinct with no universality of its acceptability when translated by teachers.

CONCLUSIONS

The culture-based multidisciplinary analysis provides the relevant instructional materials needed for the primary education in the curriculum guide for kindergarten, Grade 1-3. The key informants and experts in the field of mother tongue can be utilized to enhance the instructional materials in the primary school. However, the previous researches in the Mother Tongue Based – Multilingual Education (MTB-MLE) has varied way to interpret as to its acceptability in the primary education. It has shown the field of expertise in the mother tongue provides the distinct way to interpret the language particularly those who local writers, journalists and broadcasters. However, the language variations may be remedied through the local residents who are experts in the mother tongue with the validation of the primary education teachers for the accepted language concepts in the locality.

Interestingly, the instructional materials of the mother tongue (Ilokano) in Northern Philippines have wide disparity as to the language usage that is varied on its geographic and ethnographic considerations. Hence, the regional clustering of languages is distinct with no universality of its acceptability when translated by teachers

Although UNESCO research studies stress the fact that children with a solid foundation in their mother tongue develop stronger literacy abilities in the school language. This educational model of the mother tongue provides a social research to validate and interpret the varied terms in the first language that is acceptable on its usage to particular ethnographic and cultural experiences by the learners and teachers. In the case of the Philippines from the far flung areas of Visayas and Mindanao, it proves to justify that their parents are more likely to communicate with teachers and participate in their children's learning; it benefits disadvantaged groups, including children from rural and Indigenous communities. On the contrary, the urban areas in the Philippines are less likely to adopt the mother tongue as the Lingua France of the primary education because the quality and excellence in basic education is anchored the L3 (English Language) in preparing the pupils to learn the subjects mathematics, science and information technology.

BIBLIOGRAPHY

Ball, Jessica (2010) Educational equity for children from diverse language backgrounds: Mother tongue-based bilingual or multilingual education in the early years. Presentation to UNESCO International Symposium: Translation and Cultural Mediation, Paris: UNESCO, 22/23 February 2010, on the occasion of the 11th International Mother Language Day in collaboration with the International Association for Translation and Intercultural Studies, 2010 International Year for the Rapprochement of Cultures

Benson, C. (2002). Real and potential benefits of bilingual progammes in developing countries. *International Journal of Bilingual Education and Bilingualism, 5* (6), 303-317.

Benson, C., & Kosonen, K. (Eds.) (2013). *Language issues in comparative education: Inclusive teaching and learning in non-dominant languages and cultures.* Rotterdam: Sense Publishers.

Bialystok, E. (2001). *Bilingualism in development: Language, literacy, and cognition.* Cambridge: Cambridge University Press.

Cummins, J. (2000). *Language, power and pedagogy.* Clevedon, UK: Multilingual Matters.

Department of Education (2012) . DepEd Order No. 16, s. 2012 : Guidelines on the Implementation of the Mother Tongue Based-Multilingual Education) issued February 17, 2012.

Department of Education (2013) . DepEd Order No. 28, 2013 : Additional Guidelines to DepEd Order No. 16, s. 2012 (Guidelines on the Implementation of the Mother Tongue Based-Multilingual Education (MTB-MLE) issued July 5,2013

King, K., & Mackey, A. (2007). *The bilingual edge: Why, when, and how to teach your child a second language.* New York: Collins.

Kosonen, K. (2005). Education in local languages: Policy and practice in Southeast Asia. *First languages first: Community-based literacy programmes for minority language contexts in Asia.* Bangkok: UNESCO Bangkok.

Kosonen, K. (2005). Education in local languages: Policy and practice in Southeast Asia.

First languages first: Community-based literacy programmes for minority language contexts in Asia. Bangkok: UNESCO Bangkok.

Hovens, M. (2002). Bilingual education in West Africa: Does it work? International Journal of Bilingual Education and Bilingualism, 5(5), 249-266.

Cummins J. (2000) Language, power, and pedagogy. Bilingual children in the crossfire. Clevedon, England: Multilingual Matters

Kosonen, K. (2005). Education in local languages: Policy and practice in Southeast Asia. *First languages first: Community-based literacy programmes for minority language contexts in Asia.* Bangkok: UNESCO Bangkok.

UNESCO (1953). *The use of the vernacular languages in education.* Monographs on Foundations of Education, No. 8. Paris: UNESCO.

UNESCO (2003). *Education in a multilingual world.* UNESCO Education Position Paper. Paris: UNESCO.

UNESCO 2003, Mother Tongue Dilemma, Education Today, July-September 2003, No. 6)

UNESCO Bangkok (2005). *Advocacy brief on mother tongue-based teaching and education for girls.* Bangkok: UNESCO.

UNESCO (2007). *Strong foundations: Early childhood care and education.* Paris: Author.

UNESCO (2008a). *Mother Tongue Matters: Local Language as a Key to Effective Learning.* Paris: UNESCO.

UNESCO (2008b). *Mother tongue instruction in early childhood education: A selected bibliography.* Paris: UNESCO.

Implementation of the K to 12 Program in the Laboratory Schools (Primary School) of the College of Teacher Education, University of Northern Philippines

- Conference: International Conference on Assessing Primary Students by Approaching and Evaluating their Competency: A Possible to Pedagogic Institutions in Vietnam and Some South Asian Countries At: Tan Trao University, Trug Mon commune, Yen Son District, Tuyen Quang Province, Vietnam (May 2015)

The research study focuses on the documentary and qualitative analysis on the principles and concepts in the primary education of the K to 12 program as to its implementation in the Laboratory School of the College of Teacher Education, University of Northern Philippines. The study is delimited to the implementation of the curriculum content as to its educational principles of the K to 12 Program on the subjects Mathematics, Science, English and Mother Tongue. The educational assessment provides the comparative analysis as to the strategic direction in the Socio-Cultural Community along the ASEAN Integration in the universal access to education and best practice of the early child care development.

The curricular analysis also reflects the guiding principles of the K to 12 program to study the educational strengths of the pedagogic content of the primary education in the Philippines. The qualitative analysis provides the standard outcome of the educational accomplishments in the laboratory school as a teacher training institution. The in-service training of teachers, curricular competitions and the faculty and staff development including the academic recognition of the laboratory schools in the university. This educational research provides the extensive presentation of the curriculum guide, conceptual framework, principles and concepts of the primary education in the K to 12 program in the Philippines. Based on the findings of the study, there are educational models that can be adopted to enhance the curriculum contents and standard educational outcome that can be utilized in the laboratory schools of the teacher training institutions in the Philippines.

I. Introduction

In the basic education program, the passage of the " Enhanced

Basic Education Act of 2013 " (Republic Act No. 10533) provides educational policy (Section 2) to empower individual who has learned, through a program that is rooted on sound educational principles and geared towards excellence, the foundations for learning throughout life, the competence to engage in work and be productive, the ability to coexist in fruitful harmony with local and global communities, the capability to engage in autonomous, creative, and critical thinking, and the capacity and willingness to transform others and one's self. It creates a functional education system guided by the life-long learning through making education learner-oriented and responsive to the needs, cognitive and cultural capacity, the circumstances and diversity of learners, schools and communities through the appropriate languages of teaching and learning, including mother tongue as a learning resource.

In the Philippines, it provides the mandatory entry to basic education in consonance with the Millennium Development Goals on achieving Education for All (EFA) to provide equal opportunities for all children to avail of accessible mandatory and compulsory kindergarten education. This educational policy is provides in Republic Act 10157, or "The Kindergarten Education Law" made Kindergarten the compulsory and mandatory entry stage to basic education. This act (Section 2) ensures that all five (5)-year old children shall be given equal opportunities for Kindergarten Education to effectively promote their physical, social, emotional and intellectual development, including values formation so they will be ready for school. Furthermore, the Department of Education (DepEd) believes that Kindergarten is the transition period from informal to formal literacy (Grades 1-12) considering that age five (5) is within the critical years where positive experiences must be nurtured to ascertain school readiness.

II. Research Objectives

The study aims to determine the extent of implementation of the relevant educational policies on the K to 12 Program in the Laboratory Schools (Primary School) of the College of Teacher Education, University of Northern Philippines. The following are specific objectives of the study :

1. To identify the research studies in primary education on the implementation of the K to 12 Curriculum of the Department of Education in the Philippines.

2. To describe the educational processes, policies and structures of the primary education along: (a) Basic Principles of the Mandatory Entry to Basic Education; and (b) Language Learning Areas in Primary Education (Grade 1 and 2).

3. To present the educational significance of the K to 12 Curriculum to the Primary Education Program as implemented in Laboratory School, University of Northern Philippines

III. Research Methodology

The research design of the study provides the qualitative analysis and educational policy analysis as to the implementation of the K to 12 Basic Education Program for Kindergarten, Grade 1 and Grade 2. The educational policies to study the primary education in the Philippines include the Republic Act No, 10533 ('Enhanced Basic Education Act of 2013), and Republic Act 10157 (he Kindergarten Education Law). In addition to this information, it also review Department Order No. 14, s. 2013 issued last March 8, 2013 as to the implementing guidelines of the Grades 1 and 2 Curricula of the K to 12 Basic Education Program and per DepEd Order No. 31, s. 2012 entitled Policy Guidelines on the Implementation of Grades 1 to 10 of the K to 12 Basic Education Curriculum Effective School Year 2012-2013, the public elementary schools. These are also the prescribed policies undertaken in the Laboratory Schools of the University of Northern Philippines.

IV. Research Studies in Primary Education on the Implementation of the K to 12 Curriculum of the Department of Education in the Philippines.

Various researches support that this is the period of greatest growth and development, when the brain develops most rapidly and almost at its fullest. It is also the stage when self- esteem, vision of the world and moral foundations are established. Teachers/parents/caregivers/adults should therefore be guided to facilitate explorations of our young learners in an engaging and creative curriculum that is developmentally appropriate which immerse them in meaningful experiences.

1. Kindergarten is the transition period from informal to formal literacy (Grades 1-12) considering that age five (5) is within the critical years where positive experiences must be nurtured to ascertain school readiness.

2. Research shows that children who underwent Kindergarten have better completion rates than those who did not. Children who complete a standards-based Kindergarten program are better prepared, for primary education.

3. Education for children in the early years lays the foundation for lifelong learning and for the total development of a child. The early years of a human being, from 0 to 6 years, are the most critical period when the brain grows to at least 60-70 percent of adult size.

Provision of varied play-based activities leads them to becoming emergent literates and, helps them to naturally acquire the competencies to develop holistically. They are able to understand the world by exploring their environment as they are encouraged to create and discover, that eventually leads them to becoming willing risk takers and ready to tackle formal school work. At 5 years old, children start schooling and are given the means to slowly adjust to formal education.

Based from these research studies on basic education, it responded the nurturing the holistic development of the children as the foundation of the lifelong learning. This is the critical development of the children from 0 to 6 years to integrate innovative learning on varied play-based activities as part of the emergent learning in exploring the environment through the development of the local identity, heritage and culture.

It must be noted that UNESCO has encouraged mother tongue instruction in primary education since 1953 (UNESCO, 1953) and UNESCO highlights the advantages of mother tongue education right from the start: children are more likely to enroll and succeed in school

(Kosonen, 2005); parents are more likely to communicate with teachers and participate in their children's learning (Benson, 2002); girls and rural children with less exposure to a dominant language stay in school longer and repeat grades less often (Hovens, 2002; UNESCO Bangkok, 2005); and children in multilingual education tend to develop better thinking skills compared to their monolingual peers (e.g., Bialystok, 2001; Cummins, 2000; King & Mackey, 2007).

Research also suggests that engaging marginalized children in school through mother-tongue based, multilingual education (MTB-MLE) is a successful model (Benson & Kosonen, 2013; Yiakoumetti, 2012). Some educators argue that only those countries where the student's first language is the language of instruction are likely to achieve the goals of Education for All. Research also suggests that engaging marginalized children in school through mother-tongue based, multilingual education (MTB-MLE) is a successful model (Benson & Kosonen, 2013; Yiakoumetti, 2012)

III. Educational Processes, Policies and Structures of the Primary Education

1. Basic Principles of the Mandatory Entry to Basic Education

The Kindergarten Education Act provides the support of the basic education program of the Department of Education in the Millennium Development Goals on achieving Education for All (EFA) by the year 2015. Basic from this educational policy (Section 2), it provides the equal opportunities for all children to avail of accessible mandatory and compulsory kindergarten education that effectively promotes physical, social, intellectual, emotional and skills stimulation and values formation to sufficiently prepare them for formal elementary schooling.

This Act applies to elementary school system being the first stage of compulsory and mandatory formal education. Thus, kindergarten will now be an integral part of the basic education system of the country. Kindergarten education is vital to the academic and technical development of the Filipino child for it is the period when the young mind's absorptive capacity for learning is at its sharpest. It is also the policy of the State to make education learner-oriented and responsive to the needs, cognitive and cultural capacity, the circumstances and diversity of learners, schools and communities through the appropriate languages of teaching and learning.

Furthermore the mandate of the kindergarten under the "Enhanced

Basic Education Act of 2013" Republic Act No. 10533) provides the instruction, teaching materials and assessment in the native language of the learners. The conceptualization of the native language refers to the use of mother tongue as the first language of the learner.

(a) The curriculum shall adhere to the principles and framework of Mother Tongue-Based Multilingual Education (MTB-MLE) which starts from where the learners are and from what they already knew proceeding from the known to the unknown; instructional materials and capable teachers to implement the MTB-MLE curriculum shall be available;

(b) The curriculum shall use the spiral progression approach to ensure mastery of knowledge and skills after each level; and

(c) The curriculum shall be flexible enough to enable and allow schools to localize, indigenize and enhance the same based on their respective educational and social contexts. The production and development of locally produced teaching materials shall be encouraged and approval of these materials shall devolve to the regional and division education units.

B. Language Learning Areas in Primary Education (Grade 1 and 2)

Based on the DepEd No.31, s.2012 that mandates the implementation of the Language Learning Areas, the mother tongue is the medium of instruction for Grade 1 and 2 for all subject areas except English. This subject will be studied in the third quarter for Grade I with 30 minutes allotment and 50 minutes allotment for Grade 2.Likewise, there is also a separate Learning Area for Mother Tongue is taught in Grade 1 and 2. While Filipino as a Learning Area, is first introduced in Grade 1 during the second quarter grading period.

Table 1
Time allotment of the Learning Areas of Grade 1 and 2 for the K to 12 Curriculum in the Basic Education Program in the Philippines

Nonmenclature/ Learning Area	Time Allotment (No. of Minutes Quarterly)							
	Grade 1				Grade 2			
	1	2	3	4	1	2	3	4
1.Mother Tongue	50	50	50	50	50	50	50	50
2.Filipino	-	30	30	30	50	50	50	50
3.English	-	-	30	30	50	50	50	50
4.Mathematics	50	50	50	50	50	50	50	50
5.Araling Panlipunan	40	40	40	40	40	40	40	40
6.Music, Arts, Physical Education and Health	40	40	40	40	40	40	40	40
7. Education sa Pagpapakatao	30	30	30	30	30	30	30	30
Total	210	240	270	270	310	310	310	310

As presented in Table 1, the instructional time for the first semester is 240 minutes or four hours per day. The subject Filipino is not yet taught in the first quarter and this will be taught in the second quarter with 30 minutes time allotment from second quarter until to the fourth quarter. On the other hand, English will only be introduced in the third quarter with only 30 minutes time allotment until to the fourth quarter. The acceleration of the time allotment will be introduced in Grade 2 with 50 minutes time allotment. The total time allotment of Grade 2 is 310 minutes or five hours and 10 minutes per day for each semester.

In addition to this information, Department Order No. 14, s.2013 (Strengthening the K to 12 Basic Education Program Delivery System for Elementary Education) provides the instructional time for both Grades 1 and 2 should be able to temporarily address the urgent needs for the classrooms and teachers. Time spent for the special instructional programs is part of the required number of working hours for teachers.

V. Educational Significance of the K to 12 Curriculum to the Primary Education Program as Implemented in Laboratory School University of Northern Philippines

In Section 4 of the Enhanced Basic Education Act, the basic education shall be delivered in languages understood by the learners as the language plays a strategic role in shaping the formative years of learners. This educational policy provides the inclusion of K to 12 Curriculum to the learners in consideration of language through the contextualization and enhancement; building proficiency and integrated seamless learning.

Table 2

Educational Significance of the K to 12 Curriculum Relevant to the Learners of the Primary Education Program as Implemented in the Laboratory Schools, University of Northern Philippines

Curriculum Relevant to Learners	Curriculum	Educational Significance of the Curriculum
A. Contextualization and Enhancement	1) The students learn the alphabet, numbers, shapes, and colors through games, songs, and dances, in their Mother Tongue. It must be based on local culture, history and reality. 2) Inclusion of Disaster Risk Reduction (DDR), Climate Change Adaptation and Information and Communication Technology	The students acquire in-depth knowledge, skills, values, and attitudes through continuity and consistency across all levels and subjects.
B. Building Proficiency (Mother Tongue-Based Multilingual Education)	1) Mother Tongue is used in instruction and learning materials of other learning areas. In Kindergarten to Grade 3, the child's dominant language is used as the language of learning 2) The learners retain their ethnic identity, culture, heritage and values.	Children learn better and are more active in class and learn a second language even faster when they are first taught in a language they understand.
C. Integrated Seamless Learning	1) Basic concepts/ general concepts are first learned. 2) More complex and	This strengthens retention and enhances mastery of topics and skills as they are revisited and

	sophisticated version of the basic/general concepts are then rediscovered in the succeeding grades.	consolidated time and again. The learner allow to learn topics and skills appropriate to their developmental and cognitive skills.

As shown in Table 2 the education significance in the K to 12 curriculum in Grade 1 and 2 provides a culture-bound theme of the language development in the formal education focuses on local heritage and history including the learning of songs, poems and other local realties in the Ilocos region. In relation to the curriculum development the emphasis of the primary education prescribes the contextualization and enhancement of subject relevant to the local heritage and culture including the integration of the mother tongue. The prescriptive subjects are required to follow basic and general subjects before the presentation of more complex and sophisticated version of learning in the subjects mathematics, science and social studies and physical education and music ,arts, physical education and character education.

As prescribe by the Department of Education, these are the innovative content of the K to 12 curriculum in the primary education in the laboratory Schools of the University of Northern Philippines:

1. In the contextualization and enhancement, this provides the acquisition of the in-depth knowledge, skills, values and attitudes through the consistency across all levels and subjects. Basically, the primary education in the laboratory schools of the University of Northern Philippines emphasizes the culture-bound across the subject areas.

2. The Mother Tongue Based-Multilingual Education is a distinct subject for Grade 1 and 2 with emphasis on the Ilokano culture and history. The prescriptive subject of the mother tongue is supported by the DepEd research that Children learn better and are more active in class and learn a second language even faster when they are first taught in a language they understand.

3. The integrated seamless learning is provided in the prescriptive curriculum of DepEd that the enhancement of the mastery of the topics are presented through the study of the basic and general concepts in the K to 12 subjects in the primary grade.

Based from these learning competencies of the subjects in the primary grade, the laboratory schools of the University of Northern Philippines still cautioned the used of the mother tongue as the lingua franca in teaching the subjects in mathematics and science. The medium of instruction is still in the English language to teach the subject of mathematics and sciences. It has shown in the research studies that teaching subjects in sciences and mathematics are still effective to use the English language. This is also the case of the private schools implementing the K to 12 program utilizing English as the medium of instruction except the subject in the Mother Tongue. The use of the English language facilitates the study basic and general concepts of sciences and mathematics. The integrated seamless learning usually requires this language the high order thinking skills are applied to

However, the effectiveness of the mother tongue reflects from the understanding of the local culture, heritage and history in the study of social studies and character education under the subjects Araling Panlipunan (AP) and Edukasyon sa Pagpapakatao (EsP). The mother tongue ensures the improvement of learning competencies as to the positive experiences to revitalize the local culture, heritage and history. The utilization of the mother tongue in the general and complex ideas of the subject areas in the primary education proves to be effective means in the enhancement of the learning process in the classroom.

VI. CONCLUSION

The educational implementation of the K to 12 program supports the major development thrust promulgated by the UNESCO in consonance with the "Education for All" (EFA). The curriculum mandates the utilization of the Early Childhood Education as advocated by the UNESCO that encouraged mother tongue instruction in primary study the primary education in the Philippines include the Republic Act No, 10533 ('Enhanced Basic Education Act of 2013), and Republic Act 10157 (he Kindergarten Education Law more likely to enroll and succeed in school and parents are more likely to communicate with teachers and participate in their children's learning.

Furthermore, the implementation of the primary education laws in the Philippines supported the   Early Childhood Education of UNESCO through the Enhanced Basic Education Act (Republic Act No, 10533) and Kindergarten Education Law (Republic Act 10157).. Other than the emphasis of the Mother Tongue Based-Multilingual Education (MTB-MLE), the K to 12 curriculum in the primary education provides the acquisition of the in-depth knowledge, skills, values and attitudes through the consistency across all levels and subjects. As the enhancement of the mastery of the topics are presented in the integrated seamless learning. Basically, the primary education in the laboratory schools of the University of Northern Philippines emphasizes the culture-bound across the subject areas followed by the prescription of the standard curriculum implemented by the Department of Education.

. BIBLIOGRAPHY

Benson, C., & Kosonen, K. (Eds.) (2013). *Language issues in comparative education: Inclusive teaching and learning in non-dominant languages and cultures.* Rotterdam: Sense Publishers.

Bialystok, E. (2001). *Bilingualism in development: Language, literacy, and cognition.* Cambridge: Cambridge University Press.

Cummins, J. (2000). *Language, power and pedagogy.* Clevedon, UK: Multilingual Matters.

King, K., & Mackey, A. (2007). *The bilingual edge: Why, when, and how to teach your child a second language.* New York: Collins.

UNESCO (1953). *The use of the vernacular languages in education.* Monographs on Foundations of Education, No. 8. Paris: UNESCO.

UNESCO Bangkok (2005). *Advocacy brief on mother tongue-based teaching and education for girls.* Bangkok: UNESCO.

Chapter 12
Memorandum of Understanding (MOU) and Memorandum of Agreement (MOA) in the International Linkages and Consortia of the Teacher Education Programs in the University of Northern Philippines, UNESCO Heritage City of Vigan

1. Romchatra Foundation

MEMORANDUM OF AGREEMENT

BETWEEN

ROMCHATRA FOUNDATION (THAILAND)

and

UNIVERSITY OF NORTHERN PHILIPPINES (PHILIPPINES)

KNOW ALL MEN BY THESE PRESENTS:

This Memorandum of Agreement made and entered into by and between:

UNIVERSITY OF NORTHERN PHILIPPINES with business and postal address at Tamag, Vigan City, Ilocos Sur, Philippines, represented by DR. GILBERT R. ARCE, in his capacity as University President, hereinafter called the "UNIVERSITY" and

ROMCHATRA FOUNDATION with office address at Charoenkrung Road, Samphantawong District, BKK, Thailand represented by PHRAPROMMANGKALACHAN in his capacity as Chairman of the Board, referred hereinafter called the "FOUNDATION".

WITNESSETH:

WHEREAS, the both parties manifest the willingness to enter into academic and non-academic ventures that will redound to their mutual benefits;

WHEREAS, the UNIVERSITY is an institution of higher learning offering various programs in accordance with its mandate;

WHEREAS, one of the objectives of the UNIVERSITY is to maintain international linkages with foreign universities and entities in pursuance with the government's globalization program;

WHEREAS, the FOUNDATION is a duly recognized entity in THAILAND that oversees the operations of Confucius Classroom at Traimitwittayalai Public High School and Confucius Institute of Maritime Silk Road;

WHEREAS, the parties mutually agreed to help each other to attain their objectives in accordance with applicable laws and regulations;

NOW, THEREFORE, the UNIVERSITY and the FOUNDATION mutually agreed to the following terms and conditions:

Page 1 of 4

RIGHTS AND OBLIGATIONS

THE UNIVERSITY shall:

1. Provide lecturers, trainors, coaches, facilitators; and experts in the different fields of specialisation in education, governance, business, technology and health to conduct extension activities as deemed needed by the FOUNDATION;

2. Conduct lecture series to promote Chinese language and culture in the Philippines; and

3. Facilitate cultural exchange.

THE FOUNDATION shall:

1. Allow the use of rooms and facilities at Traimitwittayalai Public High School in the conduct off-campus lectures; and other academic and non-academic activities of the university;

2. Name the provided venue as the University of Northern Philippines Traimit Campus;

3. Donate instructional facilities and equipments as warranted; and

4. Provide lecturers to promote Chinese language and culture in the Philippines.

OTHER TERMS AND CONDITIONS

This agreement shall take effect upon the approval of the UNP-Board of Regents subject to extension or pre-termination upon mutual consent of both parties. Any pre-termination shall be in writing and notice shall be served within 30 days from the intended date of pre-termination;

This agreement may be amended or supplemented upon the mutual agreement of the parties;

Any disputes arising from this agreement shall be resolved amicably and all court actions shall be filed exclusively before the RTC, Vigan City to the exclusion of other Courts;

In case of pre-termination, any activities with prior approval shall be allowed to continue until its completion;

Any violation of the obligation shall be a ground for the termination of the agreement.

In witness whereof, parties hereunto affixed their signatures this 29th of March 2016 at Vigan City, Ilocos Sur.

Page 2 of 4

292

MEMORANDUM OF AGREEMENT

BETWEEN

ROMCHATRA FOUNDATION (THAILAND)

and

UNIVERSITY OF NORTHERN PHILIPPINES (PHILIPPINES)

KNOW ALL MEN BY THESE PRESENTS:

This Memorandum of Agreement made and entered into by and between:

UNIVERSITY OF NORTHERN PHILIPPINES with business and postal address at Tamag, Vigan City, Ilocos Sur, Philippines, represented by DR. GILBERT R. ARCE, in his capacity as University President, hereinafter called the "UNIVERSITY" and

ROMCHATRA FOUNDATION with office address at Charoenkrung Road, Samphantawong District, BKK, Thailand represented by PHRAPROMMANGKALACHAN in his capacity as Chairman of the Board, referred hereinafter called the "FOUNDATION".

WITNESSETH:

WHEREAS, the both parties manifest the willingness to enter into academic and non-academic ventures that will redound to their mutual benefits;

WHEREAS, the UNIVERSITY is an institution of higher learning offering various programs in accordance with its mandate;

WHEREAS, one of the objectives of the UNIVERSITY is to maintain international linkages with foreign universities and entities in pursuance with the government's globalization program;

WHEREAS, the FOUNDATION is a duly recognized entity in THAILAND that oversees the operations of Confucius Classroom at Traimitwittayalai Public High School and Confucius Institute of Maritime Silk Road;

WHEREAS, the parties mutually agreed to help each other to attain their objectives in accordance with applicable laws and regulations;

NOW, THEREFORE, the UNIVERSITY and the FOUNDATION mutually agreed to the following terms and conditions:

Page 1 of 4

MEMORANDUM OF UNDERSTANDING

BETWEEN

ROMCHATRA FOUNDATION (THAILAND)

and

UNIVERSITY OF NORTHERN PHILIPPINES (PHILIPPINES)

The **DR. SOMDETPHRAMAHARATCHAMONGKHONLAMUNI**, Chairman of Romchatra Foundation **(Thailand)**, with office address at Charoenkrung Road, Samphantawong District. BKK, Thailand and the **DR. ERWIN F. CADORNA**, President of **University of Northern Philippines (UNP)**, with office address at Tamag, Vigan City, Ilocos Sur 2700 Philippines desire to promote their mutual interest in promoting academic and cultural cooperation and exchange between their institutions and in pursuant to the prevailing laws and regulations in their respective countries, as well as the policies and procedures of **Romchatra Foundation and University of Northern Philippines** concerning academic and cultural cooperation and collaboration, have reached the following scope and details of the Memorandum of Understanding:

1. The two universities agree to encourage and promote cooperation and exchange on the following academic activities:
   a. Faculty, Staff and Student Exchange Programs;
   b. Joint scientific research projects and programs
   c. Joint extension and other academic related activities like lectures, workshops, fora, symposia and seminars; and
   d. Other cooperation and collaboration activities deemed of mutual benefit to both universities.
2. Specific activities to be carried out under this Memorandum of Understanding shall be negotiated, consulted and agreed upon through a Memorandum of Agreement as its implementing guidelines. The Memorandum of Agreement within general framework of the Memorandum of Understanding shall detail all

2. Maritime Silk Road Confucius Institute

Memorandum of Understanding
Between
University of Northern Philippines, Philippines
And
Maritime Silk Road Confucius Institute, Thailand

University of Northern Philippines, Philippines and Maritime Silk Road Confucius Institute, Thailand, wishing to establish relations between the two institutions, agree to cooperate with each other as follows:

Scope of the Cooperation

Subject to mutual consent, the areas of cooperation will include any program offered at either institution as thought desirable, feasible and of mutual benefits in fostering the collaborative relationship between the two institutions through such activities as:

a. Teacher-student Exchange
b. Cultural Exchange
c. Cultural Research
d. Research Cooperation
e. Summer Camp

The terms of cooperation for each specific activity implemented under this Memorandum of Understanding shall be mutually discussed and agreed upon in writing by both parties prior to the initiation of that activity. Each institution shall designate a liaison officer to develop and coordinate the specific activities and programs agreed upon.

Renewal, Termination and Amendment

This Memorandum of Understanding shall remain in force for five years from the date of the final signature and is subject to renewal or termination by a six-month written notification of either party, and shall be effective on completion of the in-session semester, unless mutually agreed upon otherwise. The Memorandum of Understanding may be amended between two parties in writing as an addendum to this agreement.

In witness whereof, the parties hereto have offered their signatures.

for Maritime Silk Road Confucius Institute   for University of Northern Philippines

Dr. Puraprommatgkalachan   Dr. Gilbert R. Arce
President   President

Date   September, 2017   Date   September, 2017

3. Tan Trao University, Vietnam

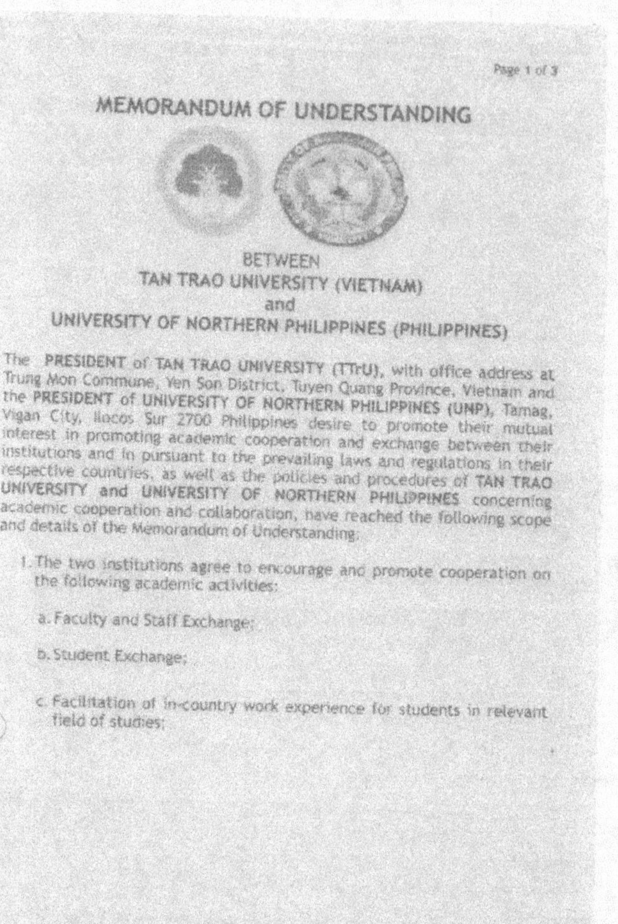

MEMORANDUM OF UNDERSTANDING

BETWEEN
TAN TRAO UNIVERSITY (VIETNAM)
and
UNIVERSITY OF NORTHERN PHILIPPINES (PHILIPPINES)

The PRESIDENT of TAN TRAO UNIVERSITY (TTrU), with office address at Trung Mon Commune, Yen Son District, Tuyen Quang Province, Vietnam and the PRESIDENT of UNIVERSITY OF NORTHERN PHILIPPINES (UNP), Tamag, Vigan City, Ilocos Sur 2700 Philippines desire to promote their mutual interest in promoting academic cooperation and exchange between their institutions and in pursuant to the prevailing laws and regulations in their respective countries, as well as the policies and procedures of TAN TRAO UNIVERSITY and UNIVERSITY OF NORTHERN PHILIPPINES concerning academic cooperation and collaboration, have reached the following scope and details of the Memorandum of Understanding:

1. The two institutions agree to encourage and promote cooperation on the following academic activities:

   a. Faculty and Staff Exchange;

   b. Student Exchange;

   c. Facilitation of in-country work experience for students in relevant field of studies;

d. Joint research and extension activities, lectures, workshops, fora, symposia and seminars;

e. Exchange of academic materials, scientific publications and other relevant scholarly information; and

f. Other cooperation and collaboration activities in education, governance, business, technology and health deemed appropriate mutually.

2. Specific activities to be carried out under this Memorandum of Understanding shall be negotiated, consulted and agreed upon through a Memorandum of Agreement as its implementing guidelines. The Memorandum of Agreement within general framework of the Memorandum of Understanding shall detail all the financial arrangements and other requirements prior to the commencement of activities.

3. Only the English version of this Memorandum of Understanding and the subsequent Memorandum of Agreement have binding effect.

4. Modifications and/or amendments to this Memorandum of Understanding shall be instigated through mutual consent.

5. Any disputes arising from the execution of this Memorandum of Understanding, both institutions on the basis of mutual trust and benefit, shall be resolved through friendly consultation.

6. In case of termination of this Memorandum of Understanding, a written notice shall be served one (1) month in advance prior to the desired termination. Under such circumstances, any on-going activity under the Memorandum of Understanding covered by a certain Memorandum of Agreement shall be allowed completion under conditions prior to the notice of termination.

7. This Memorandum of Understanding shall be in effect from the date duly signed by designated officials of the respective institutions. The

effective period of the Memorandum of Understanding shall be five years, and shall automatically be extended if any of the parties expresses in written notice desire to terminate or modify this Memorandum of Understanding.

8. That both parties execute this Memorandum of Understanding and further declare their willingness to enter into an agreement for its proper implementation.

IN WITNESS WHEREOF, the undersigned hereto affixed their signatures in this Memorandum of Understanding this 23th day of **May 2015** in Trung Mon Commune, Yen Son District, Tuyen Quang Province VIETNAM.

For:
TAN TRAO UNIVERSITY

DR. NGUYEN BA DUC
President

For:
UNIVERSITY OF NORTHERN PHILIPPINES

DR. GILBERT R. ARCE
SUC President IV

Witnessed By:

THANH THI LE TRAN
Vice President for Science Management & International Affairs

ALBERT R. TEJERO, CPA, MBA
Vice President for Finance & Administration

MEMORANDUM OF AGREEMENT

BETWEEN

TAN TRAO UNIVERSITY (VIETNAM) and UNIVERSITY OF NORTHERN PHILIPPINES (PHILIPPINES)

KNOW ALL MEN BY THESE PRESENTS:

This Memorandum of Agreement made and entered into by and between:

TAN TRAO UNIVERSITY (TTrU), with office address at **Trung Mon Commune, Yen Son District, Tuyen Quang Province, Vietnam**, represented by, **DR. NGUYEN BA DUC** his capacity as **President**, referred to as **"THE FIRST PARTY"**; and

UNIVERSITY OF NORTHERN PHILIPPINES with business and postal address at **Tamag, Vigan City, Ilocos Sur, Philippines**, represented by **DR. GILBERT R. ARCE**, in his capacity as **University President**, hereafter referred to as **"THE SECOND PARTY"**.

WITNESSETH:

WHEREAS, the both parties manifest the willingness to enter into academic and non-academic ventures that will redound to their mutual benefits;

WHEREAS, the both parties agree to pursue collaboration in research and extension programs; cultural and scientific interests; faculty, staff and student exchanges; and other activities for the advancement of global excellence in education, governance, business, technology and health;

WHEREAS, the First Party, in its desire to satisfy growing demand for global higher education in Vietnam, would like to tap the expertise of the Second Party along its mature academic programs and as a party in future innovative academic programs, subject to existing laws and legal orders of the government of Vietnam;

Page 1 of 3

WHEREAS, the Second Party, as a mature institution of learning in the Philippines, commits itself to assist the First Party, while at the same time implores its assistance to enhance further the latter's existing programs to meet global students, subject to existing laws and legal orders of the Republic of the Philippines;

NOW THEREFORE, for and in consideration of the foregoing premises, parties agree that:

OBLIGATIONS

The University shall:

1. Provide and deploy qualified student teachers in English, Science and Mathematics;
2. Conduct supervisory visit by the Center for International Studies during the stay of the student teachers in Tan Trao University;
3. Gather feedback from Tan Trao University regarding the Student-Teachers' performance as basis in improving the program;
4. Take responsibility on the expenses of the Students for one airfare, pre-departure and arrival expenses;
5. Arrange and provide temporary entrance visas for deployed student teachers.

The Tan Trao University shall:

1. Accept and provide opportunities for student teachers to apply real world teaching experiences;
2. Provide the student teachers with best mentors to enhance their teaching competencies;
3. Provide necessary compliments by securing the safety of student teachers during their stay in Tan Trao University;
4. Allow the practice teachers to have access to information related to the school needed for the training;
5. Determine the number of student teachers to be deployed at Tan Trao University in any given time;
6. Provide one way airfare, transport, accommodation and subsistence daily allowance (no less than 2.500.000 Dong per month) to the student teachers during their stay in Tan Trao University;
7. Submit student teachers performance evaluation to the University of Northern Philippines;
8. Arrange and provide extended visas for deployed student teachers as required.

Page 2 of 3

This Agreement shall take effect immediately upon signing by all parties concerned and shall remain in force unless sooner terminated by mutual consent.

IN WITNESS WHEREOF, parties hereunto affixed their signatures this 4 th day of March 2016 at Tan Trao University.

TAN TRAO UNIVERSITY
By:

DR. NGUYEN BA DUC
President , Tan Trao University

UNIVERSITY OF NORTHERN PHILIPPINES
By:

DR. GILBERT R. ARCE
SUC President IV, Univ. of Northern Philippines

WITNESSES:

PHAM THI KIEU TRANG
Coordinator, Science management and International Affaird office

GENEROSO GUDELIO P. PAJARILLO, Ph.D.
Coordinator, Center for International Studies

NGUYEN VAN GIAP
Head, Science management and International Affaird office

CHRISTOPHER F. BUENO, Ed.D.
Dean, College of Teacher Education

4.   Suan Dusit University

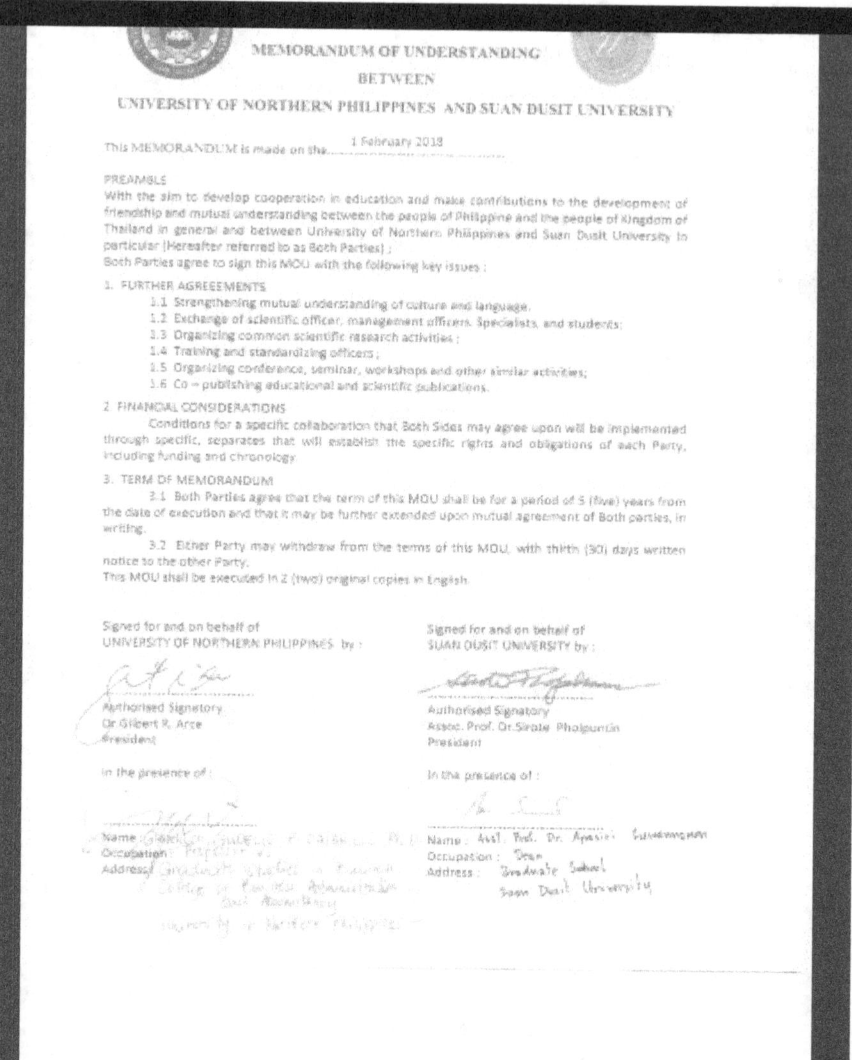

MEMORANDUM OF UNDERSTANDING

BETWEEN

UNIVERSITY OF NORTHERN PHILIPPINES AND SUAN DUSIT UNIVERSITY

This MEMORANDUM is made on the 1 February 2018

PREAMBLE

With the aim to develop cooperation in education and make contributions to the development of friendship and mutual understanding between the people of Philippine and the people of Kingdom of Thailand in general and between University of Northern Philippines and Suan Dusit University in particular (Hereafter referred to as Both Parties) ;

Both Parties agree to sign this MOU with the following key issues :

1. FURTHER AGREEEMENTS
    1.1 Strengthening mutual understanding of culture and language.
    1.2 Exchange of scientific officer, management officers, Specialists, and students;
    1.3 Organizing common scientific research activities ;
    1.4 Training and standardizing officers ;
    1.5 Organizing conference, seminar, workshops and other similar activities;
    1.6 Co – publishing educational and scientific publications.

2 FINANCIAL CONSIDERATIONS
    Conditions for a specific collaboration that Both Sides may agree upon will be implemented through specific, separates that will establish the specific rights and obligations of each Party, including funding and chronology.

3. TERM OF MEMORANDUM
    3.1 Both Parties agree that the term of this MOU shall be for a period of 5 (five) years from the date of execution and that it may be further extended upon mutual agreement of Both parties, in writing.
    3.2 Either Party may withdraw from the terms of this MOU, with thirtn (30) days written notice to the other Party.

This MOU shall be executed in 2 (two) original copies in English.

Signed for and on behalf of   Signed for and on behalf of
UNIVERSITY OF NORTHERN PHILIPPINES by :   SUAN DUSIT UNIVERSITY by :

Authorised Signatory   Authorised Signatory
Dr.Gilbert R. Arce   Assoc. Prof. Dr.Sirote Pholpuntin
President   President

In the presence of :   In the presence of :

Name :   Name : Asst. Prof. Dr. Ayasini Suwanwongkan
Occupation :   Occupation : Dean
Address :   Address : Graduate School
                                                               Suan Dusit University

5. Duangvipa School

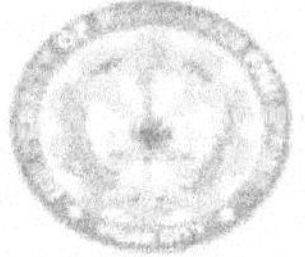

MEMORANDUM OF UNDERSTANDING

BETWEEN
DUANGVIPA SCHOOL (THAILAND)
and
UNIVERSITY OF NORTHERN PHILIPPINES (PHILIPPINES)

The **DIRECTOR** of **DUANGVIPA SCHOOL**, with office address as 146 Soi Ekachai 43, Ekachai Road, Bangbon Bangkok, Thailand 10150 and the **PRESIDENT** of **UNIVERSITY OF NORTHERN PHILIPPINES (UNP)**, Tamag, Vigan City, Ilocos Sur 2700 Philippines desire to promote their mutual interest in promoting academic cooperation and exchange between their institutions and in pursuant to the prevailing laws and regulations in their respective countries, as well as the policies and procedures of **DUANGVIPA SCHOOL** and **UNIVERSITY OF NORTHERN PHILIPPINES** concerning academic cooperation and collaboration, have reached the following scope and details of the Memorandum of Understanding:

1. The two institutions agree to encourage and promote cooperation on the following academic activities:

    a. Faculty, Staff and Student Exchange;

    b. Facilitation of in-country work experience for UNP students in relevant field of studies, and as potential career deployment;

    d. Joint research and extension activities, lectures, workshops, fora, symposia and seminars; and

    f. Other cooperation and collaboration activities in education.

2. Specific activities to be carried out under this Memorandum of Understanding shall be negotiated, consulted and agreed upon through a Memorandum of Agreement as its implementing guidelines. The Memorandum of Agreement within general framework of the Memorandum of Understanding shall detail all the financial arrangements and other requirements prior to the commencement of activities.

3. Only the English version of this Memorandum of Understanding and the subsequent Memorandum of Agreement have binding effect.

4. Modifications and/or amendments to this Memorandum of Understanding shall be instigated through mutual consent.

5. Any disputes arising from the execution of this Memorandum of Understanding, both institutions on the basis of mutual trust and benefit, shall be resolved through friendly consultation.

6. In case of termination of this Memorandum of Understanding, a written notice shall be served one (1) month in advance prior to the desired termination. Under such circumstances, any on-going activity under the Memorandum of Understanding covered by a certain Memorandum of Agreement shall be allowed completion under conditions prior to the notice of termination.

7. This Memorandum of Understanding shall be in effect from the date duly signed by designated officials of the respective institutions. The effective period of the Memorandum of Understanding shall be five years, and shall automatically be extended if any of the parties expresses in written notice desire to terminate or modify this Memorandum of Understanding.

8. That both parties execute this Memorandum of Understanding and further declare their willingness to enter into an agreement for its proper implementation.

IN WITNESS WHEREOF, the undersigned hereto affixed their signatures in this Memorandum of Understanding this ____th day of April 2016 in Bangkok, Thailand.

ACKNOWLEDGEMENT

Republic of the Philippines   )
Ilocos Sur) S. S.

BEFORE ME, a Notary Public for and in the Province of Ilocos Sur personally appeared.

Known to me and to me known to be same persons who executed the foregoing instrument which they signed and acknowledged to me as their free and voluntary act and deed, and of the entities that they represent.

This instrument consists of four (4) pages including this page wherein this Acknowledgement is written, and signed by the parties and witnesses on each page thereof.

WITNESS MY HAND AND NOTARIAL SEAL this ___MAY 1 0 2018_________ at Vigan City, Ilocos Sur.

CATALINO P. PAZ
NOTARY PUBLIC
EXPIRES DECEMBER 31, 2018
PTR NO. 842-15
IBP NO. PTR/OR-IBP-09-0305
ROLL NO. 72617/2-1 6-86
COMMISSION NO. 03-15-12-29-15
NOTARIAL SEAL V. IGAN SUR

6. Plookpanya School

MEMORANDUM OF UNDERSTANDING

BETWEEN
PLOOKPANYA SCHOOL (THAILAND)
and
UNIVERSITY OF NORTHERN PHILIPPINES (PHILIPPINES)

The DIRECTOR of PLOOKPANYA SCHOOL, with office address at 306/22 Soi Mitraphap 4, Liab Klongcholapratan Road, Nai Meaung, Mueang Nakhon Rachasima District, Thailand 3000 and the PRESIDENT of UNIVERSITY OF NORTHERN PHILIPPINES (UNP), Tamag, Vigan City, Ilocos Sur 2700 Philippines desire to promote their mutual interest in promoting academic cooperation and exchange between their institutions and in pursuant to the prevailing laws and regulations in their respective countries, as well as the policies and procedures of PLOOKPANYA SCHOOL and UNIVERSITY OF NORTHERN PHILIPPINES concerning academic cooperation and collaboration, have reached the following scope and details of the Memorandum of Understanding:

1. The two institutions agree to encourage and promote cooperation on the following academic activities:

   a. Faculty, Staff, Personnel and Student Exchanges;

   b. Facilitation of in-country work experience for UNP students in relevant field of studies, and as potential career deployment;

   c. Joint research and extension activities, lectures, workshops, fora, symposia and seminars;

   d. Exchange of academic materials, publications and other relevant scholarly information; and

e. Other cooperation and collaboration activities in education, governance, business, technology and health deemed appropriate mutually.

2. Specific activities to be carried out under this Memorandum of Understanding shall be negotiated, consulted and agreed upon through a Memorandum of Agreement as its implementing guidelines. The Memorandum of Agreement within general framework of the Memorandum of Understanding shall detail all the financial arrangements and other requirements prior to the commencement of activities.

3. Only the English version of this Memorandum of Understanding and the subsequent Memorandum of Agreement have binding effect.

4. Modifications and/or amendments to this Memorandum of Understanding shall be instigated through mutual consent.

5. Any disputes arising from the execution of this Memorandum of Understanding, both institutions on the basis of mutual trust and benefit, shall be resolved through friendly consultation.

6. In case of termination of this Memorandum of Understanding, a written notice shall be served one (1) month in advance prior to the desired termination. Under such circumstances, any on-going activity under the Memorandum of Understanding covered by a certain Memorandum of Agreement shall be allowed completion under conditions prior to the notice of termination.

7. This Memorandum of Understanding shall be in effect from the date duly signed by designated officials of the respective institutions. The effective period of the Memorandum of Understanding shall be five years, and shall automatically be extended if any of the parties expresses in written notice desire to terminate or modify this Memorandum of Understanding.

8. That both parties execute this Memorandum of Understanding and further declare their willingness to enter into an agreement for its proper implementation.

IN WITNESS WHEREOF, the undersigned hereto affixed their signatures in this Memorandum of Understanding this 21th day of October 2016 in Bangkok.

For:
PLOOKPANYA SCHOOL

MISS PATTAREE SURAROCHPRAJAK
School Director

MISS SUKANYA MUNIKOM
Deputy Director

For:
UNIVERSITY OF NORTHERN PHILIPPINES

GILBERT R. ARCE, EdD
SUC President IV

Witnessed By:

GENEROSO G. P. PAJARILLO, Ph.D.
Coordinator, Centre for International Studies

CHRISTOPHER F. BUENO, Ph.D.
Dean
College of Teacher Education

CRISTINA R. BUNDOC, DBA
Dean, CBAA

ACKNOWLEDGMENT

Republic of the Philippines   )

Ilocos Sur) S.S.

BEFORE ME, a Notary Public for and in the Province of Ilocos Sur personally appeared:

Known to me and to me known to be same persons who executed the foregoing instrument which they signed and acknowledged to me as their free and voluntary act and deed, and of the entities that they represent.

This instrument consists of four (4) pages including this page wherein this Acknowledgement is written, and signed by the parties and witnesses on each page thereof.

WITNESS MY HAND AND NOTARIAL SEAL this ______ of _____________ at Vigan City, Ilocos Sur.

7. Mulan Language School

MEMORANDUM OF AGREEMENT

BETWEEN
MULAN LANGUAGE SCHOOL HAT YAI (THAILAND)
and

UNIVERSITY OF NORTHERN PHILIPPINES (PHILIPPINES)

KNOW ALL MEN BY THESE PRESENTS:

This Memorandum of Agreement made and entered into by and between:

MULAN LANGUAGE SCHOOL HAT YAI, with office address at 3 304-306 ChockChai4 rd., Lat Phrao Bangkok Thailand 10230, represented by MS. WAKOTCHAKORN RAKKAMNERD, in her capacity as School Director, referred to as "THE SCHOOL"; and

UNIVERSITY OF NORTHERN PHILIPPINES with business and postal address at Tamag, Vigan City, Ilocos Sur, Philippines, represented by DR. GILBERT R. ARCE, in his capacity as University President, hereafter referred to as "THE UNIVERSITY".

WITNESSETH:

WHEREAS, the both parties manifest the willingness to enter into academic and non-academic ventures that will redound to their mutual benefits;

WHEREAS, the both parties agree to pursue faculty, staff and student exchanges; and other activities for the advancement of global excellence in education;

WHEREAS, the SCHOOL, in its desire to satisfy growing demand for global education in Thailand, would like to tap the expertise of the UNIVERSITY along its Teacher Education programs and as a party in future innovative academic programs, subject to existing laws and legal orders of the government of Thailand;

WHEREAS, the UNIVERSITY, as a mature institution of learning in the Philippines, commits itself to assist the SCHOOL, while at the same time implores

8. Nopparat Pattanasas School

311

MEMORANDUM OF AGREEMENT

BETWEEN

NOPPARAT PATTANASAS SCHOOL (THAILAND) and

UNIVERSITY OF NORTHERN PHILIPPINES (PHILIPPINES)

KNOW ALL MEN BY THESE PRESENTS:

This Memorandum of Agreement made and entered into by and between:

NOPPARAT PATTANASAS SCHOOL (NPS), with office address at 108/249 M.1 Rama 2 Road, Samaedam, Bangkhunthian, Bangkok, Thailand 10150, represented by MR. SORAAUS PUMGBANGKRADEE, in his capacity as Director, referred to as "THE SCHOOL"; and

UNIVERSITY OF NORTHERN PHILIPPINES with business and postal address at Tamag, Vigan City, Ilocos Sur, Philippines, represented by DR. GILBERT R. ARCE, in his capacity as University President, hereafter referred to as "THE UNIVERSITY".

WITNESSETH:

WHEREAS, the both parties manifest the willingness to enter into academic and non-academic ventures that will redound to their mutual benefits;

WHEREAS, the both parties agree to pursue faculty, staff and student exchanges; and other activities for the advancement of global excellence in education;

WHEREAS, the SCHOOL, in its desire to satisfy growing demand for global education in Thailand, would like to tap the expertise of the UNIVERSITY along its Teacher Education programs and as a party in future innovative academic programs, subject to existing laws and legal orders of the government of Thailand;

WHEREAS, the UNIVERSITY, as a mature institution of learning in the Philippines, commits itself to assist the SCHOOL, while at the same time implores its assistance to enhance further the latter's existing programs to meet global students, subject to existing laws and legal orders of the Republic of the Philippines;

Page 1 of 3

NOW THEREFORE, for and in consideration of the foregoing premises, parties agree that:

OBLIGATIONS

The University shall:

1. Provide and deploy qualified student teachers in English, Science and Mathematics;
2. Conduct supervisory visit by the Center for International Studies during the stay of the student teachers in Nopparat Pattanasas School;
3. Gather feedback from School regarding the Student-Teachers' performance as basis in improving the program;
4. Take responsibility on the expenses of the Students for one airfare, pre-departure and arrival expenses;
5. Arrange and provide temporary entrance visas for deployed student teachers; and
6. Responsible fully on the students during the entire practice teaching.

The School shall:

1. Accept and provide opportunities for student teachers to apply real world teaching experiences;
2. Provide the student teachers with best mentors to enhance their teaching competencies;
3. Provide necessary compliments by securing the safety of student teachers during their stay in Nopparat Pattanasas School;
4. Allow the practice teachers to have access to information related to the school needed for the training;
5. Determine the number of student teachers to be deployed at Nopparat Pattanasas School in any given time;
6. Provide one way airfare, transport, accommodation and subsistence daily allowance (no less than 300 baht per day) to the student teachers during their stay in Nopparat Pattanasas School;
7. Submit student teachers performance evaluation to the University of Northern Philippines;
8. Arrange and provide extended visas for deployed student teachers as required.

This Agreement shall take effect immediately upon signing by all parties concerned and shall remain in force unless sooner terminated by mutual consent.

IN WITNESS WHEREOF, parties hereunto affixed their signatures this 27th day of _____April_____ 2016 at Nopparat Pattanasas School.

Page 2 of 3

NOPPARAT PATTANASAS SCHOOL

By:

MR. SORAAUS PUNGBANGKRADEE
Director

UNIVERSITY OF NORTHERN PHILIPPINES

By:

DR. GILBERT R. ARCE
SUC President IV

WITNESSES:

MS. NOPPARAT PUNGBANGKRADEE
Vice Director

GENEROSO GUDELIO P. PAJARILLO, Ph.D.
Coordinator, Centre for International Studies

CHRISTOPHER F. BUENO, Ph.D.
Dean, College of Teacher Education

Page 3 of 3

9. National Commission for Culture and the Arts- Graduate Diploma in Cultural Education

NATIONAL COMMISSION FOR CULTURE AND THE ARTS
Philippine Cultural Education Program

MEMORANDUM OF AGREEMENT
Routing Form

UNIVERSITY OF NORTHERN PHILIPPINES
Grantee
(formerly Cebu Normal University)

GRADUATE DIPLOMA IN CULTURAL EDUCATION (LEVEL I)
Project Title

APRIL 1-MAY 31, 2018
Implementation Date

Res No. 2019-244

Grant: PhP 650,000.00

Prepared by: AMRIS P. VILLAREAL   Date: ________
Administrative Officer

JOSEPH "SONNY" E. CRISTOBAL   Date: ________
Director, PCEP

Initial Review by: RESIL SOLIS   Date: ________
Legal, NCCA

MARICHU G. TELLANO   Date: ________
Deputy Executive Director

Certified Funds: HERENCIO Y. LLAPITAN   Date: ________
Chief Accountant, NEFCA

Funds Obligated: MARLYN C. ESTRELLA   Date: ________
NCCA Budget Officer

Conforme: DR. GILBERT B. ARCE   Date: ________
Grantee

Approved /Signed by: RICO S. PABLEO JR.   Date: ________
Executive Director

Notarized by: Date: ________
Records Division

NOTE: Keep this form always on top of the MOA/MOU and attach a copy of the project document and Board
Resolution for guidance. After the MOA/MOU has been completely signed by all parties, be sure to
provide a copy o the following: voucher, project file and proponent.

Republic of the Philippines ● Office of the President
NATIONAL COMMISSION FOR CULTURE AND THE ARTS
Room 5-D 633 General Luna St., Intramuros 1002, Manila
Telephone: 63-(2) 568-4167 / Fax: 63-(2) 527-2192 local 529 / e-mail: pcep.secretariat@gmail.com /
website: http://ncca.ncc.ph/philippine-cultural-education-program-pcep/

Project: 2019 Graduate Diploma in Cultural Education (Level 8)
MOA: NCCA – University of Northern Philippines
MOA Duration: March 1, 2019 – August 31, 2019
Date of Implementation: April 1, 2019 – May 31, 2019

h. Integrate/weave in the transmission of values that would instill honesty, integrity, hard work, and concern for the environment in the various art forms, e.g. songs, literary pieces, performances, exhibitions, seminars, research, documentaries, etc., and in all other cultural activities organized for the public's appreciation in compliance with the United Nation's Millennium Development Goals (UN-MDGs);

i. As may be requested by the NCCA and upon availability of the Grantee, render free cultural services to access vulnerable groups and poor communities to free arts training rooted in pride of habitat, heritage, history, language and sensitivity to our social conditions, to generate their will for social transformation to promote a culture of peace and sustainable development;

j. Undertake the local and national promotion of the event and shall properly acknowledge the sponsorship of the NCCA in all media dissemination and all other collateral materials to promote the event. The minimum output shall be two (2) streamers exclusively acknowledging the NCCA as sponsor and placed at the strategic locations. The Commission shall be correctly spelled out: *National Commission for Culture and the Arts (NCCA)*. In the posters, flyers, invitations, press releases and programs, the NCCA logo shall be of equal size or larger than the logo of other major sponsors. Acknowledgement shall be done before, during and after the program;

k. Authorize the NCCA to include, partially or entirely the project output of the activity in the NCCA database and website (www.ncca.gov.ph) and for use in the NCCA reports or other collateral materials as the NCCA deems necessary for the promotion of culture and arts in the country. The NCCA agrees to acknowledge the source and authorship of the material used;

l. Coordinate regularly with the NCCA Staff for the implementation, monitoring and assessment of the PROJECT through letter, phone or sms text messaging. The NCCA shall assign a counterpart officer which shall coordinate and monitor on a regular basis the progress of the PROJECT;

m. Submit all liquidation reports as required by the NCCA within two (2) months after the implementation of the PROJECT. The Report of Checks Issued and Report of Disbursements shall be submitted to the NCCA NEPCA Division;

n. Submit **6 hard copies of Terminal Report** to the NCCA PCEP Secretariat. Terminal Reports shall be in accordance with the requirements of NCCA as provided for in the NCCA Guide on Terminal Report;

o. Submit A DVD containing a non-editable PDF (Portable Document File) format of the Report readable in a standard computer. The DVD must be of high quality (ex: Imation, Sony) in transparent case and properly labeled. Photos must be saved in JPG files for possible use in NCCA publications.

p. For Manuscript or Publication, the Report shall consist of 1 hardbound copy of the manuscript or book and 1 DVD containing the PDF format of the output.

q. Submit one (1) master copy of clear and broadcast quality video documentation of the project in DVD (AVI/MP4/MOV) format edited in such a ways that it can be used as instructional material for TV and classrooms, if applicable;

3. In case the GRANTEE fails to complete the project covered by this Memorandum of Agreement (MOA) without justifiable and lawful reason, or there is a material violations of the provisions of the MOA, or of COA Circular, the NCCA shall institute legal action against the GRANTEE.

4. In case the amount granted for the project was not fully utilized by the GRANTEE, it must return to the NCCA any amount unutilized, including interest, if any.

5. For its part, The NCCA must officially acknowledge its acceptance of the completed PROJECT if the results indicated in the inspection reports so warrant.

6. This AGREEMENT shall take effect on March 1, 2019, shall continue to be in force until August 31, 2019, after such time the GRANT shall have been completed with all the terms and conditions therein satisfied.

Page 3 of 5

316

Project: 2019 Graduate Diploma in Cultural Education (Level I)
MOA: NCCA – University of Northern Philippines
MOA Duration: March 1, 2019 – August 31, 2019
Date of Implementation: April 1, 2019 – May 31, 2019

7. Should there be an occurrence of any force majeure or similar condition which may delay or prevent the timely completion or fulfillment of this AGREEMENT and the attainment of its objective/s, the party with knowledge thereof shall notify the other in writing, specifying the cause and its implications and consequences upon the fulfillment of the GRANT, to enable the parties to adopt remedial measures.

8. In the event of unjustified failure of the GRANTEE to complete or fully implement the GRANT, in accordance with the terms and conditions stipulated in this AGREEMENT, or if the NCCA considered the PROJECT grossly unsatisfactory, or if there is any breach or violation thereof committed by the GRANTEE, the NCCA may forfeit the GRANT and terminate this AGREEMENT. Thereupon, the NCCA may take over the implementation/ execution of the GRANT without prejudice to holding the GRANTEE liable for the return/ reimbursement to the NCCA of the fund, or the balance thereof, received by the GRANTEE and for which it is accountable pursuant to this AGREEMENT. The GRANTEE shall also be liable under such civil action and/or criminal prosecution as may be warranted under existing laws.

9. The parties shall mutually agree upon any amendment or modification of this AGREEMENT or its renewal. No modification or amendment of this AGREEMENT shall be valid unless the same is in writing and signed by both parties. No waiver of any provision of this AGREEMENT shall be valid unless it is in writing and signed by the party against whom it is sought to be enforced.

10. Failure of a party at any time to insist upon strict performance of any condition, promise, agreement or understanding set forth herein shall not be construed as a waiver or relinquishment of the same or other condition, promise, agreement or understanding at a future time.

WHEREFORE, the parties hereto have hereunto affixed their signatures this _________ day of _________________ in the City of Manila, Philippines.

For the NCCA:

For the GRANTEE:

RICO S. PABLEO JR.
Executive Director

DR. GILBERT R. ARCE
President

Signed in the Presence of:

MARICHU G. TELLANO
Deputy Executive Director

DR. CHRISTOPHER F. BUENO
Project Director

JOSEPH J. CRISTOBAL
Director, PCEP

Certified Funds Available
in the Amount of PhP 650,000.00
CY 2019

HERENCIO V. LLAPITAN
Chief Accountant
OSH 02- 104375-7849 472- 0317

MEMORANDUM OF AGREEMENT

KNOW ALL MEN BY THESE PRESENTS:

This Memorandum of Agreement executed by and between:

The **COMMISSION ON HIGHER EDUCATION (CHED)**, an agency of the National Government organized and established under Republic Act No. 7722 otherwise known as the "Higher Education Act of 1994," with office address at HEDC Bldg., C.P. Garcia Ave., U.P. Diliman, Quezon City, represented herein by its Chairperson, **PATRICIA B. LICUANAN, Ph.D.**, herein referred to as **"FIRST PARTY"**;

-and-

The UNIVERSITY OF NORTHERN PHILIPPINES , a higher education institution with principal office at VIGAN CITY ILOCOS SUR, represented herein by its GILBERT R. ARCE, UNIVERSITY PRESIDENT herein referred to as **"SECOND PARTY"**;

and-

WITNESSETH: That,

WHEREAS, the **FIRST PARTY** is mandated by law to promote affordable quality and relevant higher education that is accessible to all; ensure academic freedom and promote its exercise and observance for the continuing intellectual growth, advancement of learning and research, development of responsible and effective leadership, education of high-level and middle-level professionals and the enrichment of the historical and cultural heritage of the Philippines;

WHEREAS, the **FIRST PARTY** is mandated by RA 10533 and its Implementing Rules and Regulations to help ensure a smooth transition to the K to 12 system by formulating appropriate strategies and mechanisms, which may cover changes in physical infrastructure or organizational and structural concerns, and partnerships between the government and other entities, along with ensuring the long-term viability of HEIs, and the alignment of higher education with the new curriculum in basic education;

WHEREAS, the **FIRST PARTY** recognizes that there is a need to provide financial support to the **SECOND PARTY** in order to upgrade its institutional capability and sustain the development efforts toward leveraging the opportunity provided by the K to 12 transition period to upgrade the Philippine higher education sector;

WHEREAS, CHED through Commission en Banc Resolution No. _____-______ (Annex "A") approved the project titled "SUSTAINING ACADEMIC EXCELLENCE IN THE TEACHER EDUCATION PROGRAM THROUGH INCLUSIVE EDUCATION AND

1

SUSTAINABLE DEVELOPMENT" (the "Project") for implementation by the **SECOND PARTY**.

NOW THEREFORE, for and in consideration of the foregoing premises, the parties hereto hereby agree as follows:

I.   ROLES AND RESPONSIBILITIES OF THE PARTIES

1. The **FIRST PARTY** shall:

    1.1.   Provide funding assistance to the **SECOND PARTY** in the amount of FOUR MILLION **Pesos (Php 4,000,000.00)** for the implementation of the Project in accordance with the approved Project Proposal (PP) (Annex "B"), Work and Financial Plan (WFP) (Annex "C").

    1.2.   Provide funding assistance to the **SECOND PARTY**, as follows:

        1.2.1.   80% of the approved budget upon signing of this document or the receipt of notice to proceed by the **SECOND PARTY**, whichever comes later;

        1.2.2.   20% of the approved budget upon 80% completion of the project, and submission of an accomplishment report indicating such progress, reviewed and endorsed by HEI head.

    1.3.   Through its Monitoring and Evaluation Team, see to it that funds provided to the **SECOND PARTY** shall be used properly and for the intended purposes specified.

2. The **SECOND PARTY** shall:

    2.1.   Ensure proper implementation of the Project;

    2.2.   Properly utilize the funds provided by the **FIRST PARTY** and see to it that these are used for the purposes for which the same are intended, in accordance with PP and WFP subject to the usual accounting and auditing rules and regulations;

    2.3.   Commence the cascading of best practices program as indicated in the submitted Proposal Design for Cascading Best Practices section of the PP;

    2.4.   Adhere to the obligations of an HEI Grantee under Article VII of the CHED Memorandum Order No. 33, series of 2016, entitled "Guidelines for Institutional Development and Innovation Grants under the K to 12 Transition Program";

    2.5.   Promptly report to the Commission the occurrence of any event or condition which might delay or prevent the timely completion of the project embraced herein, specifying in writing the amount of time

2

involved, the causes of the delay, and its subsequent implications on the entire timetable, work schedule, and budget of the project;

2.6. Request for project extension to the **FIRST PARTY** in writing, in case the need arises. The said request shall be subject for approval by the CHED Commission En Banc. It shall be understood that the grant extension does not bring with it additional funding from the **FIRST PARTY**;

2.7. Issue an Official Receipt for every amount received from the CHED;

2.8. Deposit the funds received from the **FIRST PARTY** with any government authorized depository bank nearest the program site;

2.9. Separately keep and maintain any/all necessary accounting ledgers/records for the project which shall be voluntarily submitted whenever required and subjected to monitoring and evaluation of the CHED Authorized Representative/s and furnish fully the certified true copies of any/all required documents;

2.10. Submit progress reports to the **FIRST PARTY** quarterly or as required;

2.11. Submit accomplishment/terminal report to the **FIRST PARTY** within sixty (60) days after the completion of the project.

2.12. Submit a liquidation report to the **FIRST PARTY**, certified correct by an accountant and approved by the head of the institution within sixty (60) days after the completion of the project. Private HEIs must have their reports audited by an external auditor.

2.13. Return to the CHED any/all unused balance of the project fund, including any/all income/interest earned/generated from the same, upon completion of the project within forty-five (45) but not more than sixty (60) calendar days, pursuant to **Executive Order No. 338**;

2.14. Abide by the provisions of **COA Circular No. 94-103** which is made an integral part hereof and other government laws, rules and regulations directly or indirectly pertaining to projects funded either fully or partly by government agencies

2.15. Adhere to the prescribed accounting entries for booking up property/equipment purchased out of project funds.

II.   **INTELLECTUAL PROPERTY/OWNERSHIP**

Any equipment and/or output resulting from the conduct of the project under grant shall be owned by the UNIVERSITY OF NORTHERN PHILIPPINES through a donation by the Commission in accordance with the provisions of Republic Act No. 10055 and other related laws, rules and regulations. The UNIVERSITY OF

3

NORTHERN PHILIPPINES shall ensure due acknowledgement of the contribution of the CHED through its Institutional Development and Innovation Grant.

## III.	PENALTY CLAUSE

The agreement shall be implemented as agreed upon in accordance with the terms and conditions stipulated herein. Failure on the part of either/any party to comply with the provision of this Agreement will warrant its discontinuance and/or administrative, civil, and/or criminal actions against responsible officers and employees of the Erring Party.

## IV.	WAIVER OF ACCOUNTABILITIES

Upon successful completion of the Project, including implementation and the submission of the final deliverables, the SECOND PARTY shall be relieved of all accountabilities under this MOA and the program after the CHED, through its K to 12 Transition Program Management Unit, has conducted and inspection determining or verifying that all final deliverables have been submitted by the SECOND PARTY.

## V.	SEPARABILITY CLAUSE

In the event that one or more provisions contained herein shall be held invalid, illegal, or unenforceable in any respect and for any reason, the remaining provisions shall remain valid, legal and, enforceable.

## VI.	DOCUMENTS COMPRISING THIS AGREEMENT

All appendages hereto attached are hereby expressly made an integral part of this agreement by reference, excluding inconsistencies with any/all part, terms, and conditions contained in this Memorandum of Agreement.

## VII.	EFFECTIVITY OF THE AGREEMENT

This Agreement shall take effect upon the receipt of the first tranche of funds by the SECOND PARTY for the project implementation, and shall be in effect for a period of 12 months.

(signature page follows)

4

IN WITNESS WHEROF, the parties hereunto have affixed their respective signatures this _______ day of DEC 19 2016 at _______________ , Philippines

COMMISION ON HIGHER
EDUCATION
FIRST PARTY

UNIVERSITY OF NORTHERN
PHILIPPINES
SECOND PARTY

By:

By:

PATRICIA B. LICUANAN, Ph.D.
Chairperson

GILBERT R. ARCE, Ed. D.
President

Signed in the presence of:

KAROL MARK R. YEE
Program Director
CHED K to 12 Transition
Program Management Unit

CHRISTOPHER F. BUENO, Ph.D.
Dean, College of Teacher Education
University of Northern Philippines

CERTIFIED AS TO AVAILABILITY OF FUNDS

MRYA PAZ B. MANALO
Chief Accountant
Higher Education Development Fund
Commission of Higher Education

CERTIFIED TRUE COPY

Republic of the Philippines
UNIVERSITY OF NORTHERN PHILIPPINES
Vigan City

EXCERPTS FROM THE MINUTES OF THE SECOND QUARTER REGULAR BOARD MEETING OF THE UNP BOARD OF REGENTS HELD AT THE CONFERENCE ROOM OF THE OFFICE OF THE CHED CHAIRPERSON , HEDC BUILDING, PRES. C.P. GARCIA AVENUE, UP DILIMAN, QUEZON CITY ON JUNE 9, 2016

BOARD RESOLUTION NO. 51, S. 2016

A RESOLUTION APPROVING THE MEMORANDA OF UNDERSTANDING FORGED BETWEEN THE UNIVERSITY OF NORTHERN PHILIPPINES AND DUANGVIPA SCHOOL (THAILAND) AND WITH NOPPARAT PATTANASAS SCHOOL (THAILAND)

WHEREAS, the memoranda of understanding were inked by the President of the University of Northern Philippines located at Barangay Tamag, Vigan City, Ilocos Sur, Philippines and the authorized representatives of Duangvipa School (Thailand) located at 146 Soi Ekachai 43, Ekachai Road, Bangbon, Bangkok, Thailand 10150 and Nopparat Pattanasas School (Thailand) located at 108/249 M.1 Rama 2 Road, Samaedam, Bangkhontian, Bangkok, Thailand 10150.

WHEREAS, these MOU are on faculty/staff exchange, facilitation of in-country work experience of UNP students in relevant field of studies and as potential career deployment and joint research and extension activities, lectures, workshops, fora, symposia, seminars, and other cooperation and collaboration activities in education;

WHEREAS, the memoranda of understanding possess mutual interest in promoting academic cooperation and exchange between the University of Northern Philippines and Duangvipa School (Thailand) and Nopparat Pattanasas School (Thailand) pursuant to the prevailing laws and regulations of the Republic of the Philippines and Thailand as well as policies and procedures of the aforementioned educational institution;

WHEREAS, the memoranda of understanding were presented to the UNP Board of Regents during the Second Quarter Regular Board Meeting held at the Conference Room of the Office of CHED Chairperson on June 9, 2016;

NOW THEREFORE, BE IT RESOLVED AS IT IS HEREBY RESOLVED, that the UNP Board of Regents approves the memoranda of understanding inked by the President of the University of Northern Philippines located at Barangay Tamag, Vigan City, Ilocos Sur, Philippines and authorized representatives of Duangvipa School (Thailand) located at 146 Soi Ekachai 43, Ekachai Road, Bangbon, Bangkok, Thailand 10150 and Nopparat Pattanasas School (Thailand) located at 108/249 M.1 Rama 2 Road, Samaedam, Bangkhontian, Bangkok, Thailand 10150 on faculty/staff exchange, facilitation of in-country work experience of UNP students in relevant fields of studies and as potential career deployment and joint research and extension activities, lectures, workshops, fora, symposia, seminars, and other cooperation and collaboration activities in education;

ADOPTED during the Second Quarter Regular Board Meeting of the UNP Board of Regents held at the Conference Room of the Office of the CHED Chairperson, 4th Floor, HEDC Building, Pres. C.P. Garcia Avenue, UP Diliman, Quezon City on June 9, 2016.

APPROVED

Certified True and Correct:

WILBERTO P. TABUTOL
University/Board Secretary

Attested:

GILBERT R. ARCE, ED. D.
Vice Chairperson, UNP BOR
President, UNP

Board Resolution No. 51, Series of 2016   Page 1

Republic of the Philippines
UNIVERSITY OF NORTHERN PHILIPPINES
Vigan City

EXCERPTS FROM THE MINUTES OF THE SECOND QUARTER REGULAR BOARD MEETING OF THE UNP BOARD OF REGENTS HELD AT THE CONFERENCE ROOM OF THE OFFICE OF THE CHED CHAIRPERSON , HEDC BUILDING, PRES. C.P. GARCIA AVENUE, UP DILIMAN, QUEZON CITY ON JUNE 9, 2016

BOARD RESOLUTION NO. 52, S. 2016

A RESOLUTION APPROVING THE MEMORANDA OF AGREEMENT FORGED BETWEEN THE UNIVERSITY OF NORTHERN PHILIPPINES AND DUANGVIPA SCHOOL (THAILAND), NOPPARAT PATTANASAS SCHOOL (THAILAND), AND ROMCHATRA FOUNDATION (THAILAND)

WHEREAS, the memoranda of agreement were inked by the University of Northern Philippines located at the Quirino Blvd., Tamag, Vigan City, Ilocos Sur, Philippines and Duangvipa School (Thailand) located 146 Soi Ekachai 43, Ekachai Road, Bangbon, Bangkok, Thailand; Nopparat Pattanasas School (Thailand) located at 108/249 M.1 Rama 2 Road, Samaedam, Bangkhuntian, Bangkok, Thailand 10150; and Romchatra Foundation (Thailand) located at Charoenkrung Road, Samphantawong District, Bangkok, Thailand;

WHEREAS, the memoranda of agreement were signed by Dr. Gilbert R. Arce in his capacity as President of the University of Northern Philippines, Ms. Chavalee Sakulismpaiboon in her capacity as Director of the Duangvipa School; Mr. Soraaus Pungbangkradee in his capacity as Director of the Nopparat Pattanasas School; and Mr. Phraprommangkalachen in his capacity Chairman and President of the Romchatra Foundation;

WHEREAS, the memoranda of agreement are on faculty\staff exchange, facilitation of in-country work experience for UNP students in relevant fields of studies and as potential career deployment and joint research and extension activities, lectures, workshops, for a, symposia and seminars and other cooperation and collaboration activities in education;

WHEREAS, this was presented to the members of the UNP Governing Board during the Second Quarter Regular Board Meeting held at the Conference Room, Office of the CHED Chairperson, 4th Floor, HEDC Building, Pres. C.P. Garcia Avenue, UP Diliman, Quezon City on June 9, 2016;

NOW THEREFORE: BE IT RESOLVED AS IT IS HEREBY RESOLVED, that the UNP Board of Regents approves the memoranda of agreements were inked by the University of Northern Philippines located at the Quirino Blvd., Tamag, Vigan City, Ilocos Sur, Philippines and Duangvipa School (Thailand) located 146 Soi Ekachai 43, Ekachai Road, Bangbon, Bangkok, Thailand; Nopparat Pattanasas School (Thailand) located at 108/249 M.1 Rama 2 Road, Samaedam, Bangkhuntian, Bangkok, Thailand 10150; and Romchatra Foundation (Thailand) located at Charoenkrung Road, Samphantawong District, Bangkok, Thailand on faculty\staff exchange, facilitation of in-country work experience for UNP students in relevant fields of studies and as potential career deployment and joint research and extension activities, lectures, workshops, for a, symposia and seminars and other cooperation and collaboration activities in education;

As of 9 October 2017

i. The sending university shall conduct the pre-departure orientation for the participating students.

j. SEAMEO Secretariat will issue e-Certificate of Completion only for the students who completely submit their blog address and evaluation form to the person in charge of SEAMEO Secretariat.

k. The 5th evaluation meeting will be conducted in Tadulako University, Palu, Indonesia in 3-4 April 2018. The next batch of program of SEA-Teacher 2018 will be discussed at the meeting.

Signed in Chiang Mai, Thailand on the 9th day of October 2017 and Witnessed by SEAMEO Secretariat, Thailand.

LETTER OF AGREEMENT
AMONG UNIVERSITIES OF INDONESIA-PHILIPPINES-THAILAND
UNDER THE PROJECT "PRE-SERVICE STUDENT TEACHER EXCHANGE IN SOUTHEAST ASIA"
(SEA-TEACHER PROJECT)

Herewith partners:

Southeast Asian Ministers of Education Organization (SEAMEO) Secretariat, a regional intergovernmental organization established in 1965 among governments of Southeast Asian countries to promote regional cooperation in education, science and culture, located in Bangkok, Thailand, represented in this document by its Director, Dr. Ir. Gatot Hari Priowirjanto. The participating universities below agree to join the project.

Indonesia Universities:

1. Halu Oleo University
2. Indonesia University of Education, Bandung
3. Institut Teknologi Sepuluh Nopember, Surabaya
4. Islamic University of Indonesia, Yogyakarta
5. Lambung Mangkurat University, Banjarmasin
6. Pakuan University, Bogor
7. Pasundan University, Bandung
8. Pattimura University,
9. Sebelas Maret University, Surakarta
10. Sepuluh Nopember Institute of Technology, Surabaya
11. Sriwijaya University, Palembang
12. State University of Makassar, Makassar
13. STMIK Bina Insani, Kota Bekasi
14. Syiah Kuala University, Banda Aceh
15. Tadulako University, Palu
16. Tanjungpura University, Pontianak
17. Universitas Muria Kudus
18. Universitas Negeri Padang, Padang
19. University of Bengkulu

As of 9 October 2017

20. University of Borneo, Tarakan
21. University of Jember, Jember
22. University of Lampung, Bandar Lampung
23. University of Mataram, Mataram
24. University of Muhammadiyah Prof. Dr Hamka, Jakarta
25. Universitas Muhammadiyah Purwokerto, Purwokerto
26. University of PGRI Yogyakarta, Yogyakarta
27. University of Sarjanawiyata Tamansiswa, Yogyakarta
28. Yogyakarta State University, Yogyakarta
29. Kalimantan Islamic University, Banjarmasin

Philippines Universities:

1. Ateneo De Naga University, Naga City
2. De La Salle University, Manila
3. Far Eastern University, Manila
4. Iloilo Science and Technology University, Iloilo City
5. Mindanao State University-Iligan Institute of Technology, Iligan City
6. Pangasinan State University, Pangasinan
7. Philippine Normal University, Manila
8. Roosevelt College Inc., Cainta, Rizal
9. Saint Louis University, Baguio City
10. Saint Mary's University, Nueva Vizcaya
11. Technological Institute of the Philippines, Quezon City
12. University of San Carlos, Cebu City
13. University of San Jose-Recoletos, Cebu City
14. University of Southeastern Philippines, Davao City
15. West Visayas State University, Iloilo City
16. Central Luzon State University, Nueva Ecija
17. Tarlac Agricultural University, Camiling Tarlac

CERTIFIED TRUE AND CORRECT

Dr Gatot Hari Priowirjanto
Director
SEAMEO Secretariat

Thailand Universities:
1. Buriram Rajabhat University, Buriram
2. Chiang Mai Rajabhat University, Chiang Mai
3. Chiang Rai Rajabhat University, Chiang Rai
4. Khon Kaen University, Khon Kaen
5. Lampang Rajabhat University, Lampang
6. Nakhon Pathom Rajabhat University, Nakhon Pathom
7. Nakhon Ratchasima Rajabhat University, Nakhon Ratchasima
8. Nakhon Si Thammarat Rajabhat University, Nakhon Si Thammarat
9. Phetchaburi Rajabhat University, Phetchaburi

As of 9 October 2017

10. Phranakhon Rajabhat University, Bangkok
11. Phranakhon Si Ayutthaya Rajabhat University, Phra Nakhon Si Ayutthaya
12. Pibulsongkram Rajabhat University, Phitsanulok
13. Rajabhat Maha Sarakham University, Maha Sarakham
14. Suan Sunandha Rajabhat University, Bangkok
15. Suratthani Rajabhat University, Surat Thani
16. Udon Thani Rajabhat University, Udon Thani
17. Valaya Alongkorn Rajabhat University, Patum Thani
18. Loei Rajabhat University, Loei

Agree as follows:

To join the SEA Teacher Project among Indonesia, Philippines and Thailand Universities. The participating universities agree that:

a. The 5ʰ batch of exchange will start **22 January – 18 February 2018** for 1 month (30 Days)(equivalent to 2 credit semester) for practicum (teaching experience) in the school networks of receiving universities.

b. The sending university of pre-service students shall provide support in arranging for the air fare, meals/ pocket money, health, accident, and travel insurance of the participating students.

c. The major/specialization will be but not limited to Math, Science, English, Economics, Physical Education, Elementary School, Social Studies, Pre-School.

d. The receiving university will be responsible in providing schools as a practicum place and provides opportunities for students in particular teaching hours and other arrangement as stated in the SEA-Teacher guidelines.

e. The receiving university will be responsible for accommodation and transportation service from and to the nearest airport.

f. The receiving university must provide mentor for participating students.

g. The agreement will be implemented in reciprocal way.

h. The eligibility of the students will be ensured by the sending and receiving universities.

As of 9 October 2017

Signed by

Indonesia Universities:

Dr Jamludin
Dean of Teacher Training and Education
Halu Oleo University

Prof Dr H Didi Suherdi, M Ed
Head
English Language Education Department
Indonesia University of Education

Prof Dr Basuki Widodo
Dean
Faculty of Mathematics, Computation and Data Science
Institut Teknologi Sepuluh Nopember

Irma Windy Astuti
Head
English Language Education Department
Islamic University of Indonesia

Mr Arief Budiman
Director International Office
Lambung Mangkurat University

Drs Deddy Sofyan, M Pd
Dean
Faculty of Teacher Training and Education
Pasuan University

Dr Cartono
Vice Dean for Academic Affairs
Faculty of Education
Pasundan University

Prof Dr Theresia Laurens
Dean
Faculty of Teacher Training and Education
Pattimura University

As of 9 October 2017

Signed by

Indonesia Universities:

Dr Jamludin Dean of Teacher Training and Education Halu Oleo University	Prof Dr H Didi Suherdi, M Ed Head English Language Education Department Indonesia University of Education
Prof Dr Basuki Widodo Dean Faculty of Mathematics, Computation and Data Science Institut Teknologi Sepuluh Nopember	Irma Windy Astuti Head English Language Education Department Islamic University of Indonesia
Mr Arief Budiman Director International Office Lambung Mangkurat University	Drs Deddy Sofyan, M Pd Dean Faculty of Teacher Training and Education Pakuan University
Dr Cartono Vice Dean for Academic Affairs Faculty of Education Pasundan University	Prof Dr Theresia Laurens Dean Faculty of Teacher Training and Education Pattimura University

330

As of 9 October 2017

Signed by

Indonesia Universities:

Dr Jamludin
Dean of Teacher Training and Education
Halu Oleo University

Prof Dr H Didi Suherdi, M Ed
Head
English Language Education Department
Indonesia University of Education

Prof Dr Basuki Widodo
Dean
Faculty of Mathematics, Computation and Data Science
Institut Teknologi Sepuluh Nopember

Irma Windy Astuti
Head
English Language Education Department
Islamic University of Indonesia

Mr Arief Budiman
Director International Office
Lambung Mangkurat University

Drs Deddy Sofyan, M Pd
Dean
Faculty of Teacher Training and Education
Pakuan University

Dr Cartono
Vice Dean for Academic Affairs
Faculty of Education
Pasundan University

Prof Dr Theresia Laurens
Dean
Faculty of Teacher Training and Education
Pattimura University

331

As of 9 October 2017

Signed by

Indonesia Universities:

Dr Jamludin
Dean of Teacher Training and Education
Halu Oleo University

Prof Dr H Didi Suherdi, M Ed
Head
English Language Education Department
Indonesia University of Education

Prof Dr Basuki Widodo
Dean
Faculty of Mathematics, Computation and Data Science
Institut Teknologi Sepuluh Nopember

Irma Windy Astuti
Head
English Language Education Department
Islamic University of Indonesia

Mr Arief Budiman
Director International Office
Lambung Mangkurat University

Drs Deddy Sofyan, M Pd
Dean
Faculty of Teacher Training and Education
Pakuan University

Dr Cartono
Vice Dean for Academic Affairs
Faculty of Education
Pasundan University

Prof Dr Theresia Laurens
Dean
Faculty of Teacher Training and Education
Pattimura University

Republic of the Philippines
UNIVERSITY OF NORTHERN PHILIPPINES
Tamag, Vigan City
2700 Ilocos Sur

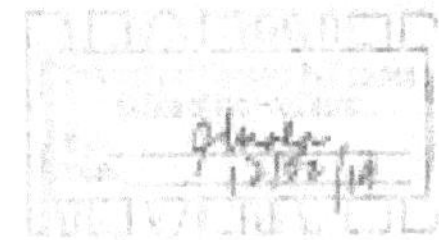

College of Teacher Education
Website: www.unp.edu.ph Mail: deancte@yahoo.com
Tel. #: (077) 674-0789

December 2, 2019

Dr. Erwin F. Cadorna
President
University of Northern Philippines
Vigan, Ilocos Sur

Sir:

Greetings!

This is to submit the modest results of the Board Licensure Examination for Professional Teachers (BLEPT) conducted last September 2019 for the Bachelor of Elementary Education, Bachelor of Secondary Education and Bachelor Science in Industrial Education in the College of Teacher Education. The national passing rate for Elementary Education is 31.34 percent and Secondary Education is 79.21 percent.

Furthermore, this is the overall breakdown of the first taker passers for the Bachelor of Secondary Education including Bachelor of Science Industrial Education and Bachelor of Secondary Education:

Degree	First Taker Passers	Failed	Total	Percentage Rating for Passers (%)
A. Bachelor of Elementary Education	92	7	99	92.99
B. Bachelor of Secondary Education	141	37	171	79.21

For the specific breakdown, may I present the program performance of the elementary, secondary and industrial education to appreciate the academic impact of the innovations and reforms conducted by the college for the last four (4) years in academic admission, maintain quality and excellence in the Teacher Education program.

Degree	First Taker Passers	Failed	Total	Percentage Rating for Passers (%)
A. Bachelor of Secondary Education				
English	16	2	18	88.88
Filipino	15	2	17	88.23
Math	15	1	16	93.75
Science	24	1	25	96.00
MAPEH (Physical Education)	21	4	25	84.00
Social Studies	14	4	18	77.70
B. Bachelor of Elementary Education				
General Education	70	6	76	95.65
Early Childhood Education	22	1	23	95.65
C. Bachelor of Science in Industrial Education				
Electronics Technology	3	0	3	100.00
Practical Arts	4	0	4	100.00

333

It must be noted that the college pursues the universal access to tertiary education has provided the education assistance of the poor parents (farmers, fishermen and other professionals with low income) that given the opportunity to study in the college from Ilocos Sur and Ilocos Norte. However, the poor but deserving students have passed through the admission policy for the College Admission Test (CAT) of 78 percent which is now 80 percent and Teaching Aptitude Test (TAT) passers to compensate the access to education program in the Teacher Education. The college further strengthened the local review classes and forging partnership with the CBRC as outsource provider in the BLEPT.

The aforementioned educational reforms provided the conduit of well-prepared LET takers to ensure the high passing rate. Furthermore, the presence of the highly competent and experience professionals contributed to the foundation of the students' pedagogical and content knowledge. It has already utilized the 21" century skills and the outcome-based education in the curriculer to ensure the needed pedagogical, technological and content knowledge are integrated in the learning competence to ensure the achievement of quality and excellence in tertiary education. This is in conformance with the risk register of ISO 9001:2015 to ensure the desired percentage average for the BLEPT passers.

In the case of the teaching competence, education and experience to ensure quality and excellence academic impact complies with QMS standards (ISO: 9001:2019) and maintaining the Center of Development that achieve to modest result of the BLEPT last September19, 2019. Likewise, the faculty members who handled the professional subjects have the teaching competence, relevant experience, dedication and commitment to ensure the graduates to be fully competent and expert in their field of specialization. Finally, the faculty members ensure that the management of learning by the pedagogical and classroom-based requirements are fully fulfilled for client satisfaction based on the approved learning design and regulatory measures of CHED

These academic reforms and innovations including the compliance of the QMS Standards and best practices of the Center of Development of the college have achieved the modest result of the BLEPT ratings that justifies the quality and excellence in the teacher education program in the University of Northern Philippines.

Thank you for your support to continually achieve the Center of Development for the Teacher Education program.

Very truly yours,

CHRISTOPHER F. BUENO, PhD
Dean, College of Teacher Education

Copy furnished: Office of the Vice President for Academic Affairs

ABOUT THE AUTHOR

The author is the Dean with the academic rank of Professor 6 of the College of Teacher Education, University of Northern Philippines, UNESCO Heritage City of Vigan. He was recipient of the Distinguished World Book Awards 2013 during the World Research Festival 2013 Award (IAMURE), Marco Polo Hotel, Davao City. He is an author and editor to the various published Amazon books in the field of Social Sciences, Education and Public Administration.

As to his recent accomplishments in the College of Teacher Education, he work out the granting of the Center of Development and the CHED Grants on "Sustaining Academic Excellence in the Teacher Education Program through Inclusive Education and Sustainable Development "- Grantee under CMO No. 33, series of 2016.

He initiated and implemented sustained International Linkages and Consortia in response to the strategic location of the College of Teacher Education, University of Northern Philippines at the UNESCO Heritage City of Vigan (Seven Wonder City of the World) to support cultural heritage and the Socio-Cultural Blueprint of ASEAN integration:

1) Editor of the Technical Assistance for Book Publication entitled "Belt and Road Initiative of the Maritime Silk Road Confucius Institute" (2017) and "One Belt One Road: Universal Perspectives in World Peace and Development through Change, Innovation, Idealism and Freedom" (2016) for Dr. Phraprommangkalachan, President Romchatra Foundation and Maritime Silk Road Confucius Institute of Hanban published in Amazon.

2) The establishment of the Learning Resource Center contributes to the sustained partnership and linkages of Romchatra Foundation as the associate member of the Maritime Silk Road Confucius Institute with the substantial contributions of the College of Teacher Education on the following areas:

a) The technical assistance of the book publications of the "One Belt One Road Initiative" of the Maritime Silk Road Confucius Institute. These books are internationally published in the Amazon (Create Independent Publishing Company) sold in the ASEAN countries including Europe and America.

b) The Hanban publications of the Maritime Silk Road Confucius Institute with the participation of the University of Northern Philippines as the Associate Member in ASEAN Foreign Universities.

d) The participation of the 11th Global Confucius Institute Conference held at Kunming, Yunnan Province, China from December 10-11, 2016 which the University of Northern Philippines provided the books to be distributed in the Members and Officials of the ASEAN Confucius Institute including Dali University in China.

3. The academic facilitation and collaboration of the Memorandum of Understanding (MOU) and Memorandum of Agreement (MOA) of Tan Trao University, Vietnam which was signed last March 10, 2016 for the research dissemination and student exchange program that deployed qualified students teachers for the College of Teacher Education and provided student teachers of Tan Trao University to apply real world teaching experience on cultural diversity. There was a substantial financial logistics support utilized in the bringing sustained student exchange program for Vietnam.

a) The academic collaboration of the International Conference with the theme " Assessing Primary Students by Approaching and Evaluating their Competence-A Possible Approach to Pedagogic Institutions in Vietnam.

b) The participation of student exchange program of two (2) BSEd students in the fourth-month internship to teach English Language for the faculty and students of Tan Trao University in 2016.

c) Student Exchange Program- The Vietnamese students were exposed to the CTE Best Practices in classroom instruction, Ilokano language and culture (MTB-MLE), teacher education extra-curricular activities last May 5-30, 2017. The accepted Vietnamese students were specialized in primary schools, literature education, physical and environment science, land and environment science.

d) Pre-Service Teacher Exchange Program of Tan Trao University with the participation of the Senior High School Teachers in providing academic support of the K to 12 curricula, Ilocano culture, Vigan Cultural Heritage activities and English Language Proficiency class for the Vietnamese students.

4. The participation of the SEA Teacher Program under the Southeast Asia Minister of Education Organization (SEAMEO) in the implementation of twinning student exchange program for their academic exposures with extra-curricular activities, cultural heritage experiences in the UNESCO Heritage City of Vigan. The participating Foreign Universities for the Pre-service Student Teachers Exchange Program in Southeast Asia are the following:
   a) Indonesia University of Education (UPI), Bandung Indonesia
   b) Sebelas Maret University (UNS), Surukarta, Indonesia,
   c) Nakon S. Thammarat Rajabhat (NSTRU), Thammarat,Thailand
   d) Buriram Rajabhat University (BRU), Buriram University

5. Active Role as Global Collaborator in the International Linkages of the Romachatra Foundation in Thailand and the eventual establishment of Maritime Silk Road Confucius Institute Learning Resource Center, at the College of Teacher Education (4th Floor, CTE Academic Building)
   a) Academic Collaboration and Student Exchange Program- Mulan Language School Hat Yai, Bangkok Thailand
   b) Student Exchange Program - Plookpanya School, Nai Meang Nakhon Rachasima District, Thailand 3000
   c) Student Exchange Program-Tan Trao University, Tuyen Quang Province, Vietnam
   d) Pre-Service Student Teacher Exchange in Southeast Asia (SEA-Teacher) a project of Southeast Asian Ministers of Education Organization (SEAMEO)

6. International Distinguished World Book Awardee and Book Amazon Publications in the Field of Social Sciences, Education and Public Administration

a) *Contemporary Republic: The Emerging Political and Economic Philosophy of the 21st Century* Amazon Independent Publishing Inc. (August 2012)
   ISBN-13:978-1479157808/ISBN-10:1479157805
   http://www.amazon.co.uk/Contemporary-Republic-Christopher-FusterBuenp/dp/1479157805/ref=sr_1_4?s=books&ie=UTF8&qid=1365511739&sr=1-4

b) *2013 Contemporary Republic: The Space Age Philosophy and Culture of the 30th Century.* Amazon Independent Publishing Inc. (June 2013)
   ISBN-10: 1490386793 / ISBN-13: 978-1490386799
   http://www.amazon.com/2013-Contemporary-Republic-Philosophy-Culture/dp/1490386793

d) *Culture : From Primitive Society to the Space Age*
   Amazon Independent Publishing Inc. (June 2013)
   ISBN-10: 1490431985/ ISBN-13: 978-1490431987
   http://www.amazon.com/Culture-From-Primitive-Society-Space/dp/1490431985

e) *Political Science : The Modern View of Government, State and Politics*
   Amazon Independent Publishing Inc. (August 2012)
   ISBN-13: 978-1479178124/ ISBN-10:1479178128
   http://www.amazon.co.uk/Political-Science-Modern-Government-Politics/dp/1479178128/ref=sr_1_1?s=books&ie=UTF8&qid=1365511739&sr=1-1

f) *Socio-Anthro: Sociology and Anthropology*
   Amazon Independent Publishing Inc. (August 2012)
   ISBN-13: 978-1479199402 / ISBN-10: 1479199400
   http://www.amazon.co.uk/Socio-Anthro-Christopher-Fuster-Bueno-PhD/dp/1479199400/ref=sr_1_5?s=books&ie=UTF8&qid=1365511739&sr=1-5

g) *Economics for Nursing, Medicine and Allied Health Professions.*
   Amazon Independent Publishing Inc. (August 2012)
   ISBN-13:978-1479152711 /ISBN-10: 1479152714
   http://www.amazon.co.uk/Economics-Nursing-Medicine-Allied-
   Professions/dp/1479152714/ref=sr_1_3?s=books&ie=UTF8&qid
   =1365511739&sr=1-3

h) *Jose P. Rizal : The National Hero*
   Amazon Independent Publishing Inc. (August 2012)
   ISBN: 10:147913062 /ISBN-13:978-1479130368
   http://www.amazon.co.uk/Jose-P-Rizal-National-
   Hero/dp/1479130362/ref=sr_1_2?s=books&ie=UTF8&qid=13655
   11739&sr=1-2

i) *Historical and Cultural Management of the UNESCO Heritage City of Vigan*
   2017 Galda Verlag, Glienicke Bibliografische Information der
   Deutschen Nationalbibliothek Die Deutsche Nationalbibliothek
   verzeichnet diese Publikation in der Deutschen
   Nationalbibliografie; detaillierte bibliografische Daten sind im
   Internet über http://dnb.ddb.de abrufbar ISBN 978-3-941267-
   72-5 (Print) and ISBN 978-3-941267-73-2 (Ebook)
   https://www.nlb.gov.sg/biblio/205261583

   Furthermore, he was designated to work in various
administrative positions of the University as the Secretary for Teacher
Enhancement and International Affairs (2002-2004), Assistant Director
of Extension Office for Programs and Projects (2004-2005), Assistant
Director of the Special Projects and International Affairs (2006-2008),
Special Assistant to the Vice President for External Affairs and Alumni
Relations (2009-2011) , ASCU-SN Secretariat in the Course Book
Writing Development Project (2007-2011),and Discipline Chair in
Social Sciences (2005-2009), Core Faculty and Extension Coordinator of
the Graduate School Program (2001-2012) .

   In his professional membership designations, he was the Executive
Vice President for 2018-2020 (National Level) Board of Trustees, State
Universities and Colleges , Teacher Educators Association (SUCTEA) ;
Vice Chairman, Region 1 Teacher Education Council (R1TEAC) as the
Professional Association for Department of Education CHED in
Region 1 ; Adviser, SUCTEA Region I; Former Public Relations
Officer (PRO) for 2016-2018 (National Levell) Board of Trustees, State

Universities and Colleges Teacher Educators Association (SUCTEA).